PRAISE for
Pince-Nez Press School Guidebooks

"Finally someone is asking the right questions."
—Admission Director of a San Francisco independent school

"No other resource provides as much information on private schools."
—Parent

"Ninety percent of the questions we are asked in the admission process are answered in your book."
—Admission Director, Bay Area independent school

"A big thank you for creating these very helpful books for parents."
—Parent, San Francisco

"[If you have] a child vying for acceptance into a private school [it] is as fascinating as a Crichton novel...."
—*Nob Hill Gazette*

"I found this book to be a very vital tool in my search for just the right school for my child."
—Parent, Palo Alto

"Parents rely very heavily on the information in your books."
—Admission Director, San Francisco independent school

"Pince-Nez Press of San Francisco publishes several books that are outstanding for parents looking for schools for their children. All of these meticulously researched, independent guides, written by parents and educational consultants, contain no advertising, and schools do not pay to be in them. Rather they are based upon visits to the schools, extensive questionnaires and interviews with the school heads and admission directors."
—*Bay Area Parent* magazine

Private K-8 Schools of San Francisco and Marin (5th Edition)
by Betsy Little, MBA, MA, and Paula Molligan, MBA, MA

© 2006 Pince-Nez Press, LLC

Cover design, page design and page layout by Idintdoit Productions

ISBN 1-930074-15-8
Library of Congress Catalog Card No.: LCCN: 2005905167
Printed in the United States.

Pince-Nez Press
1459 18th Street, PMB 175
San Francisco, California 94107
415.267.5978
www.pince-nez.com
info@pince-nez.com

Private K–8 Schools

of

San Francisco & Marin

• fifth edition •

Betsy Little, MBA, MA

Paula Molligan, MBA, MA

Pince-Nez Press

To our families with love

CONTENTS

SCHOOLS BY COUNTY

San Francisco

Adda Clevenger Jr. Preparatory and Theater School
Brandeis Hillel Day School
Cathedral School for Boys
Children's Day School
Chinese American International School
Convent of the Sacred Heart Elementary School
Corpus Christi Elementary School
Discovery Center School
Ecôle Notre Dame des Victoires*
French-American International School
The Hamlin School
Hillwood Academic Day School*
Holy Name of Jesus School
Holy Trinity Orthodox School*
Katherine Delmar Burke School
Kittredge School
Krouzian-Zekarian-Vasbouragan Armenian School
The Laurel School
Lisa Kampner Hebrew Academy
Live Oak School
Lycée Français La Pérouse
Megan Furth Academy at Sacred Heart/St. Dominic*
Mission Dolores Catholic School
Our Lady of the Visitacion School*
Presidio Hill School

St. Anne School
St. Anthony Immaculate Conception School*
St. Brendan School*
Saint Brigid School
St. Cecilia Elementary
Saint Charles Borromeo School*
St. Elizabeth School*
St. Finn Barr School*
St. Gabriel School
St. James School
St. John's School
St. Mary's Chinese Day School
Saint Monica School
St. Paul's Elementary School
St. Peter's School
St. Philip School
St. Stephen School*
St. Thomas More School*
St. Thomas the Apostle School*
Saint Vincent de Paul School
Sts. Peter and Paul Elementary School*
San Francisco Adventist School*
San Francisco Day School
San Francisco Friends School
The San Francisco School
San Francisco Waldorf School
School of the Epiphany*
Star of the Sea School*
Stuart Hall for Boys
Synergy School
Town School for Boys
Voice of Pentecost Academy*
West Portal Lutheran School
Zion Lutheran Day School

Marin

Brandeis Hillel Day School
Cascade Canyon School
Lycée Français La Pérouse
Marin Christian Academy
Marin Country Day School
Marin Horizon School
Marin Montessori School
Marin Primary & Middle School
Marin Waldorf School
Montessori de Terra Linda
Mount Tamalpais School
North Bay Christian Academy*
Our Lady of Loretto School*
Ring Mountain Day School
St. Anselm School*
St. Hilary School*
St. Isabella School*
Saint Mark's School
St. Patrick School*
St. Raphael School*
St. Rita School*
San Domenico School

* Indicates short entry at back of book

SCHOOLS BY TYPE

Independent Schools (Nonprofit, members CAIS)

Brandeis Hillel Day School, Marin
Brandeis Hillel Day School, San Francisco
Cathedral School for Boys
Children's Day School (provisional member)
Chinese American International School
Convent of the Sacred Heart Elementary School
French-American International School

The Hamlin School
Katherine Delmar Burke School
Live Oak School
Lycée Français La Pérouse, Marin and San Francisco
Marin Country Day School
Marin Horizon School
Marin Primary & Middle School
Mount Tamalpais School
Presidio Hill School
Saint Mark's School
San Domenico School
San Francisco Day School
San Francisco Friends Schools
The San Francisco School
Stuart Hall for Boys
Town School for Boys

Other Nonprofit Schools
Cascade Canyon School
The Laurel School
Marin Montessori School
Marin Waldorf School
Montessori de Terra Linda
Ring Mountain Day School
Synergy School
San Francisco Waldorf School

Proprietary Schools
Adda Clevenger Junior Preparatory and Theater School for Children
Discovery Center School
Hillwood Academic Day School*
Kittredge School

Catholic Schools
Convent of the Sacred Heart Elementary School
Corpus Christi School

Ecôle Notre Dame des Victoires*
Holy Name of Jesus School
Megan Furth Academy at Sacred Heart/St. Dominic*
Mission Dolores Catholic School
Our Lady of Loretto School*
Our Lady of the Visitacion School*
St. Anne School
St. Anselm School*
St. Anthony Immaculate Conception School*
St. Brendan School*
Saint Brigid School
St. Cecilia Elementary
Saint Charles Borromeo School*
St. Elizabeth School*
St. Finn Barr School*
St. Gabriel School
St. Hilary School*
St. Isabella School*
St. James School
St. John's School
St. Mary's Chinese Day School
Saint Monica School
St. Patrick School*
St. Paul's Elementary School
St. Peter's School
St. Philip School
St. Raphael School*
St. Rita School*
St. Stephen School*
St. Thomas More School*
St. Thomas the Apostle School*
Saint Vincent de Paul School
Sts. Peter and Paul Elementary School*
San Domenico School
School of the Epiphany*
Star of the Sea School*
Stuart Hall for Boys

Jewish Schools
Brandeis-Hillel Day School, Marin
Brandeis-Hillel Day School, San Francisco
Lisa Kampner Hebrew Academy

Other Religious Schools
Cathedral School for Boys
Holy Trinity Orthodox School*
Krouzian-Zekarian-Vasbouragan Armenian School
Marin Christian Academy
North Bay Christian Academy*
San Francisco Adventist School*
Voice of Pentecost Academy*
West Portal Lutheran School
Zion Lutheran Day School

All Girls
Convent of the Sacred Heart Elementary School
The Hamlin School
Katherine Delmar Burke School

All Boys
Cathedral School for Boys
Stuart Hall for Boys
Town School for Boys

Elementary Schools with Preschools
Children's Day School
Chinese American International School
French-American International School
Krouzian-Zekarian-Vasbouragan Armenian School
The Laurel School
Lisa Kampner Hebrew Academy
Lycée Français La Pérouse, Marin and San Francisco

Marin Christian Academy
Marin Horizon School
Marin Montessori School
Marin Primary & Middle School
Marin Waldorf School
Montessori de Terra Linda
Ring Mountain Day School
Saint Paul's Elementary School
St. Raphael School*
Sts. Peter and Paul Elementary School*
San Domenico School
The San Francisco School
San Francisco Waldorf School
Voice of Pentecost Academy*

Elementary Schools with High Schools
Convent of the Sacred Heart Elementary School
French-American International School
Lisa Kampner Hebrew Academy
Lycée Français La Pérouse, San Francisco
San Domenico (girls day/boarding high school)
San Francisco Waldorf School
Stuart Hall for Boys
Voice of Pentecost Academy*

INTRODUCTION

The information contained in this Guide is based upon (1) information provided by the schools in response to a questionnaire sent to the schools; (2) interviews with admission directors and principals; (3) visits to most of the schools (usually up to a two-hour visit per school including classroom visits); and, in some cases, (4) publicly available information on the schools. The additional schools listed in the back of the Guide, as well as any new schools between the revisions, are invited to provide full information in the next edition. Schools do not pay to be included in this Guide—it is not advertising. Quotations are used to note qualitative information provided by the schools. Should a school choose not to answer any part of the questionnaire it is noted as N/P (not provided), and if the information requested is not applicable it is noted as N/A. Quotations from schools may be altered by use of abbreviations or by editing or use of punctuation to shorten length of quote to meet space restrictions.

This Guide is intended to provide a starting point for parents in the private school search. No one school is best for all students; consequently, no attempt is made to rank or rate schools. Moreover, what families are looking for in a school will vary considerably. Some may be looking for a school that sends a good number of graduates to particular high schools while others may be interested in a spiritual environment or a particular educational philosophy. It is important for families to consider the fit between their student and family needs and a school's offerings.

Some parents seek advice from educational consultants who specialize in narrowing school choices that fit a family's individual needs. Consultants specialize in knowing the ethos and culture of a school and can save a great deal of time and money in recommending the best school placement.

Private Schools

In the lexicon of this Guide, "private schools" mean schools established and controlled by a non-governmental agency or individual and are supported by endowment and tuition. Within this very broad category are schools that are set up as non-profit, tax-exempt corporations with boards of trustees known as independent schools; privately owned tax-paying schools known as proprietary schools; and religiously affiliated schools. Most depend on tuition, fees and outside funding sources to finance most of their expenses. Annual fund appeals, contributions, and various fund-raising activities make up the difference in a school's operating budget. Most schools look for 100% parent participation in their annual appeals as the percentage makes a statement in attracting outside funding for grants and foundation support. These organizations look to the financial contributions of the school's current parents, faculty and alumni as a reflection of satisfaction with the school.

Approximately 10% of students in California attend private schools. This varies by geographic area. Over the past 20 years in San Francisco the percentage has remained fairly stable at 25% (Source: http://www.demographers.com) and in Marin the percentage is approximately 20% (http://www.demographics.marin.org).

Regulation of Private Schools

Although California private schools are not regulated by the California Department of Education, most private schools are members of national education associations which require adherence to strict guidelines for membership. In addition, many schools participate with outside agencies for accreditation. Private schools are not held to the public school minimum of 175 instructional days per academic year, nor to a minimum number of hours in the school day. Private schools must comply with all state and local regulations relating to health, fire safety, earthquake safety, business licenses, and other matters. All school employees must also have a criminal check and be fingerprinted. They are not required to hire credentialed teachers. Private schools need only follow very general curriculum guidelines promulgated by the State Department of Education.

California law requires private elementary and secondary schools to file an affidavit with the California Department of Education. Any school with an enrollment of six or more students must be registered and a full list of these schools is available at www.cde.ca.gov/privates-chools/data.html. The only effect of the filing is to deem students enrolled in the school "non-truant." It is not "accreditation."

Types of Private Schools

Private schools fall within three broad categories: independent, proprietary and religiously affiliated.

Non-Profit Independent Schools

Although any school may call itself an "independent school," members of associations such as the California Association of Independent Schools (CAIS) and the National Association of Independent Schools (NAIS), are non-profit organizations governed by their own boards of trustees as opposed to being governed by a central diocese, church's board of trustees, or some other off-site entity. The NAIS requires that its members be "primarily supported by tuition, charitable contributions, and endowment income rather than by tax or church funds." To be eligible for NAIS membership, schools must be independently governed by a board of trustees, practice nondiscriminatory policies, be accredited by an approved state or regional association, and hold not-for-profit 501(c)(3) tax-exempt status. (For more information, see the NAIS web site at www.nais.org and the CAIS web site at www.caisca. org.)

Generally, a board of trustees provides oversight of the school's administration. The trustees are composed of parents, community leaders, and others dedicated to the school's mission. Trustees are normally invited to serve as volunteers for terms of two to four years, and board meetings are typically closed to non-members.

CAIS explains independent schools as "pre-collegiate, non-profit institutions governed by boards of trustees and supported by tuition revenue, charitable contributions, and endowment income. Throughout the accreditation process, schools hold themselves publicly accountable to all who seek assurance that they meet high standards of educational quality, operation, and staff competence." Schools cannot apply for membership until they have been in operation for five years, be incorporated as a non-profit, and meet CAIS standards and those of a visiting committee of the CAIS Board.

According to the NAIS, its member schools "stress social responsibility and service to the community in their policies and programs and encourage enrollment from all segments of the community."

Independent schools may have religious affiliations and each school is responsible for its own curriculum. As tax-exempt organizations, they may be eligible for grant and/or foundation monies. Most independent schools expect parents to make tax-deductible contributions to the school and/or be involved in fundraising activities.

Elementary schools in the Bay Area that are members of the Bay Area Directors of Admissions (BADA) have established "principles of good practice" surrounding admissions. They share admission forms, deadlines, and notification dates. BADA member schools do not solicit donations for their schools from applicant families during the application period. Current members included in this Guide are: Brandeis Hillel Day Schools, The Katherine Delmar Burke School, Cathedral School for Boys, Chinese American International School, Convent of the Sacred Heart Elementary School, French American International School, The Hamlin School, Live Oak School, Marin Country Day School, Marin Horizon School, Marin Primary & Middle School, Mount Tamalpais School, Presidio Hill School, Saint Mark's School, San Domenico School, San Francisco Day School, San Francisco Friends School, the San Francisco School, Stuart Hall for Boys, and Town School for Boys.

Proprietary Schools

Proprietary schools operate on a profit basis and may be corporations, partnerships, or sole proprietorships. These schools pay taxes like any other business. Donations to them are not tax-deductible though some schools set up foundations to receive donations. Generally, they do not have boards of trustees, but they may have parent committees to advise owners on a broad range of topics. A number of proprietary schools are owned and run by one individual with a distinct vision. In such a school, parents should be absolutely certain that they agree and can fully support the vision of the director. Parents should also get assurances that the school would be able to continue to function if the director became ill or otherwise unable to direct the day-to-day activities.

Religiously Affiliated Schools

Few generalities can be made about religious schools except that they seek to instill moral values. Religiously affiliated schools, both Christian and non-Christian, vary in degree as to the level of sectarian integration of the curriculum. Religious affiliation varies from one school to another with some schools requiring membership of a particular religion as an admission requirement and others welcoming students without regard to religion. Families choose religiously affiliated schools for a variety of reasons including: family or cultural tradition; appreciation for the concurrent teaching of values alongside academics; and a perception of higher academic standards, higher standards of behavior, and a better peer group.

Catholic: All the Catholic schools in this Guide fall within the Archdiocese of San Francisco. There are three types of Catholic schools: parochial schools, which are attached to a parish; independent Catholic schools, which are non-profit organizations with their own boards of trustees; and Archdiocesan schools, which were parochial schools until their parishes closed.

Catholic parochial schools do not necessarily have a high percentage of Catholic students. Some schools that once primarily served the needs of parish families are now serving neighborhood populations that may or may not be Christian. Nevertheless, all students are required to take religion classes and attend mass.

Catholic schools establish their own curricula following guidelines published by the San Francisco Archdiocese. Although each school is afforded limited autonomy, the Archdiocese dictates most procedural and legal matters. Some parochial schools have an advisory school board on which parents may serve, and most have parent-teacher committees. Schools within the Archdiocese normally share admissions deadlines and dates on which they send out notification letters.

Christian: The term "Christian school" is used in this Guide to refer to schools that are independent and are governed by a self-perpetuating board. Some may be a ministry of a particular congregation.

Jewish: Jewish day schools are designed to provide students an academic program which includes Judaic studies within a Jewish cultural environment. Students learn to appreciate and celebrate Jewish practices and philosophies.

Public Schools

The Bay Area has many excellent public grade schools. Public schools are funded by local, state and federal dollars. They are controlled by the local board of education and owned by the public. Information on public schools can be obtained from each school district or from the Department of Education in Sacramento. Numerous web sites provide information on Bay Area public grade schools.

Charter schools are publicly funded schools that are granted a high degree of autonomy. In California there are over 200 charter schools. They are unique in that they can control their own budgets, staffing, and curriculum (Source: www.education.umn.edu). The charters may be granted by a local school board or the California State Board of Education. These schools must adhere to the terms of their charter or their charter can be revoked. Lotteries are used to determine admission with priority for enrollment based on factors such as district residency, participation in establishing the school, employee status, etc. The lottery establishes a waitlist for any openings that may develop. Families can obtain information on charter schools by calling their local school districts or visiting district web sites.

Accreditation and Associations

"Accreditation certifies to other educational institutions and to the general public that an institution meets established criteria or standards and is achieving its own stated objectives" (Source: www.acswasc.org). Criteria often include student assessment and support, curriculum review, promotion of student learning, academic standards, financial stability, and physical and human resources. Accreditation is optional; schools are not required to be accredited, however, certain exceptions apply to schools receiving public funds. Public schools have the option of refusing to accept credits from schools that are not accredited. The main accrediting agency for schools below the college level in California is the Accrediting Commission for Schools, which is an arm of the Western Association of Schools and Colleges (ACS/WASC). The accreditation process requires extensive documentation of a school's goals and objectives; a self-evaluation performed by the school staff and community; and an on-site visit to the school by a team of educational professionals. The evaluating team validates the internal study, evaluates its findings, and recommends a term of accreditation to the Commission. Schools that seek accreditation may apply for candidate or interim status with ACS/WASC. All schools are subject to a full review every six years. If a school has not met all ACS/WASC criteria, it may receive a shorter term of accreditation requiring additional reports and visits. If parents have questions about accreditation, they may contact the Accrediting Commission for Schools at (650) 696-1060.

Another accrediting organization in California is the California Association of Independent Schools known as CAIS. To be a voting member of CAIS a school must be accredited by CAIS. It is an association of over 180 schools in California wherein each school's accountability is open for public review to assure the school meets high standards in their quality, operations, and staff. Schools complete a self-study which is evaluated by an on-site visit of education professionals. Schools are accredited for a maximum of six years, and must complete an interim report between accreditation visits to track the school's adherence to any CAIS recommendations. CAIS is a collaborative partner with WASC and NAIS. CAIS can be reached at (310) 393-5161.

The Association of Christian Schools International (ACSI) accredits Christian schools, although Christian schools may also apply for joint ACSI/WASC accreditation or be only ACSI accredited. Any questions regarding accreditation may be directed to (719) 528-6906.

The National Lutheran School Accreditation (NLSA) organization offers Lutheran schools the opportunity to go though a voluntary self-study and evaluation accreditation process. It evaluates Lutheran schools not only on the quality of a school's academics and programs, but it also looks at the spiritual dimension of the school. NLSA is governed by the National Accrediting Commission that is comprised of representatives from various participating Lutheran districts. Over 500 schools are currently accredited by this organization.

Some schools, both non-profit and proprietary, choose not to go through the accreditation process because of the cost and the time involved. In addition, each school must pay the expenses—including airfare, hotel, and meals—for a team of three to four evaluators to study the school for two to three days. Schools involve parents, students, faculty, administration and board members in their self-evaluation documentation. Accreditation not only serves as an indicator of the quality of the school, but also serves as a tool for self-improvement. Schools that do not seek accreditation often consider their "stamp of approval" to be satisfied parents and successful high school placement, as well as the school's longevity.

The National Association of Independent School (NAIS) includes 1,200 independent schools in both the United States and overseas. NAIS provides Principles of Good Practice for ethical behavior and advocates broad access in affirming principles of justice and equity. It is a membership organization, not an accrediting organization, with a national voice on behalf of member schools and acts as a center for collective action. The voting membership comes from non-profit schools that have been established for over five years. These schools must be accredited by an independent organization recognized by NAIS and demonstrate financially sound operations and non-discriminatory practices. In addition, voting members must also be associated with a state or regional level independent school association. For further information call (202) 973-9700.

The Association of Waldorf Schools North America's (AWSNA) mission is to strengthen and support independent Waldorf schools as well as Waldorf teacher education institutes.

Similarly, the Association of Montessori Internationale (AMI) is a professional organization that adheres to traditional Montessori programs. The American Montessori Society (AMS) has incorporated more recent methods and materials into its programs. Parents should be aware that the word "Montessori" is not trademarked, thus anyone can use it.

The National Catholic Educational Association (NCEA) is a membership organization that provides individual, affiliate, and institutional memberships to Catholic education. It is a voluntary association of institutions and educators affiliated with religious education programs, elementary and secondary schools, colleges and universities. It represents over 200,000 Catholic educators serving almost eight million students. The NCEA promotes the educational and religious mission of the Catholic Church, advocates Catholic education, and fosters collaboration within its membership. The Western Catholic Education

Association (WCEA) works collaboratively with WASC for school improvement and accreditation of Catholic school members.

The National Association of Episcopal Schools (NAES) is independently incorporated and is a voluntary membership organization. It provides professional support and advocates for those who serve "Episcopal schools, Early Childhood Education programs and school exploration/establishment/expansion efforts throughout the Episcopal Church U.S.A. As a voluntary membership services organization, NAES does not accredit Episcopal schools, nor does it establish or have statutory oversight of the academic and religious programs or governance of any Episcopal school" (Source: http://www.naes.org/about/).

The Friends Council on Education (FCE) founded in 1931 promotes Quaker education and supports Friends education in maintaining their values-based learning.

The Jewish Education Service of North America (JESNA) is an organization devoted to advancing Jewish learning. It works to recruit talented educators, identify and disseminate models of excellence in education, and develop creative new approaches to expand the impact of Jewish education.

The Torah Umesorah is a national society for Hebrew day schools founded in 1945. Over 600 schools with enrollments totaling 170,000 students belong to this nationwide organization of Orthodox day schools.

Many schools in the San Francisco area belong to the Bay Area People of Color in Independent Schools (POCIS). POCIS is a committee of NAIS and is organized to support national and regional goals for the betterment of people of color in independent schools (Source: www.ba-pocis.org). Summerbridge and Making Waves serve middle school students who face limited opportunities for academic success. Both programs provide a purposeful curriculum that is interactive and implemented by high school and college student mentors.

Schools also may be members of the Educational Records Bureau (ERB) or the Secondary School Admission Test Board (SSATB). The ERB is a non-profit organization that has 1450 members from public and private schools in 41 states and 32 countries. The ERB publishes tests known such as the Comprehensive Testing Program (CTP 4) and the Independent School Entrance Examination (ISEE). To be a member of ERB, a school must be accredited.

The Secondary School Admission Test Board (SSATB) is a non-profit organization that not only provides the SSAT examination, but also supports professional development of its members with publications and meetings.

The International Boys School Coalition (IBSC) provides a means for educators to talk about the importance and relevance of educating boys. The National Coalition of Girls Schools (NCGS) is an association of girls independent, private and public day and boarding schools in the United States and abroad. The NCGS promotes the value and benefit of all-girl schools.

The Council of International Schools (CIS) members are accredited schools. CIS is a non-profit corporation which is registered in the United States but is administered in the United Kingdom.

The French Ministry of Education requires education standards to be followed in U.S. schools teaching French nationals. The Ministry sends a representative to make sure the teaching conforms to teaching programs, pedagogies, and examinations applicable in French schools. The schools must conform to the French criteria.

The schools in this guide were asked to list membership organizations. Most of these organization acronyms are listed in the back of this guide. For the most part, these are all collaborative associations that enhance the respective educational goals of each interest.

Fundamentals of Admission

Keeping a Perspective

Parents always worry whether they are doing the right thing for their child. It is easy for parents to get caught up in the whirlwind of private school admissions and lose perspective. The best advice for parents is to relax about the process as well as the outcome. Try not to become overly focused on any one school. A child's future success is not guaranteed because of admission to any given school. Admission decisions can be based on uncontrollable factors and do not necessarily mean the child is not qualified. Although admission to a particular school may appear tantamount in importance at the time, in reality there are always viable alternatives in both public and private sectors. Parents are encouraged to keep a healthy perspective throughout the admission process.

Beginning the Application Process

Parents should begin contacting schools in August to request the school's application information. This information will include all pertinent steps and dates. The private school admission process usually begins with school tours as early as October and ends the following March when notification letters are sent. Application deadlines are generally in December-January. Most schools adhere to a very strict policy regarding application and notification deadlines. Late applications are reviewed on a space available basis.

Parents may also choose to attend a "Kindergarten Information Night" which is usually held in October each year in San Francisco and Marin for parents interested in private schools. The San Francisco event is hosted by the Jewish Community Center. For further information, call (415) 292-1200. The Marin County Information Evening is hosted on a rotating basis so parents are encouraged to contact any one of the independent schools in Marin for specific information. Schools set up booths with their information and admission directors meet with parents/guardians and answer their questions.

For parents/guardians who apply to numerous schools, the admission process can be very stressful and the time commitment tantamount to a part-time job. It is especially difficult for parents/guardians with demanding or inflexible work schedules because of the amount of time needed for required appointments. Most schools mandate that parents/guardians attend a one to three hour tour that is usually held on a weekday when classes are in session. Evening open houses are available at some schools. If parents choose to apply, schools generally require both parents/guardians have a personal interview with the admission director. In addition, parents/guardians may have to: bring their child to the school for an interview or a screening/observation or class visit during a weekday or Saturday which will last from one to three hours; complete an application; provide references and narrative evaluations from their child's current teacher(s); and pay a nonrefundable application fee of up to $150 for each child per school.

Transfer Students

Transfer students share the same application, financial aid deadlines and notification dates as Kindergarten applicants. Many schools may accept applications year-round depending on space availability. For the most part, school year openings are rare and many schools are reluctant to enroll a new student mid-year. Schools do not usually know the number of openings available for grades one through eight until a few weeks before they make admission decisions.

Most schools will require a class visit for transfer students. The class visit is a very important determinant in the admission decision. Schools want to make sure the applicant is a good fit for their program academically and behaviorally. The school visit provides an opportunity for interaction in a classroom setting. It is also an opportunity for the applicant to get a feel for the school and meet potential classmates.

Admission Standards

Schools were asked if they have minimum admission requirements. This information should help families focus on realistic school possibilities based on their child's individual profile.

Admission committees attribute a great deal of importance in evaluating an application to the parent and/or student interview, student visit, recommendation(s), screening/test scores, academic achievement at any prior school, extra and co-curricular activities, and interests. Schools are looking to complement their current populations.

Student Profiles

On paper, it can appear that all schools cater to the "best and the brightest" and offer a rigorous curriculum. Some parents have commented that it seems there is no place for "average" students. The category question of "What sort of student do you best serve?" is designed to give a sense of the "breadth" of students, in terms of abilities and varied talents/potential that the school serves.

Tours

It is essential to begin the process early. At some schools, parents are expected to submit the application and fee prior to the interview and/or tour. School tours are time-consuming and often inconveniently scheduled but essential because they provide an opportunity to see the school in action. Schools that seem a perfect match on paper can become out-of-the-question after an on site visit. Differences in school missions and philosophies are evident in classroom instruction. Seeing a variety of grade levels allows parents to get a better picture of a school's program. Parents should be observant of such things as: the level of participation and active engagement of the students both in and out of the classroom; student-teacher and student-student rapport; general sense of order; and the variety of work displayed.

Application

Application and financial aid forms are available from schools in early fall. Many application forms request student and parent input as well as teacher recommendations. Parents may be asked to write short commentaries addressing topics such as why the school is a match for the child; the student's strengths and challenges; and special circumstances or other pertinent information. Some schools ask older applicants to describe their interests or hobbies, challenges and strengths, and co-curricular activities. Parents and students are encouraged to start early as this process can be time-consuming.

If a school is a member of the BADA group, the member schools will share recommendation forms required from the applicant's current preschool or elementary school teacher(s). The forms ask teachers to evaluate various aspects of a student's academic and personal qualities.

Catholic schools may require an Annual Parishioner/Church/Temple Certification Form. If a school does not require this certification form it advisable to submit one if applicable. Most certification forms ask a pastor, minister or rabbi to certify that a family is registered, involved, and/or contributes to the parish/church/temple. Some forms ask parents to describe the family's spirituality in the event the family is not of any particular faith and does not attend a church.

Although being a member of the Catholic Church is not mandatory for admission consideration, most parish schools give preference to Catholic students within parish boundaries, and then to Catholic students outside the parish.

Jewish day school students are generally members of congregations or Jewish community centers. Jewish schools use different requirements of Judaic backgrounds and practices in identifying potential candidates for admission. Not all Jewish schools require that a student be Jewish. Applicants may be required to provide a Jewish professional recommendation provided by a rabbi, Jewish Studies teacher, cantor, or Jewish youth group leader.

Other religiously affiliated schools may have specific religious membership requirements. Generally schools include this information in their admission information.

Some schools seek additional letters of recommendation. However, families should be very selective about the kind and type of additional information they submit. One admission director said, "The thicker the file, the thicker the student." Another admission director gave this rule of thumb, "If you are tempted to send extras, ask this: 'Does it demonstrate specific talents or abilities that won't come through in the application packet or process, and are those talents or abilities pertinent to the school's programs?'"

Admission Screening and Testing

Most schools have cut-off dates for Kindergarten admission. Although the State of California mandates that a child turns five by December 1, most private schools encourage applicants with birth dates after September 1 to wait a year. The dates given in this guide under "K age requirement" refer to the age the child must be for the first day of Kindergarten—not the age at the time of application. If applicants are "not yet ready for Kindergarten," schools will encourage the parent/guardian to give the child "the gift of time" by waiting a year and reapplying. The median entry age for the many competitive independent schools approximates five years, seven months on the first day of Kindergarten. Parents should give serious consideration to this issue as a child who starts school too early may develop academic and/or social issues in middle school.

Admission screenings for young applicants range from one-on-one interviews to group play; and from general observations to standardized developmental assessments. Many schools look for "developmental readiness," to determine if a child's chronological age is in sync with the child's developmental age. This may include an assessment of a child's language, listening, motor and social skills. In order to reduce multiple assessments of an individual child, some schools share screening results. This information will be included in a school's admission literature.

Parents worry about how well their child will perform. Coaching or prepping for these screenings is not recommended. It is important a child be well-rested and healthy for the screening. Developmental readiness is like growing hair-a child will either be ready or not.

Generally, older applicants are required to spend a half/full day visiting the school, take a standardized test and have an individual or group interview. Sometimes schools interview candidates and administer an assessment on the same date the student visits the school. Other times, schools will have a separate date for the assessment and/or the interview. Individual schools require different admission tests for entry consideration. Grades are automatically submitted to the applicant's school after the parents sign a transcript release form contained in the admission information.

Admission Deadlines and Notification Letters

The application deadline generally ends in January. Interviews and student visits may be held as late as February, and the majority of schools mail acceptance notification letters in mid-March. The Bay Area Directors of Admissions (BADA) schools share the same mailing date in mid March; Catholic schools also share a mailing date which is usually February-March. Oftentimes, Catholic school notification letters are mailed before the BADA school letters. Parents are asked to make a commitment within a week of the notification date and the timing of the notification letters can be problematic. Schools will ask for a nonrefundable deposit to secure a student's space for the fall. Deposits generally range from $300-$2,500 and are required to guarantee a student's place until the next payment is due in June or July.

Parents and students do not have to attend every open house and every event the school offers. Attending school events, however, gives parents and students an excellent opportunity to learn more about a school and its student body. This research aids in making informed decisions.

Admission Directors' Advice to Parents

"Parents may have unrealistically high expectations of their children. We urge parents to set aside their own desires—such as those based upon social status, family expectations, or legacies—and to focus on what is best for their student. We recommend families talk first about realistic choices in terms of finances, geography, type of school (coed or single sex, religiously affiliated, etc.) and begin the search with these parameters in mind. Parents need to know that competition is keen for admissions to Bay Area schools as we clearly do not have enough spaces for all the qualified students that apply."

"Start early! The biggest mistake parents make is not being organized: call in time to schedule a school visit and request an application packet. Adhere to all application deadlines. Never suggest anything that could be interpreted as a bribe. Schools are looking to work in partnership with families and want to accept students that will be successful within their school environment."

Schools seek a "balanced class," considering many factors such as gender, age, and academic achievement, etc. Admission decisions can be the result of many uncontrollable factors such as sibling applicants, legacies, gender balance, and more. Schools cannot possibly take all the qualified candidates that apply and must make very difficult decisions. Be respectful of the process and of a school's decision.

Interviews

Through the interview process, prospective parents and/or students have an opportunity to meet one-on-one with a school representative who is usually the Director of Admission. If possible, each parent should attend the interview. This meeting provides a chance for the school representative to personalize the process and help determine if there is a match between a family's needs/expectations and a school's offerings. Similarly, a family has an opportunity to get an impression of the school. Schools are looking for parents who will be team players and who will work in partnership with them.

Preferences

Schools with preschools give preference to current preschoolers for Kindergarten spaces. In addition, schools oftentimes give preference to siblings of current enrollees, legacies and/or faculty children. Even if the numbers seem discouraging, it is advisable to apply as admission directors do not truly know the number of openings available until after the application deadline.

Admission Etiquette and Tips

Parents should relax, be on time for the interview and meet all deadlines. It is advisable to call the school a few weeks before the deadline to make sure all required documentation is in order. Avoid excessive or solicitous contact which might be perceived as overkill by the school. Avoid submitting more information than requested by the school.

Parents need to trust their intuition. All the research in the world is often not as reliable in choosing a school as a parent's intuition. Once parents have visited all prospective schools, and if one school is clearly a family's first choice, parents are encouraged to communicate this preference to the respective admission director. It is not a guarantee of admission but it will be noted.

What to Look for in a Grade School

Single Sex or Coed

There are advocates for both single sex and coed school environments. Both groups have research to support their positions. The pros and cons of single sex or coed schools should be investigated and considered by families and students. It is important to be aware of the choices available and remain open to exploring both options.

Religious Affiliation

Religiously affiliated schools require varying levels of religious participation. Parents should inquire as to the extent and content of the religion programs. Some school programs are designed to embrace a specific religious venue and mandate that the student be affiliated with their sect or identify themselves as so.

Standardized Test Scores

With an increased emphasis over the last decade on standards and accountability in education, standardized testing has become a fact of life from nearly preschool on—and a highly controversial topic. Private schools do not publish standardized test scores, but suggest prospective parents gauge the strength of a school's program by the successes of their students i.e. Johns Hopkins Talented Youth designees, high school placement, science fair winners, mathletes, etc. During the admission process, these schools selected students with strong aptitude and achievement, and thus, the comparative norms among private schools are skewed. Standardized test scores are primarily used by private independent schools as internal mechanisms for the assessment of their programs and students.

Endowment

Just as a savings account enhances a family's financial security, so does a school's endowment. The interest on an endowment can be used for capital improvements, financial aid, faculty salaries and the like. Most schools solicit donations for building their endowments. If a school has a 501(c) 3 nonprofit designation donations are tax deductible.

Enrollment

Schools in this guide range from 40 to 655. Smaller schools may offer a more intimate setting with more individual attention and parental involvement while larger schools may provide more extensive facilities and programs as well as larger peer groups.

Average Class Size

Average class size in this guide varies from 8 to 35 students. It is important to ask a school about the number of students, teachers and teacher aides in the classroom. This statistic is different than the ratio of teacher to students found in the Faculty section of this Guide.

School Year

Most schools are open from late August to early or mid-June. There are many schools that have an extended school year or offer academic and/or recreational summer programs.

Student Body

Each school in this guide was asked to provide the ethnic makeup of its student body. This information may be important to parents who are looking for a school with ethnic diversity.

Cost

The schools included in this guide charge tuition ranging from $1,650 to more than $19,000 annually. Parents should expect tuition increases from 1% - 10% annually regardless of the overall state of the economy. In addition to tuition, there can be additional fees for: field trips, uniforms, outdoor education, books, etc. Schools in this guide were asked to identify approximate projected costs for family budgeting purposes. Most schools require parents to make an initial non-refundable deposit applicable to tuition upon acceptance to the school. Payment options for the remainder of tuition vary from school to school. Some schools allow parents to pay monthly while other schools have one or multiple installment payment plans. In addition, some schools offer sibling discounts. Many schools offer tuition refund plans which provide insurance for tuition payments should a student need to leave during the school term.

Parents need to consider the cost of extended daycare programs, after-school enrichment classes and/or the expense of vacation coverage in cost forecasts. When parents choose a school, they are usually making a nine-year financial commitment. The schools included in this guide were asked to provide the approximate annual tuition increase that parents can anticipate. Most schools try to provide timely notification of tuition and fee increases.

Indexed Tuition/Flexible Tuition/Financial Aid

Paying for private school tuition presents a challenge to many families. Schools are concerned about being able to serve an economic cross section of students. In order to broaden economic diversity, more and more schools are offering indexed, flexible tuitions or financial aid. Most aid awarded is need-based. Indexed tuition, flexible tuition and financial aid decisions are based on a family's assets, family size, discretionary expenses, current and other educational expenses, as well as any extraordinary circumstances. This money is NOT a loan; consequently, it is not expected to be repaid. Unless a school is using its own criteria, most schools participate in the School Scholarship Service (SSS). Aid using this service is based on a family's ability to pay as demonstrated by the information provided by parents on the Personal Financial Statement (PFS) form from SSS. Both custodial as well as non-custodial parents need to provide the necessary financial information. Should one parent not be able to comply, an explanation will be required. All parents will be asked to include their most recent tax return and applicable attachments, and W-2's or a Business/Farm statement if they are self-employed. This information is necessary whether parents/guardians are separated, divorced or not married.

While each family is expected to contribute to tuition to the maximum extent that is economically feasible, the schools do not expect tuition levels to be the same for all. Financial aid, indexed or flexible tuition funding is distributed from a school's operating budget, unrestricted endowment income, or specifically targeted funds. Schools encourage families to apply for financial aid if they have any concerns regarding their ability to pay full tuition. A financial aid administrator notes: "You know what the answer is if you do not apply for aid."

Aid forms are available with admission applications and are expected to be submitted by a deadline date. Schools do not guarantee funding as the number of requests usually exceed the available funds. Consequently, they cannot fund all the deserving families and students that apply for aid. The schools try to be as equitable as possible giving first priority to their current families. Most of the time parents receive the aid offer with the acceptance notification letters. Usually the school will continue the financial aid award for the term of the student's enrollment assuming family circumstances remain unchanged. Generally, tax returns and relevant attachments, W-2's, Business and Farm Statements, as well as the form for divorced or separated parents are required each year. Because of limited funding, schools want to make sure that need is demonstrated annually.

The Catholic school financial aid applications are processed by the Archdiocese, which offers limited financial aid grants.

Private scholarship funds are also available for students. Parents must show evidence of qualifying income status for funding eligibility. One of these sources is The BASIC Fund (Bay Area Scholarships for Inner city Children) which grants up to $1500 per child wishing to attend a registered K-8 private school (415-986-5650, www.basicfund. org). Grants are based on household size and income, and the child must meet all academic and admission requirements of a registered private school. Currently, The BASIC Fund supports over 3500 students in Alameda, Marin, San Francisco and San Mateo counties. The program is referred to as "Helping Hand" and promotes a partnership with parents and their involvement with their child's school. The application deadline is usually the April 15th following the school notification letters. If a grant is awarded, the BASIC Fund will pay the school directly on the family's behalf.

The Guardsmen Scholarship Program (415-561-2700, www. guardsmen.org) grants a maximum of $2,000 for students entering K-6 private schools in the Bay Area. Presently The Guardsmen supports 194 students. Students who are currently in the program will be supported through Grade 12 subject to an annual application, funding availability, a minimum 2.0 GPA, and family income eligibility. The application deadline is April 15 and the tuition assistance payment is made directly to the school.

If a family receives funding from either The BASIC Fund or The Guardsmen, they are not eligible to receive scholarship funding from the other. Families are, however, eligible for school based financial aid. The family will be responsible to the school for any tuition costs and fees in excess of the scholarship.

The SMART Program (Students Mentoring and Resource Team) offers full tuition grants as well as uniform and book costs to economically disadvantaged San Francisco public school children. These grants are for children entering sixth grade through eighth grade. Students apply in March of fourth grade and the selection process continues through fifth grade. "Candidates must demonstrate strong academic potential, sincere motivation and a commitment to participate in a year-round program." The SMART program "provides students with high-quality academic and extracurricular opportunities as well as a network of ongoing support to ensure a smooth transition into their new schools and to promote a successful academic experience for each child" (415-865-5400, www.thesmartprogram.org).

Conventional loans that DO need to be repaid can be researched on the following sites: www.slmededucationloans.com, www.tuition-pay.com, www.teri.org, www.estudentloan.com, www.prepgate.com, www.afford.com, www.yourtuitionsolution.com (Source: www.finaid.org). Other sources might include home equity loans, 401 K borrowings, personal loans, low interest credit card loans, and gifts. Parents should explore other funding sources such as from grandparents and other family members. Currently monetary gifts for tuition and other school expenses are not subject to gift tax if the tuition is paid directly to the school based on a school invoice. Always check with tax professionals for current regulations.

Mission Statement/Academic Program

Private schools in California are required to follow only general guidelines promulgated by the State in establishing their curricula. Under these guidelines, they are required to "offer instruction in the several branches of study required to be taught in the public schools of the state" (Education Code, Section 48222). The branches of education are broadly defined, leaving schools more latitude than guidance. For example, private schools are required to teach mathematics, including concepts, operational skills, and problem solving in grades one through six. Beyond these general mandates, each school makes its own curriculum decisions or implements the curriculum requirements or guidelines of its governing organization.

It is important that parents understand and support the mission, philosophy and academic program of any school their children attend. To this end, schools were asked for their mission statement or educational philosophy and for a description of their academic program.

The mission statement or philosophy describes the school's overall approach to education. Often such statements are very general. The language should, however, give an indication of the relative importance in the program of academics, spiritual education, character development, physical education, and other aspects of education. Parents should ask questions of the school to make sure they agree with and can support the curriculum. This is especially true if parents send a child to a religious school. Parents should consider how religion affects academic content in terms of faith-based topics and discussions, religious themes, family life perspectives, etc.

Parents need to be aware that teaching philosophies and methods have changed significantly over the past twenty years. Parents who experienced a traditional education may be surprised to find a plethora of pedagogical innovations that may include such practices as cooperative learning, peer tutoring, inventive spelling, use of calculators and laptops, and project based learning.

Schools were asked about subject offerings including music, drama, art, PE and foreign languages and the hours per week of instruction. Many schools are devoting considerable resources offering up-to-date technology, and computer training and classes in keyboarding, digital media, web design, etc. are common. Conversely, some schools choose to exclude computers from their classrooms based on philosophical reasons.

Parents who have strong feelings about what and how they expect their child to learn—whether in math, reading, writing, science, art, or other subjects—should make sure they select a school that will meet their expectations.

Homework

In this guide, the schools have provided average homework time. Parents should take into consideration that this is just an average and homework time varies considerably from child to child. An increasing number of schools are posting homework assignments on the Internet or sending them home via e-mail to increase communication between home and school.

High Schools

Parents should consider a grade school's high school placement in gauging a K-8 program's effectiveness. High school admission reflects numerous factors such as students' academic, athletic, artistic qualifications; curricular and co-curricular high school offerings; economic, geographic considerations; and college placement, etc. High schools may prefer students from one particular school more than another, or they may seek students from a variety of K-8 schools to create a more diversified student body.

A useful source to help evaluate high schools is *Private High Schools of the San Francisco Bay Area (3rd Ed.)*, by Betsy Little and Paula Molligan. The book profiles 65 private high schools throughout the Bay Area with information on SAT scores, college placement, costs, etc. See the back of this guide for more information.

Faculty

Schools were asked for teachers' ethnicity, educational qualifications, and the teacher/student ratio. Private schools are required by law to have a criminal check of all employees, but teachers are not required to hold a California teaching credential. Many private school teachers are credentialed for the State of California while others hold credentials from other states. Private schools may use their discretion about teacher qualifications. For instance, schools may choose to hire a PhD in biology to teach science without regard to a specific credential. Most private schools require teachers to have earned at least a bachelor's degree. Faculty qualifications are often described in school literature.

Private schools set their own policies concerning continuing teacher education/training. Teachers may be required to attend teacher in-service days and participate in various professional activities such as conferences and graduate level college courses.

The teacher/student ratio is sometimes deceiving. Parents are advised to get further explanations from the school for the teacher/student ratio. Check whether schools use full-time faculty or include aides in their statistic. Also ask if a portion of the class is separated or grouped together for certain subjects to accurately judge the effective teacher/student ratio. Find out if and how frequently full or part-time aides are used in the classroom.

Special Subject Teachers

This category refers to teachers whose area of expertise is in a given subject. These teachers are trained professionals for that specific discipline.

Middle School

Many schools separate older students in a middle school section which may begin as early as fifth grade. Typically, these programs feature a curriculum specific to early adolescents. This may include departmentalization, accelerated classes, advisory groups, special elective course offerings, interscholastic sports, etc. Accelerated classes may be offered in a variety of subjects, and more often than not, schools are providing tracking in mathematics.

It is important for parents of all entry applicants to view classes in upper grades in order to observe what a school is building towards. Parents need to keep in mind that high schools use academic records primarily from sixth through eighth grade in determining admission eligibility.

Middle school programs usually sponsor a variety of social activities which can include hiking, bowling, pizza socials, school dances, ice skating, and the like. These activities are typically chaperoned by teachers and/or parent volunteers and are designed to promote positive social adolescent interactions.

Support Services

Schools were asked about student support services that include licensed counselors, counselor/student ratio and the number of learning specialists on staff. In addition, schools were asked to describe their support for learning differences and their high school placement program. As with the faculty/student ratio, these statistics can be misleading. Parents should inquire if the counselor's duties are primarily as advisors to faculty or if they work directly with students individually or in small group settings.

Similarly, parents should investigate available support for children with learning differences. Learning differences are often masked and not always apparent in young children, but become evident in middle school. Thus, parents of early grade applicants might not know if their child will need these services.

A learning difference or disability affects the way children of average to above average intelligence process, receive or express information. With intervention and support a child can learn compensatory strategies. If a child has learning differences, it is important to choose a school that makes accommodations and provides the necessary support. The extent of services offered varies among the schools. Each school in this Guide was asked what special programs or resources it has for children with learning disabilities or differences. Some schools give students additional support such as: study guides, extra time on tests, an accommodated curriculum and/or tutorial assistance. If no programs or resources are provided by the school, students may be referred to outside tutors. Additional charges for many of these programs may be assessed and parents should inquire about the costs.

If parents are aware of any specific learning issues, it is advisable to discuss them with the respective admission director in order to ascertain if the school is an appropriate fit. Some of the schools in this Guide do an excellent job accommodating a broad range of student abilities.

High school placement services can range from no services to a full-time counselor. Admission to Bay Area high schools is extremely competitive and a daunting task for adolescents and parents. As a result, many families appreciate the assistance of school placement professionals.

Student Conduct and Health

Schools were asked to describe their discipline/behavior policy as well as their preventative education and awareness programs. Schools described programs and/or policies such as: character development, diversity, harassment, etc. Parents should be comfortable with the behavior standards of an individual school so they can support the school's policies.

Private schools do not face the constraints that public schools do in removing students whose behavior is harmful to themselves or to other students. Private school reaction to discipline issues can be swift when necessary because they are not required to undergo a lengthy appeal process.

Schools were also asked about their preventative education programs such as drug/alcohol awareness, sex education classes, health issues and the like. This education is sometimes integrated within a specific discipline such as science and other times it is taught as a separate course.

Athletics

Most schools in this Guide offer students physical education classes two to five times a week taught by a PE specialist. Many offer competitive sports beginning as early as third grade through intramural teams, private school leagues or the Catholic Youth Organization (CYO).

Campus Life

Many Marin County schools offer campuses with park-like settings. Most San Francisco schools have limited outdoor facilities often using rooftops, paved playgrounds or nearby parks for outdoor sports. Most schools in both locations offer lovely buildings, spacious well-equipped classrooms, libraries, computer labs, a gym, and auditorium or gathering space that accommodate the student body.

School libraries vary considerably in number of volumes, use of technology, square footage and ambience. Many educators view a library as a focal point of an elementary school and consider it an integral part of a school's academic life. Parents should take note of how welcoming a library appears to children and if it encourages participation. In addition, parents should inquire about library accessibility, library staffing and scheduled library time for students.

Most schools have designated computer labs staffed by technology specialists. In addition, some schools offer class sets of laptops and desktops for general classroom use. Educators use computers as a tool for learning. Many campuses have wireless networks and offer advanced courses in technology.

Extended Day Programs

Parents should examine extended care facilities with the same care they give to the classroom. The extended day programs sometimes use common school areas such as classrooms and gyms or they are housed in a separate designated facility. It is advisable to learn about the facilities, the staffing qualifications, programs offered, age groupings, space availability, the cost and vacation coverage. Some extended day programs offer relaxed free play in a home-like environment, and others can pack a child's afternoon full of sports, language classes, and individual tutoring. Costs of extended care range from free to more than $18 per hour. Drop-in care can cost more. The cost of after-school enrichment classes are usually in addition to extended day fees.

Extended care programs also vary in terms of flexibility. They may be limited to children who sign up for the entire semester or year, or they may allow occasional or drop-in use. Some schools automatically send children who are not picked up by dismissal time to the extended care program and charge the parents for "drop-in" care. Others send the children to the school office to wait for parents. At some schools, parents pay in advance for extended care and unused hours are not refunded; other schools allow parents to pay for hourly use.

Extended care programs should be evaluated for not only for age-appropriate programs but also for age-appropriate security. Parents are encouraged to ask about fenced play yards, locked doors or gates leading to the play yards, and sign-in/sign-out procedures, etc. Parents should check daycare availability for vacation and holiday coverage.

Summer Programs

Nearly all of the schools in this guide operate on a nine and one-half-month calendar from late August or early September to early or mid-June. Many schools have summer programs, but only a few offer summer programs that last the entire summer. If schools offer summer programs they are generally open to the public as well as to their current students.

Parent Involvement

All schools would like parents to participate in their fundraising efforts. Indeed, for schools to be attractive for grant and foundation support the schools must show a high level of parent, faculty and alumni participation. Pledges or donations are encouraged because schools often depend on these funds to bridge the difference between tuition and actual educational costs. Schools count on families donating funds at appropriate giving levels. Many schools allow parents to make monthly payments toward their pledges or donations. If schools have required parent participation it is noted.

One of the signs of a good school is parent involvement. Schools often require parents to give a certain amount of time volunteering for activities such as fundraising, auctions, school maintenance, newsletters, field trips, etc. Sometimes schools offer weekend or evening opportunities and permit parents to pay a fee in lieu of volunteer hours.

What Sets the School Apart from Others

This category provided each school the opportunity to characterize its uniqueness. Parents should take special note of this category as an indicator of how a school differentiates itself from other schools.

Editor's Notes

1. This guide does not include schools primarily serving children with special needs. Parents should seek recommendations from school placement specialists as to these schools.

2. The information set forth in this guide was gathered in Spring-Summer, 2005. Information was requested only from K-8 schools or schools that are in the process of expanding to K-8.

3. Schools that would like to be included in future editions of this book may contact Pince-Nez Press at (415) 267-5978 or info@pince-nez.com.

4. Unless otherwise indicated, financial aid information relates to financial aid provided by or through the school, not aid from other sources.

5. Much of the information in this guide reflects a compilation and condensation of the information provided by the schools. Quotations represent qualitative information provided by the school. These quotations might be altered by editing including the use of abbreviations, and punctuation to shorten the length of quotes to meet space restrictions.

6. San Francisco geographical districts noted by the editor after each school's address are based upon areas of the city recognized by the City Planning Department. If a second designation is given it is because the school is close to another district or because the second designation is a commonly used term for the area.

7. We have worked hard to make sure the information in this guide is accurate as of the date of printing. Schools change their programs and costs regularly so parents should rely on a school's most up-to-date information. School's inclusion in this guide is at the editor's discretion and invitation. Schools that did not respond to the survey in a timely fashion, or chose not to participate are listed in the back of the guide.

8. Schools are secular unless otherwise noted.

Acronyms and Abbreviations

ACS	Accrediting Commission for Schools
ALA	American Library Association
AEFE	L'Agence pour l'Enseigement Français à l'Etranger
AMI	Association Montessori Internationale
AMS	American Montessori Society
ASCD	Association for Supervision and Curriculum Development
ASCI	Associated Christian Schools International
AWSNA	Association of Waldorf Schools, North America
BAAD	Bay Area Admissions Directors (High Schools)
BADA	Bay Area Directors of Admissions (Grade Schools)
BADH	Bay Area Division Heads
BAIHS	Bay Area Independent High Schools
BAISHA	Bay Area Independent School Head Association
BAISL	Bay Area Independent School Librarians
BAMA	Bay Area Montessori Association
BASIC Fund	Bay Area Scholarships for Inner city Children
BJE	Bureau of Jewish Education
CAIS	California Association of Independent Schools
CASE	Council for Advancement and Support of Education
CAT	California Achievement Test
CBSA	California Boarding School Association
CIS	Council of International Schools
CTBS	California Test of Basic Skills
DARE	Drug Abuse Resistance Education
EPGY	Education Program for Gifted Youth
ERB	Educational Records Bureau
ESHA	European School Heads Association
ETS	Educational Testing Service
FCE	Friends Council on Education
G	Grade(s)

GLSEN	Gay, Lesbian, and Straight Educators Network
hr(s)	hour(s)
HS	High School
IBO	International Baccalaureate Organization
IBSC	International Boys School Coalition
IEP	Individual Education Plan
IMC	Instructional Media Center
ISAL	Independent School Athletic League
ISBOA	Independent Schools Business Officers Assn.
ISEE	Independent Schools Entrance Exam
ITBS	Iowa Test of Basic Skills
JESNA	Jewish Education Service of North America
LC-MS	Lutheran Church, Missouri Synod
min.	minute(s)
N/A	Not Available or Not Applicable
N/P	Not provided
NAES	National Association of Episcopal Schools
NAIPS	National Association of Independent Private Schools
NAIS	National Association of Independent Schools
NCEA	National Catholic Educational Association
NCGS	National Coalition of Girls Schools
NIPSA	National Independent Private School Association
NLSA	National Lutheran Schools Association
PE	Physical education
PEJE	Partnership for Excellence in Jewish Education
PFS	Personal Financial Statement
POCIS	Bay Area People of Color in Independent schools
PPSL	Peninsula Parochial Sports League
SAT	Stanford Achievement Test
SF	San Francisco
SMART	Students Mentoring and Resource Team
SPCAL	South Peninsula Catholic Athletic League
SSAT	Secondary School Admission Test
SSATB	Secondary School Admission Test Board
SSS	School Scholarship Service

TABS	The Association of Boarding Schools
TBA	To be announced
WASC	Western Association of Schools and Colleges
WCEA	Western Catholic Education Association

HIGH SCHOOL ABBREVIATIONS

Independent schools

Athenian: The Athenian School (Danville, coed)
Bay School: The Bay School (SF, coed)
Bentley: Bentley School (Lafayette, coed)
Branson: The Branson School (Ross, coed)
Castilleja: Castilleja School (Palo Alto, girls)
College Prep: The College Preparatory School (Oakland, coed)
CSH: Convent of the Sacred Heart High School (SF, girls)
Crystal: Crystal Springs Uplands School (Hillsborough, coed)
Drew: Drew College Preparatory School (SF, coed)
Head-Royce: The Head-Royce School (Oakland, coed)
IHS: International High School (SF, coed)
Lick: Lick-Wilmerding High School (SF, coed)
Lycée: Lycée Français La Pérouse (SF & Marin, coed)
MA: Marin Academy (San Rafael, coed)
Marin School: The Marin School (Sausalito, coed)
Menlo: Menlo School, (Atherton, coed)
Sacred Heart: Sacred Heart Preparatory (Atherton, coed)
San Domenico: San Domenico School (San Anselmo, girls)
SF Waldorf: San Francisco Waldorf High School (SF, coed)
Sonoma Academy (Santa Rosa, coed)
Sterne: Sterne School (SF, coed)
Stuart Hall: Stuart Hall High School (SF, boys)
University: University High School, (San Francisco, coed)
Urban: The Urban School of San Francisco (SF, coed)
Wheery: Wheery Academy (Redwood City, coed)
Woodside: Woodside International School (SF, coed)
Woodside Priory: Woodside Priory School, (Portola Valley, coed)

Catholic Schools
Bellarmine: Bellarmine College Preparatory (San Jose, boys)
ICA: Immaculate Conception Academy (SF, girls)
MC: Marin Catholic College Preparatory (Kentfield, coed)
Mercy–Burlingame: Mercy High School (Burlingame, girls)
Mercy–SF: Mercy High School (SF, girls)
Mitty: Archbishop Mitty High School (San Jose, coed)
Note Dame: Notre Dame High School (Belmont, girls)
Presentation: Presentation High School (San Jose, girls)
Riordan: Archbishop Riordan High School (SF, boys)
SHCP: Sacred Heart Cathedral Preparatory School (SF, coed)
St. Francis: St. Francis High School (Mountain View, coed)
St. Ignatius/SI: St. Ignatius College Preparatory (SF, coed)
St. Lawrence: St. Lawrence Academy (Santa Clara, coed)
Serra: Junipero Serra High School (San Mateo, boys)

Jewish Schools
JCHS: Jewish Community High School of the Bay (SF, coed)
Lisa Kampner Hebrew Academy (SF, coed)

[Ed. Note: Information on these and other private (independent and
parochial) Bay Area high schools can be found in *Private High Schools
of the San Francisco Bay Area (3rd Ed.)*, authored by Little and Molligan and published by Pince-Nez Press. See back of this book for more
information.]

Private Boarding Schools
Andover: Phillips Academy Andover (MA)
Avon: Avon Old Farms School (CT)
Cate: Cate School (CA)
Choate: Choate Rosemary Hall (CT)
Colorado Rocky Mountain School (CO)
Dana: Dana Hall School (MA)
John Cooper School (TX)
Deerfield: Deerfield Academy (MA)

Ethel Walker: The Ethel Walker School (CT)
Exeter: Phillips Exeter Academy (NH)
Foxcroft: Foxcroft School (VA)
Groton: Groton School (MA)
Gunnery: The Gunnery (CT)
Hawaii Preparatory Academy (HI)
Hotchkiss: The Hotchkiss School (CT)
Kent School (CT)
Lawrence Academy (MA)
Middlesex: Middlesex School (MA)
Midland: Midland School (CA)
Proctor: Proctor Academy (NH)
St. Andrew's School (DE)
St. Mark's: St. Mark's School (MA)
St. Paul's: St. Paul's School (NH)
Santa Catalina: Santa Catalina School (CA)
Stevenson: Robert Louis Stevenson School (CA)
Thacher: The Thacher School (CA)
Vanguard: Vanguard Academy (FL)

Foreign Private Schools
Lycée International (Paris, France)

Public Schools
Alameda: Alameda High School (Alameda)
Aragon: Aragon High School (San Mateo)
Burlingame: Burlingame High School (Burlingame)
Burton: Phillip and Sala Burton High School (magnet, SF)
Capuchino High School (San Bruno)
CAT: City Arts and Technology High School (charter, SF)
Christian High School: Alma Heights Christian Academy (Alma Heights)
Deer Valley: Deer Valley High School (Antioch)
Drake: Sir Francis Drake High School (San Anselmo)
El Camino: El Camino High School (South San Francisco)
Galileo: Galileo High School (magnet, SF)

Gateway: Gateway High School (charter, SF)
Golden Gate: Golden Gate High School (charter, SF)
ISA: International Studies Academy (SF)
June Jordan School for Equity (SF)
Leadership: Leadership High School (charter, SF)
Lincoln: Abraham Lincoln High School (SF)
Lowell: Lowell High School (magnet, SF)
Marin School of the Arts (Novato)
Marin School of Art and Technology (Novato)
Novato High School (Novato)
Tamalpais: Tamalpais High School (Mill Valley)
Redwood: Redwood High School (Larkspur)
San Marin: San Marin High School (Novato)
San Mateo: San Mateo High School (San Mateo)
San Rafael: San Rafael High School (San Rafael)
SOTA: San Francisco School of the Arts (magnet, SF)
Terra Linda: Terra Linda High School (San Rafael)
Terra Nova: Terra Nova High School (Pacifica)
Thurgood Marshall: Thurgood Marshall Academic High School (magnet, SF)
Washington: George Washington High School (SF)
Wallenberg: Raul Wallenberg High School (SF)
Westmoor: Westmoor High School (Daly City)

SCHOOLS

ADDA CLEVENGER JUNIOR PREPARATORY AND THEATER SCHOOL FOR CHILDREN
180 Fair Oaks Street (at 23rd) (Mission/Noe Valley)
San Francisco, CA 94110
(415) 824-2240
www.addaclevenger.org

Carol Harrison, Head of School, acjp@pacbell.net
George Nearon, Director of Admission, acjp@pacbell.net

General
Coed K-8 day school. Founded in 1980. For profit. **Member:** N/P. **Enrollment:** Approx. 150. **Average class size:** 14. **Accreditation:** "The school has been in operation 25 years and has not sought accreditation." **Endowment:** N/P. **School year:** Year-round. **Instructional days:** 200 +8 required performance days. **School day:** Begins at 8:30 a.m. Dismissal is 4:15 p.m. for K-4, 5 p.m. for G5, 5:30 p.m. for G6-8.

Student Body
Ethnicity: "Diverse student body."

Admission
Applications due: For K, Sept.-March; for G1-8, throughout the year on a space-available basis. **Application fee:** $100. **Application process:** Parents attend a Saturday afternoon information meeting hosted by teachers and parents. They are then invited by appointment to visit when classes are in session. Classroom visits are scheduled Tuesdays and Thursdays from 8:40 to 10:30 a.m. **No. of applications:** N/P. **No. of K spaces:** 24-30. **Percentage of K class made up of school's preschool class:** N/A. **Admission evaluation requirements for K:** Readiness for a full day (8:30 a.m. to 4:15 p.m. with rest time, but

no nap time) and first grade level curriculum—to be determined by parents and Director. **Other grades:** Students attend school two full days. Teachers evaluate placement and make recommendations based on their observations. Interviews with parents and students are part of this process. **Preferences:** N/P. **What sort of student do you best serve?** "Students of above average learning ability who have a good attention span and an eagerness to learn."

Costs

Latest tuition: $13,290 ($12,000 tuition plus fees). **Sibling discount:** $800 for each sibling. **Tuition includes:** Lunch: No; Transportation: No; Laptop computer: No; Other: All fees are included in tuition. **Tuition increases:** Approx. 4-6% annually, if any. Increases are not automatic. **Other costs:** Approx. $350+ for uniforms, and costs for field trips, personal costume items and dance shoes; tickets to professional and high school productions; concert tours/music festivals (G6–8 Concert Group and/or Show Choir); and speech tournament fees (Junior High). **Percentage of students receiving financial aid:** "None. We are able to charge a moderate tuition because all students pay the same amount. Exception: Family emergency, short term basis." **Financial aid application deadline:** N/A. **Average grant:** N/A. **Percentage of grants of half-tuition or more:** N/A. **Donations:** The school requests admission donations to the annual December holiday concert and summer graduation concert.

School's Mission Statement

"The mission of the Adda Clevenger School is to serve children who are able to accomplish more than they are allowed to do in a regular classroom, where the teacher must pay close attention to students who require more repetition. Quick learners often do not get their time's worth out of the school day. We believe that all normal learners have the potential to become gifted and talented if given the opportunity. At Adda Clevenger an environment has been designed to stimulate, challenge and inspire students to open as many doors as possible and to provide opportunities to develop their talents to the fullest. By eighth grade they should be well prepared to qualify for admission to college preparatory high schools."

Academic Program

Philosophy: "The philosophy of the school is best expressed by James J. Gallagher, an educator especially interested in the needs of gifted children, who writes, 'We can create giftedness through designing enriched environments and opportunities, or we can destroy it by failing to create those environments and opportunities.' The curriculum is designed to cover subjects appropriate to the formal education of children, exceeding state requirements. No special agendas are served. After a short evaluative session Kindergarten children begin first grade level work including science, social studies, handwriting, creative expression, art, acrobatics, music and dance. A systematic phonics-based program is used to teach reading and spelling. The K-4 math program emphasizes acquisition of basic computational skills, moving to more complex concepts including pre-algebra and geometry. Eighth grade students complete Algebra 1 and some begin second year high school math during the eighth grade year. Because the international tradition of a longer school day and year is followed, students are able to enjoy the challenges of a full performing arts curriculum as well as accelerated academics and sports. The creative and performing arts program consists of writing, art, improvisational and performance drama, dramatic literature, dance, floor gymnastics, chorus and show choir, private vocal instruction, music theory and hand bell choir." **Foreign languages:** "A variety of languages for fun and as needed in the choral music program." **Computer training:** "Computers are used sparingly at school. The goal of formal education should be to help each child develop to full potential his/her own natural computer. Sitting in front of a man-made computer probably is not the best means to that end. We encourage the use of computers at home at an early age, but do not require it." **No. of computers available for students:** N/A. **No. of hours weekly of:** Art- Lower School 1.5-3, Upper School varies; Drama- varies according to age; Music- 1.5 (K) to 8.5 (G6-8) including theory, performance rehearsals and individual vocal coaching; Computers- N/A; Foreign language- N/A; PE- daily. **Outdoor education:** N/P. **Grading:** Two formal annual assessment reports sent to parents, both letter and narrative, with course summaries once or twice each school year. Letter grades begin in K. **Average nightly homework:** "Age appropriate.

Many students complete homework in supervised extended care classes." Posted on the Internet: No. **Percentage of students participating in Johns Hopkins Center for Talented Youth Program:** "None, as it conflicts with our year-round schedule." **Other indicators of academic success:** "Individual assessment by teachers, test scores (of questionable value), acceptances to college preparatory high schools, academic achievement and awards at both high school and college level." **High schools attended by latest graduating class:** Lowell, University, Lick, Urban, JCHS, SHCP, CSH, IHS, Mercy-SF, San Domenico, Drew, Crystal, Notre Dame Belmont.

Faculty

Ethnicity: "Diverse ethnicity includes Russian, Chinese, Filipino, Spanish, Swiss, Polish and American." **Percentage of teachers with graduate degrees:** 75%. **Percentage with current California credential:** N/P. **Faculty selection/training:** Teachers are selected based on experience with and special interest in subjects they are hired to teach. They need to be able to work independently and as a team. Many of the classes are team taught. All new teachers receive on the job training from faculty members who are experienced with Adda Clevenger teaching methods. Requirements in lieu of credential are BA/MA, significant teaching experience or demonstrated knowledge of assigned subjects, and references. **Teacher/student ratio:** Approx. 1:10 in K-4; approx. 1:14 in G5-8. **Special subject teachers:** "All teachers specialize in the subjects they teach." **Average teacher tenure:** 8 years.

Middle School

Description: G6-8. **Teacher/student ratio:** Ranges from 7-24 students in a class, depending on subject. **Elective courses offered:** N/P. **Achievement tracking in:** Math and English. **Student social events:** Back to school picnic/swim party; trips to Europe, Ashland, New York, Columbia (California); annual Halloween party at Pier 39 and on the Bay; Raging Waters in San Jose during Intersession; lunches downtown before attending theater; parties a Mel's after attending high school performances; graduation and dinner and show (Teatro ZinZanni or Beach Blanket Babylon).

Student Support Services

No. of Licensed Counselors on staff: N/P. **Counselor/student ratio:** N/P. **Learning specialists on staff:** None. **Learning differences/disabilities support:** None. **High school placement support:** A Placement Counselor assists students and parents. During Intersession (last two weeks of August, first week of September) high school teachers and former high school admissions directors give workshops on the admissions process including essay and interview preparation for seventh and eight grade students. Test prep classes are part of the Math and English courses during Intercession and the first semester of eighth grade. Students take the SSAT at the end of seventh grade and again in eighth grade.

Student Conduct and Health

Code of conduct: N/P. **Prevention education and awareness addressed in:** "This is part of the social studies/current events curriculum. We have an annual visit from a member of AA who talks about alcohol and drug abuse. This also is covered from time to time by the current events magazine used in social studies classes. Sex education is considered the parents' responsibility, but does enter the classroom whenever a topic such as teen pregnancies, AIDS, etc. is featured in the same student news magazine designed for seventh to ninth grade students."

Athletics

Sports offered: Gymnastics, basketball, dancesport, and age-appropriate sports games. **Team play begins in:** N/A.

Campus/Campus Life

Campus description: The school is located in a historic twelve thousand square foot building (circa 1908) in San Francisco's Noe Valley. On the ground floor there are four classrooms, a small library, a large art room, an auditorium and stage. The upper floor has four classrooms, a dance studio, music/chorus room, offices, and a resource room. **Library:** Small, approximately 800 volumes. Children also use the local public library. **Sports facilities:** Two fenced-in playgrounds with a basketball court. **Theater/Arts facilities:** Auditorium, stage, dance studio, music rehearsal room, art room. **Computer lab:** No. **Science lab:** Yes. **Lunch program:** No. **Bus service:** No. **Uniforms/dress code:** Dress code. **Opportunities for community service:** Yes.

Extended Day

Morning care: Begins at 7:30 a.m. **After-school care:** Until 6 p.m. **Grade levels:** All. G5-8 are in class until 5:30 daily. **Cost:** $64.40 to $128.80. **Drop-in care available:** Yes. **Coverage over major holidays:** No. **Homework help:** Yes. **Snacks:** Not provided. **Staff/student ratio:** N/P. **After-school classes:** For students in K-4, the school day lasts until 4:15 p.m., then they have homework class, sports or visit the art room. Students in G5-8 are in regularly scheduled academic and performing arts classes until 5 p.m. or 5:30 p.m. daily. Cost: $50 monthly for G5-6 after 4:15. No charge for middle school students.

Summer Programs

The school's three-week Creative Summer Day Camp (non-academic) is optional, but included in tuition. It involves art, sports, music, dance, drama, and rehearsals for the gymnastics demos and musical to be performed for parents on the last day. Children help paint backdrops, make props, etc. **Cost:** Included in tuition.

Parent Involvement

Parent/teacher communication: Newsletters and e-mail. Parent/teacher conferences scheduled at parents' or teachers' request. **Participation requirements:** Parents are required to support and attend all student performances. There are many opportunities for parent involvement and all are strictly voluntary. Members of the Parent Association assist with the annual dinner, dance, and auction held in conjunction with the San Francisco Sinfonietta. **Parent education programs offered?:** No.

What Sets the School Apart From Others

"While there are many excellent private academic schools in San Francisco, Adda Clevenger stands alone in providing a double curriculum—accelerated academics and performing arts. All students are members of the Adda Clevenger Youth Chorus of San Francisco. Middle School choristers twice have been invited to sing at the White House; have been on European concert tours—in the summer of 2004 they participated in the Salzburg Music Festival and ten concerts in Switzerland and Italy; on March 6, 2005 they performed at Carnegie Hall, New York, in the National Middle School Honor Choir. Summer, 2006, they will travel to England to participate in the Ninth Annual International Children's Choir Festival at Canterbury and London. Every year all students take part in three full musical productions ranging from Gilbert and Sullivan operettas to Broadway musicals and dance shows. There are choral concerts held in December and June, and gymnastics demonstrations in July. As part of their training, children in Middle School attend many live performances during the year. They also compete in two speech tournaments. At Adda Clevenger, children get more from their time spent in school."

How Parents/Students Characterize School

Parent comment(s): "Please visit school on Parent Information Day. Parents host the meeting and are happy to tell you why they chose and why they remain at Adda Clevenger."
Student comment(s): "On class tour days students enjoy talking with visitors and 'showing off' their school."

BRANDEIS HILLEL DAY SCHOOL, MARIN
180 N. San Pedro Road
San Rafael, CA 94903
(415) 472-1833 *fax (415) 491-1317*
www.bhds.org

Dr. Henry Shreibman, Head of School
Susan Levinson, Director of Admission, slevinson@bhds.org

General
Co-ed K-8 Jewish day school. Founded in 1963. Independent. Nonprofit. **Member:** CAIS, BADA, SSAT, ERB. **Enrollment:** Approx.

200. **Average class size:** 18. **Accreditation:** CAIS (6-year term: 2000-06). **Endowment:** $7.2 million. **School year:** Sept.-June. **Instructional days:** 174. **School day:** 8:20 a.m. to 3:15 p.m. for G1-8, 8:20 a.m. to 2 p.m. for K.

Student Body
Ethnicity: N/P.

Admission
Applications due: Jan. (call for date). **Application fee:** $75. **Application process:** N/P. **No. of applications:** N/P. **No. of Kindergarten spaces:** 22-26. **Percentage of K class made up of school's preschool class:** N/A. **Admission evaluation requirements for K:** Screening, recommendations, parent interview. **Other grades:** Test scores, report cards, school visit, screening. **Preferences:** N/P. **What sort of student do you best serve?** "Intellectually curious, tolerant, socially aware."

Costs
Latest tuition: $17,400 for K-7, $18,400 for G8. **Sibling discount:** None. **Tuition includes:** Lunch: No; Transportation: No; Laptop computer: No; Other: Field trips and outdoor education. **Tuition increases:** N/P. **Other costs:** None. **Percentage of students receiving financial aid:** 30%. **Financial aid application deadline:** Jan. (call for date). Financial aid is based on need. **Average grant:** N/P. **Percentage of grants of half-tuition or more:** N/P. **Donations:** The school expects 100% participation from parents.

School's Mission Statement
"The mission of Brandeis Hillel Day School is to serve the Jewish community by providing children with an outstanding academic program in general and Judaic studies within a dynamic and diverse Jewish cultural environment."

Academic Program
Philosophy: "Our academic program is both challenging and age-appropriate which together create an environment for each child to excel." **Foreign languages:** Hebrew. **Computer training:** "All students

have access to a multi-media lab and media information library." **No. of computers available for students:** 60. **No. of hours weekly of:** Art- 1; Drama- 1; Music- 1; Computers- varies; Foreign language- 5; PE- 2-3. **Outdoor education:** G4-8. **Grading:** Varies by grades; letter grades begin in G4. **Average nightly homework:** Varies. Posted on the Internet: Yes. **Percentage of students participating in Johns Hopkins Center for Talented Youth Program:** N/P. **Other indicators of academic success:** "Test scores, high school and colleges attended." **High schools attended by latest graduating class:** Branson, MA, Urban, Redwood, San Rafael, Sonoma Academy, Terra Linda, JCHS, Drake, Tamalpais, and University.

Faculty

Ethnicity: N/P. **Percentage of teachers with graduate degrees:** 50%. **Percentage with current California credential:** 45%. **Faculty selection/training:** Experience, degrees, credentials, enthusiasm, commitment. **Teacher/student ratio:** 1:9. **Special subject teachers:** Art, music, technology, drama, PE. **Average teacher tenure:** 10-15 years.

Middle School

Description: "Our middle school endeavors to reach students on the academic, social and emotional levels by engaging students in interdisciplinary projects, by hiring teachers who understand the particular needs of middle school students, and by offering a challenging and rigorous program. Commences in G6." **Teacher/student ratio:** 1:9. **Elective courses offered:** Band, music, art, drama, musical theater, technology. **Achievement tracking in:** All academic areas. **Student social events:** Dances, a middle school retreat, and joint activities with the school's SF campus.

Student Support Services

No. of Licensed Counselors on staff: One part-time. **Counselor/student ratio:** N/P. **Learning specialists on staff:** One. **Learning differences/disabilities support:** Full-time learning specialist. **High school placement support:** "The high school placement counselor works with 8th grade families to find the best high school fit for the student."

Student Conduct and Health

Code of conduct: Discipline/behavior policy. **Prevention education and awareness addressed in:** Drugs, sex, health, and harassment programs.

Athletics

Sports offered: Cross-country, basketball, track and field. **Team play begins in:** G3 (intramural).

Campus/Campus Life

Campus description: N/P. **Library:** 7,500 volumes, 24 wireless laptops. **Sports facilities:** Gymnasium, sports fields, pool. **Theater/Arts facilities:** Yes. **Computer lab:** Yes. **Science lab:** Yes. **Lunch program:** Yes. **Bus service:** No. **Uniforms/dress code:** Dress code. **Opportunities for community service:** "We provide all of our students with community service opportunities."

Extended Day

Morning care: Begins at 8 a.m. **After-school care:** Until 6 p.m. **Grade levels:** K-5. **Cost:** $6.50/hour. **Drop-in care available:** Yes. **Coverage over major holidays:** No. **Homework help:** Yes. **Snacks:** Not provided. **Staff/student ratio:** 1:10. **After-school classes:** Yes. **Cost:** N/P.

Summer Programs: N/P.

Parent Involvement

Parent/teacher communication: Conferences, website, e-mail, newsletter. **Participation requirements:** Voluntary. **Parent education programs offered?:** Yes.

What Sets the School Apart From Others

"Through a rigorous and nurturing program that uniquely integrates academics, values, technology and the arts, Brandeis Hillel Day School students become accomplished, independent, and creative thinkers who develop a life-long love of learning."

How Parents/Students Characterize School

Parent comment(s): "A place where families are welcomed into an inclusive, challenging, thoughtful and diverse Jewish community."
Student comment(s): "I love going to school."

Brandeis Hillel Day School, San Francisco

655 Brotherhood Way (at 19th Avenue) (Lakeshore/Park Merced)
San Francisco, CA 94132
(415) 406-1035   fax (415) 584-1099
www.bhds.org

Dr. Henry Shreibman, Head of School, hshreibman@bhds.org
Chaim Heller, Head of SF Campus, cheller@bhds.org
Tania Lowenthal, Director of Admission, tlowenthal@bhds.org

General

Co-ed K-8 community Jewish day school. Founded in 1963. Independent. Nonprofit. **Member:** CAIS, BADA, JESNA, ERB and SSAT. **Enrollment:** Approx. 380. **Average class size:** 21. **Accreditation:** WASC/CAIS (6-year term: 2000-06). **Endowment:** $7 million. **School year:** Sept.-June. **Instructional days:** 181. **School day:** 8:15 a.m. to 3:15 p.m.

Student Body

Ethnicity: 93.2% Caucasian (non-Latino), 3% Asian, 3% Latino, .8% African-American.

Admission
Applications due: Jan. 31st. **Application fee:** $75. **Application process:** School tours for K are conducted during regular school hours from September to January. Open houses are held in the fall for K and in February for middle school. Upon receipt of an application BHDS schedules an admission screening and parent interview. Notifications are mailed on a common date in cooperation with other Bay Area independent schools. **No. of applications:** N/P. **No. of K spaces:** 44.

Percentage of K class made up of school's preschool class: N/P. **Admission evaluation requirements for K:** Screening, recommendations. **Other grades:** School visit, test scores, school grades. **Preferences:** N/P. **What sort of student do you best serve?** "A student that thrives in an academically challenging environment and a 'radically kind' social atmosphere."

Costs

Latest tuition: $17,400 for K-7, $18,400 for G8. **Sibling discount:** No. **Tuition includes:** Lunch: No; Transportation: No; Laptop computer: No; Other: Books, materials, supplies, outdoor education trips, yearbook. **Tuition increases:** Approx. 4-8% annually. **Other costs:** None. **Percentage of students receiving financial aid:** 30%. **Financial aid application deadline:** Approx. Jan. 31st (call for date). Financial aid is based on need and the schools' resources. **Average grant:** N/P. **Percentage of grants of half tuition or more:** N/P. **Donations:** Voluntary donations for the annual fund, capital campaign, and auctions.

School's Mission Statement

"To serve the Jewish community by providing children with an outstanding academic program in general and Judaic studies within a dynamic and diverse Jewish cultural environment."

Academic Program

Philosophy: "We are deeply committed to the intellectual, social, spiritual and physical growth of our students. We also expect our children to develop compassion, tolerance and mutual respect for others. We guide them to become responsible citizens in our community and in the world." **Foreign languages:** Hebrew; Spanish as an elective. **Computer training:** "Technology is used as a tool to help students access the world and enhance their studies. Beginning in first grade, all classes have equal lab time. iMac computers, digital scanners and cameras, laser printers and educational software are available to provide opportunities for students to learn." **No. of computers available for students:** One per student in the computer lab and additional laptops for students through the portable "airport." **No. of hours weekly of:** Art- 1-2; Drama- 1-2; Music- 1-2; Computers- varies with class and project based curriculum; Foreign language- Hebrew daily, Spanish - elective; PE- 3. **Outdoor education:** "In 4th-8th grades, students participate in extended class trips. Our educational mission is to integrate a strong academic and cultural program with a challenging outdoor experience and travel. In the 4th grade students explore California's Gold Country; 5th graders go to the Northern California coast for a science and outdoor camping experience; 6th graders participate in a four-day outdoor science camp at Yosemite National Park. 7th graders attend the Ashland Shakespeare Festival and go river rafting in southern Oregon; in the 8th grade, students take a week-long trip to Washington DC as a culmination of their social studies coursework." **Grading:** Letter grades begin in G5. **Average nightly homework:** None in K; 10-20 min. for G1; 20-30 min. for G2; 30-45 min. for G3; 45 min.-1 hr. for G4; 1 to 1-1.5 hrs. for G5-6; 2 hrs. for G7-8. Posted on the Internet: Yes, for middle school. **Percentage of students participating in Johns Hopkins Center for Talented Youth Program:** Over 60%. **Other indicators of academic success:** "ERB, Geo Bee." **High schools attended by latest graduating class:** Drew, IHS, JCHS, Lick, Urban, Hebrew Academy, SHCP, SI, Mercy, CAT, Gateway, Lincoln, Lowell, SOTA, Aragon, Burlingame, San Mateo, Terra Nova.

Faculty

Ethnicity: 73.3% Caucasian (non-Latino), 20% other, 6.7% Latino, 3% multi-racial. **Percentage of teachers with graduate degrees:** N/P. **Percentage with current California credential:** N/P. **Faculty selection/training:** "We hire the best teachers for the job. We recruit from professional organizations. BHDS has an extensive professional development program and all teachers are encouraged to participate." **Teacher/student ratio:** 1:9. **Special subject teachers:** Art, music, drama, PE, library, ESL, computers. **Average teacher tenure:** 8 years.

Middle School

Description: "Commences in G6. We recognize the changing needs of the emerging adolescent. Within our family-like atmosphere where there are many adults to provide support and nurturance, our students thrive. They continue to consolidate their scholastic achievements and to develop their problem-solving abilities. Our interdisciplinary curriculum weaves together an awareness of past and present connections and future possibilities." **Teacher/student ratio: 1:9. Elective courses offered:** Art studio, band, cooking, creative writing, drama, self defense, ethnobotany, journalism, yearbook, debate, track and fitness. **Achievement tracking in:** Language arts, math, social studies, science, Hebrew and Judaic Studies. **Student social events:** Dances, retreats, interaction with other schools through community service.

Student Support Services

No. of Licensed Counselors on staff: One full-time. **Counselor/student ratio:** N/A. **Learning specialists on staff:** The Dean of Faculty whose job it is to work with high achieving students and the ESL teacher. **Learning differences/disabilities support:** "The resource specialist works with students, parents, and staff to provide appropriate education for children identified with specific learning disabilities." **High school placement support:** "The High School Admissions Team assists eighth grade students and parents through the process. The vast majority of our students are accepted by their first and second choices to the finest public and private high schools."

Student Conduct and Health

Code of conduct: "Students are expected to behave in ways that promote physical safety and well-being, respectful to themselves and others, responsible for school property, promote positive learning environment and be sincere, honest and committed learners." **Prevention education and awareness programs:** These programs cover substance abuse, sex education, sex, health, harassment, and anti-bullying.

Athletics

Sports offered: Cross-country, soccer, basketball, volleyball and baseball. **Intermural team play begins:** G6. Member of ISAL.

Campus/Campus Life

Campus description: "The San Francisco Frank and Jennie Gauss Campus, completed in 1983, opened a new state-of the-art building for the 2002-2003 academic year. Located in a suburban type setting on two acres, the site includes the San Francisco Jewish Community Center Preschool and is next to Congregation Beth Israel-Judea. In the new building there are eight classrooms, two for kindergarten and six for grades one through three. The building also houses a 2,800 square foot library and a Judaic Studies room, acoustically designed music room and a multimedia/technology seminar space. In addition, the campus also includes science and computer labs, a regulation-size gymnasium, art studios, a learning resource center, and large playing fields, as well as fourth through eighth grade classrooms. There are plans to build a cultural art center, cafeteria and new gymnasium." **Library:** "The goal is to instill a genuine love of and respect for books and literature. In the process, students are taught how best to use the resources of the library for academic and personal needs—everything from learning how to check out a book to writing a research paper. The library's collection includes over 25,000 volumes." **Sports facilities:** Gymnasium, sports field. **Theater/Arts facilities:** Yes. **Computer lab:** Yes. **Science lab:** Yes. **Lunch program:** Yes. **Bus service:** Yes. **Uniforms/dress code:** No. **Opportunities for community service:** "We regard service to the community as a BHDS value, as students gain a sense of belonging to a larger community. The goals of our community service program include showing students that one person can make a difference, putting acts of kindness into action through work in our community, promoting student leadership in the school and the community at large."

Extended Day

Morning care: Begins at 7:45 a.m. **After-school care:** Until 6 p.m. **Grade levels:** K-5. **Cost:** $6.50/hour. **Drop-in care available:** Yes. **Coverage over major holidays:** No. **Homework help:** Yes. **Snacks:** Provided. **Staff/student ratio:** N/P. Middle-school students may stay after school to do their homework, with supervision, free of charge. **After-school classes:** Drama, movie making, gymnastics, cooking/baking, self-defense, chess, piano/trumpet; painting/drawing/mixed media, magic, Spanish. Cost: $120-$165 for 10-week session.

Summer Programs
The school offers Shakespeare camp and other camps. Please contact the school for current offerings. **Cost:** N/P.

Parent Involvement
Parent/teacher communication: Conferences, website, e-mail, voice-mail, newsletter. **Participation requirements:** "All parents are members of the Brandeis Hillel Day School Parent Association. The Parent Association is an active organization through which parents become involved, support BHDS and develop community. While it is not required for our parents to volunteer, in addition to the PA there are many committees and opportunities to do so. BHDS is proud of its active parent volunteer." **Parent education programs offered?:** Yes.

What Sets the School Apart From Others
"In addition to academic excellence, BHDS is committed to educating children to be caring members of the Jewish community, to value and appreciate the Jewish heritage and to become ethically responsible human beings."

How Parents/Students Characterize School
Parent comment(s): "BHDS is not only a school of academic excellence, it also has soul." **Student comment(s):** "I was very well prepared for high school in math, science and language arts. I was also given invaluable social tools to deal with the challenges of high school. My BHDS friends are friends for life"

CASCADE CANYON SCHOOL
2626 Sir Francis Drake Boulevard
Fairfax, CA 94930
(415) 459-3464 *fax (415) 459-6714*
www.cascadecanyonschool.org

Peggy Tunder, Primary School Director, cascade@marin.k12.ca.us
Zoe Ghazi, Elementary School Director, cascade@marin.k12.ca.us
Linda Franco, Middle School Director, cascade@marin.k12.ca.us

General

Coed K-8 day school. Founded in 1981. Independent. Nonprofit. **Member:** N/P. **Enrollment:** Approx. 66. **Average class size:** 14. **Accreditation:** None. **Endowment:** N/A. **School year:** Sept.-June. **Instructional days:** 180. **School day:** 8:30 a.m. to 3 p.m.

Student Body

Ethnicity: 98% Caucasian (non-Latino), 2% Asian.

Admission

Applications due: Ongoing. **Application fee:** $75. **Application process:** Parents visit the school and submit an application. Student visits are then scheduled. **No. of applications:** Varies. **No. of K spaces:** 10. **Percentage of K class made up of school's preschool class:** N/A. **Admission evaluation requirements for K:** Student's visit, minimum age requirement of 5 years old. **Other grades:** Parent-director phone meeting, parent observation of class followed by student visitation. **Preferences:** N/A. **What sort of student do you best serve?** "Self-motivated, independent, and cooperative."

Costs

Latest tuition: $10,200. **Sibling discount:** 10% per child. **Tuition includes:** Lunch: No; Transportation: No; Laptop computer: No. **Tuition increases:** Approx. 7%/yr. **Other costs:** Approx. $325 for books, $500 other fees. **Percentage of students receiving financial aid:** None. **Financial aid application deadline:** N/A. **Average grant:** N/A. **Percentage of grants of half-tuition or more:** N/A. **Donations:** A minimum of 40 hours of service per family or a $500 donation in lieu of participation; two annual fundraisers or $500 in lieu of participation.

School's Mission Statement

"Cascade Canyon School is dedicated to maintaining a small student/teacher ratio and to offering an integrated and balanced curriculum that exposes students to the joys of learning as a lifelong pursuit and leads students to become independent thinkers, strong leaders, and active participants in global community who are respectful of others, flexible in responding to challenge and appreciative of diversity."

Academic Program

Philosophy: "Cascade Canyon School was founded in 1981 to provide an educational community that nurtures and challenges each student academically, physically, and creatively." **Foreign languages:** French, sign language. **Computer training:** N/P. **No. of computers available for students:** "Two in each class." **No. of hours weekly of:** Art- 1-2; Drama- 1; Music- 1; Computers- N/P; Foreign language- 2-3; PE- 2-3. **Outdoor education:** Varies. **Grading:** N/P. **Average nightly homework:** 30-90 min. Posted on the Internet: No. **Percentage of students participating in Johns Hopkins Center for Talented Youth Program:** N/A. **Other indicators of academic success:** N/P. **High schools attended by latest graduating class:** Drake, Novato School of Art & Technology, Lycée International.

Faculty

Ethnicity: N/P. **Percentage of teachers with graduate degrees:** N/P. **Percentage with current California credential:** N/P. **Faculty selection/training:** N/P. **Teacher/student ratio:** 1:10 in K, 1:14 in G1-8. **Special subject teachers:** Art, French, history, library, map/geography, music, PE, science, sign language, theater. **Average teacher tenure:** 8 years.

Middle School

Description: G6-8, departmentalized for science, French, sign language, art and geography. **Teacher/student ratio:** 1:14. **Elective courses offered:** N/P. **Achievement tracking in:** None. **Student social events:** "Transitions Program for G8 students. Students participate in activities that help strengthen personal, family, and community relationships, as well as build character and decision-making skills."

Student Support Services

No. of Licensed Counselors on staff: None. **Counselor/student ratio:** N/A. **Learning specialists on staff:** None. **Learning differences/disabilities support:** N/P. **High school placement support:** By Middle School Director.

Student Conduct and Health

Code of conduct: N/P. **Prevention education and awareness programs:** Sex and health for G4-8, and sex, health and drugs for G7-8.

Athletics

Sports offered: Soccer, basketball and volleyball. **Team play begins in:** G1 (intramural).

Campus/Campus Life

Campus description: N/P. **Library:** Over 1,000 books, references and videos. **Sports facilities:** Playground, basketball court. **Theater/Arts facilities:** Outdoor theater, costume and prop department, and an indoor workshop space with a stage. **Computer lab:** No. **Science lab:** Yes. **Lunch program:** Yes. **Bus service:** No. **Uniforms/dress code:** None. **Opportunities for community service:** Available in all grades.

Extended Day: None.

Summer Programs: None.

Parent Involvement

Parent/teacher communication: Conferences, website, e-mail, newsletter, written evaluation. **Participation requirements:** A minimum of 40 hours service is required per family. **Parent education programs offered?:** None.

What Sets the School Apart From Others

"Multi-grade learning, small class size, Transition Program, outdoor education, cross-age community activities."

How Parents/Students Characterize School

Parent comment(s): N/P.
Student comment(s): N/P.

CATHEDRAL SCHOOL FOR BOYS

1275 Sacramento St. (at Jones next to Grace Cathedral)(Nob Hill)
San Francisco, CA 94108
(415) 771-6600 fax (415) 771-2547
www.cathedralschool.net

Canon Headmaster Michael Ferreboeuf, Head of School,
ferreboeuf@cathedralschool.net
Cathy Madison, Director of Admission, madison@cathedralschool.net

General

K-8 boys day school. Founded in 1957. Independent. Episcopal. Nonprofit. **Member:** CAIS, NAIS, NAES, BADA. **Enrollment:** Approx. 245. **Average class size:** 24 in K-4, 16 in G5-8. **Accreditation:** WASC/CAIS (6-year term: 2000-06). **Endowment:** $10 million. **School year:** Sept.-June. **Instructional days:** 177. **School day:** Begins at 8:20 a.m. Dismissal is 2:15 p.m. for K, 2:30 p.m. for G1, 2:40 p.m. for G2, 3 p.m. for G3-4 and 3:25 p.m. for G5-8.

Student Body

Ethnicity: 37% Caucasian (non-Latino), 27% Asian, 15% other, 12% Latino, 5% multi-racial, 4% African-American.

Admission

Applications due: Early January (call for date). **Application fee:** $75. **Application process:** Tours are available 2 weekday mornings from the end of September to mid-January. Parent interviews for K applicants are not required but may be requested. Applicants are screened for developmental readiness on a Saturday in January. **No. of applications:** Approx. 100-130. **No. of K spaces:** 24. **Percentage of K class made up of school's preschool class:** N/A. **Admission evaluation requirements for K:** Developmental readiness screening and preschool evaluation. **Other grades:** Requirements include school visit, grades, test scores, teacher recommendation and reports from specialists when appropriate. Parent interviews are required for G1-8 applicants. **Preferences:** Children of graduates and siblings. **What sort of student do you best serve?** "Boys who are eager and ready to learn."

Costs

Latest tuition: $17,400. **Sibling discount:** None. **Tuition includes: Lunch:** No; **Transportation:** No; **Laptop computer:** Available at school in G5-8; **Other:** Outdoor education, field trips, books, art, music and instrumental music lessons. **Tuition increases:** Approx. 7.5% annually. **Other costs:** Uniforms (available new or used at the Cathedral School shop). School pictures and gym shirts are the only other fees. **Percentage of students receiving financial aid:** 18%. **Financial aid application deadline:** Feb. (call for date). Financial aid is based on need. **Average grant:** $10,500. **Percentage of grants of half-tuition or more:** 70%. **Donations:** All voluntary.

School's Mission Statement

"To provide an excellent education for boys at the elementary level. ◆ To attract a diverse student body of strong academic potential. ◆ To provide a school committed to intellectual inquiry and rigor, centered in the Episcopal tradition, respectful of and welcoming to people of all religious traditions and beliefs. ◆ To develop civic responsibility through exemplary programs of outreach and service. ◆ To create a community bonded by open-heartedness, hope, compassion and concern."

Academic Program

Philosophy: "Cathedral School for Boys, founded in 1957, strives to provide education in the best traditions of the Episcopal Church and in consonance with the mission of Grace Cathedral. We believe that this education is derived from three main sources: the highest academic and personal standards humanely applied; a diverse community united in its concern for the school and for the world; and an active engagement with religion and the spiritual dimension. Academically, the school sets high standards in literacy, basic skills, self-discipline, the joy of learning, and the pursuit of wisdom. We set equally high standards in good behavior, caring, mutual respect, truth-telling and honor, and emphasize these qualities in all aspects of school life. Art, music, drama and physical education are integral parts of the curriculum. We prepare boys to enter demanding secondary schools confidently; we recognize that there are a variety of learning styles and paces among able students, and we try to teach accordingly. Teachers focus on learning styles which are boy-friendly: hands-on, active study which allows for movement and vigor. We affirm the integrity of childhood and the elementary curriculum, and do not try to replicate secondary school studies." **Foreign languages:** Mandarin or Spanish in G5-8. Latin is required in G7-8. **Computer training:** Integrated into curriculum. A Tech Lab is available; a roving lab of laptops are used in G5-8 classrooms. **No. of computers available for students:** 100. **No. of hours weekly of:** Art-K-4 daily in classroom and 45 min./week in art studio, G5-8 art studio once a week for 85 minutes; Drama- 1-2 average; Music- 3x/week in Chapel, 1 hr. K-4 and 2 hrs. G5-8; Foreign language- 40 min. daily; PE- 40 min. daily. **Outdoor education:** Week-long trips once a year for G5-8; international language trips. **Grading:** A-F, beginning in G6. **Average nightly homework:** Varies by grade from 1.5 hours to 2 hours per night. Nothing assigned Friday is due Monday. Posted on the Internet: Yes. **Percentage of students participating in Johns Hopkins Center for Talented Youth Program:** N/P. **Other indicators of academic success:** N/P. **High schools attended by latest graduating class:** Bay School, Branson, Bentley, Gateway, IHS, Lick, Lowell, SI, Stuart Hall, Tamalpais, University, Proctor, Midland, Thatcher.

Faculty
Ethnicity: 81% Caucasian (non-Latino), 10% Asian, 4% Latino, 2% African-American, 2% multi-racial, 1% other. **Percentage of teachers with graduate degrees:** 56%. **Percentage with current California credential:** 95%. **Faculty selection/training:** BA and 3 years experience required. **Teacher/student ratio:** 1:8.5. **Special subject teachers:** Science, Latin, art, computer, music, Mandarin, Spanish, chaplain, PE, library and research skills. **Average teacher tenure:** 9 years.

Middle School
Description: Begins with 5th grade when students are added and then divided into two smaller groups. Two homerooms of 15-16 boys transition into a departmentalized schedule in 5th grade. Grades 6-8 are fully departmentalized including double periods once a week in all major disciplines, including art and science. The program is project-based with an emphasis on an integrated curriculum. Each boy has an advisor and meets with his advisor and parents in Parent Teacher con-

ferences. **Teacher/student ratio:** 1:9. **Elective courses offered:** Varies per quarter. Courses have included Hoops, Mah Jong, Brunch Bunch, Jazz Combo, Strategy Games, Bowling, Film Review, SSAT Prep Verbal, SSAT Prep Math, Digital Video, and Guitar Workshop. **Achievement tracking in:** Math G7-8; math enrichment G5-6. **Student social events:** Eighth grade dances twice a year with other independent schools; Play Day once a year with 4 other independent schools.

Student Support Services
No. of Licensed Counselors on staff: None. Full-time Chaplain. **Counselor/student ratio:** N/A. **Learning specialists on staff:** One. **Learning differences/disabilities support:** Parent group and part-time learning specialist on staff; parent education events. **High school placement support:** "The Head of the Upper School is the High School Placement Advisor and works extensively with parents and students to prepare for and manage the process, including SSAT prep, student interview and essay prep and counseling regarding appropriate choices. Students attend both local and boarding schools."

Student Conduct and Health
Code of conduct: "Cathedral School for Boys has very few formal rules. It is assumed that boys will conduct themselves in a manner respectful of the rights of others and appropriate to their own active membership in a school community. Boys are expected to: be mindful of their own and others' safety and well being, taking care to be friendly and kind all around; be respectful of others, of their work and property; be responsible for their belongings and accountable for their work; and courteously cooperate in the maintenance of good order and of an environment conducive to learning. Discipline at CSB is described as 'caring justice.' Caring justice fits the school's desire to create a safe, morally aware environment for all that respects the rights and needs of individuals. We believe that effective discipline combines clear, consistent expectations with compassion and sensitivity towards the unique lives of each boy, and we relate the disciplinary consequences to the action, not the boy." **Prevention education and awareness programs:** "A human development curriculum is being expanded to include appropriate health education at every grade level, including nutrition, adolescence,

sex, drug and alcohol education. Advisory groups made up of 6-7 boys meet every week; outside speakers address these topics; and the physical education program also includes these topics."

Athletics

Sports offered/team play begins: Boys in G5-8 engage in basketball (winter, ISAL) and cross-country (fall, ISAL); boys in G6-8 play soccer (fall, ISAL) and golf (spring, ISAL); boys in G7-8 play baseball and volleyball (spring, ISAL). There is a no-cut policy, and there are two teams or more per grade level. Golf and volleyball are dependent upon other league participants.

Campus/Campus Life

Campus description: The campus includes a large building containing 14 classrooms, a library, a science lab, an art studio, and a music studio. **Library:** Contains over 12,000 volumes, 17 computers, and a full-time librarian. **Sports facilities:** Gymnasium, roof playground. **Theater/ Arts facilities:** Large room with a stage for drama and assemblies. **Computer lab:** Yes. **Science lab:** Yes. **Lunch program:** Yes. **Bus service:** No. **Uniforms/dress code:** The school uniform is a blue shirt and grey pants with a navy sweater bearing the school crest. Upper School boys wear a school tie. **Opportunities for community service:** Every grade does community service, arranged for by the Chaplain. Students in G7-8 go off campus for placement once a week for one quarter to various sites, *i.e.*, retirement homes, tutoring in schools, environmental projects. There are food drives, special projects and other opportunities throughout the year.

Extended Day

Morning care: Begins at 7:30 a.m. **After-school care:** Until 6 p.m. **Grade levels:** K-6 (G7-8 by arrangement). Cost: $6.50/hour for regular care, pre-paid two times a year. **Drop-in care available:** With 24 hrs. notice, or less in an emergency. **Coverage over major holidays:** No coverage on Labor Day, Thanksgiving Thursday and Friday, President's Day, Martin Luther King, Jr. Day, and Memorial Day. During the 3 school breaks at Christmas, Winter Break in February and Spring Break the school offers camps from 9 a.m.–5 p.m. **Homework help:**

Yes, in a supervised study hall. **Snacks:** Provided. **Staff/student ratio:** 1:10. **After-school classes:** Vary each quarter. Might include Aikido, science exploration, cooking, theater arts, chess, movie making. All students may take these classes, but boys in the extended day program have priority. Parents do not pay for extended care during class hours. Cost: Call for fees.

Summer Programs

The school offers a full summer program for both boys and girls. Call for a brochure.

Parent Involvement

Parent/teacher communication: Formal conferences are held twice during the school year, and informally, if necessary. Calls are returned promptly and e-mail is utilized as well. Homework is posted on the website. The website also provides school information, activities, and a newsletter weekly. Lower School teachers also send home a weekly newsletter. **Participation requirements:** The only requirement is an 8 hour shift at the Cathedral School Shop. **Parent education programs offered?:** Speakers, workshops and various discussion groups are held throughout the year sponsored by either the Headmaster, FrED (Friends for Education and Diversity), the Parent Association parent education group or the Learning Differences Parent Support group.

What Sets the School Apart From Others

"We are an Episcopal school which means that we are an inclusive community that embraces all religious backgrounds, and is made up of differences of all kinds, ethnic, cultural, and socio-economic. Our families include LGBT families, and many other combinations of loving adults raising children. We are a small school and are very intentional about how we teach to boys. Our faculty, who love and understand boys, does extensive continuing education, and we continue to learn from the latest research regarding education and the teaching of boys. The environment is warm, collegial and safe with an atmosphere of support and encouragement for every boy to succeed, finding his strengths, acknowledging his weaknesses, and giving his best."

How Parents/Students Characterize School

Parent comment(s): "By far the best aspect of our experience at CSB has been the humane, caring faculty and the tremendous personal investment they are willing to put into each boy."

Student comment(s): "I think writing the term paper we had to do in History really prepared me for the hard work to come in high school and college."

CHILDREN'S DAY SCHOOL

333 Dolores Street (between 16th and 17th Sts.) (Mission/Castro)
San Francisco, CA 94110
(415) 861-5432 *fax (415) 861-5419*
www.cds-sf.org

Rick Ackerly, Head of School
Aimee Giles, Director of Admission, aimeeg@cds-sf.org

General

Co-ed PS-8 day school. Founded in 1983. Independent. Nonprofit. **Member:** CAIS, NAIS. **Enrollment:** Approx. 275. **Average class size:** N/P. **Accreditation:** CAIS (provisional). **Endowment:** N/A. **School year:** 9-month calendar. **Instructional days:** 175. **School day:** 8:30 a.m. to 2:45 p.m. for K, 8:30 a.m. to 3 p.m. for G1-4, and 8:15 a.m. to 3:30 p.m. for G5-8.

Student Body

Ethnicity: 65% Caucasian (non-Latino), 12% multi-racial, 10% Latino, 8% Asian, 5% African-American.

Admission

Applications due: Mid-Jan. (call for date). **Application fee:** $50. **Application process:** Attend a 1.5 hour tour or an evening open house in October-January. Depending on the grade applying for and the number of openings, the applicant and his or her family may be invited for a visit. **No. of applications:** Approx. 50. **No. of K spaces:** Approx. 4. **Percentage of K class made up of the school's own preschool class:** 90%. **Admission evaluation requirements for K:** Teacher recommendation, student visit. **Other grades:** Teacher recommendation(s), grades, standardized test scores, student visit. **Preferences:** Siblings and children of faculty/staff/board. **What sort of student do you best serve?** "The CDS educational and academic environment is designed to meet the needs of a wide range of children with varying intelligences and interests. Our students are happy, confident, curious children who are eager to learn. CDS students exhibit a high degree of social responsibility and routinely make a difference in the world around them. They work and learn collaboratively with other students of all ages and are appreciative and respectful of differences in others. They show caring of themselves, others and their environment and are academically skilled with an average ERB score in the 90th percentile."

Costs

Latest tuition: Sliding scale tuition from $1,650 to $16,500. **Sibling discount:** None. **Tuition includes:** Books and all other required instructional expenses. Lunch: No; Transportation: No; Laptop computer: No. **Tuition increases:** 6-7% annually. **Other costs:** None. **Percentage of students receiving financial aid:** 40% students are on sliding scale. **Financial aid application deadline:** Mid-Jan. (call for date). Financial aid is based on need. **Average grant:** $8,250. **Percentage of grants of half-tuition or more:** 50%. **Donations:** "It is our ongoing goal to encourage wide community ownership and investment in CDS. We rely on voluntary contributions to support our operating budget as well as to fund improvements to our school facility. Parents are encouraged to participate in our Annual Fund and other fundraising initiatives, and we ask that all families contribute at a level consistent with their financial capabilities."

School's Mission Statement

"The mission of Children's Day School is to educate children to their full potential by nurturing and challenging them intellectually, physically, socially and morally. We believe that education is an enterprise through which children share in and contribute to the intellectual, cultural, social and moral resources of the larger community. Moreover, we believe children are best able to develop their own powers of thought and understanding through active participation in personally and socially meaningful work. We are therefore committed to an educational program that is project based, integrated across academic disciplines and grounded in the practice of social responsibility. Our curriculum is designed to encourage a love of learning and to foster an attitude of caring for self, for others, for ideas, for the natural environment and for the human-made world. As a community, Children's Day School strives to be compassionate and generous, to value diversity and to promote justice and respect for all people regardless of age, gender, race, economics, ethnicity, culture, religion, sexual orientation, abilities or family circumstance."

Academic Program

Philosophy: "Our challenging curriculum promotes academic excellence, encourages creative exploration and critical thinking and creates an enduring love of learning. Using an inquiry-based curriculum grounded in contemporary research and theory, we nurture the development of the whole child—intellectually, personally and socially. What makes our academic program unique is the way in which students are taught and how we measure success. Throughout the school day, children work individually and in groups learning that inquiry and interaction leads to exciting new discoveries. Interdisciplinary projects involve students in problem-solving investigations that foster and teach collaborative learning skills. We measure our success by the success of each individual student. Elementary and middle school students are involved in parent-teacher conferences to set individual goals at the beginning of each school year." **Foreign languages:** Spanish starting in preschool. **Computer training:** Part of classroom instruction. **No. of computers available for students:** "Computers in each classroom." **No. of hours weekly of:** Art- 2; Drama- 2 (beginning in G5); Music- 1; Computers- varies by grade; Foreign language- Spanish-speaking teacher in PS-K, 1.5 hrs. in K-4, 3 hrs. in G5-8: PE- 2; Environmental Education (EE): 1. **Outdoor education:** Varies by grade. **Grading:** A-F; letter grades begin in middle school (G5). **Average nightly homework:** 10 min. in G1; 20 min. in G2; 30 min. in G3; 40 min. in G4; 50-120 min. in G5-8. Posted on the Internet: No. **Percentage of students participating in Johns Hopkins Center for Talented Youth Program:** N/P. **Other indicators of academic success:** "Our primary focus is daily evaluation in the classroom. Teachers create benchmarks for progress and assemble portfolios of student work to provide parents with concrete assessments of their child's progress in each academic discipline. Written progress reports are prepared 2-3 times a year and parent-teacher conferences are held twice a year. The Educational Records Bureau (ERB) standardized test is given to students from third through eighth grades." **High schools attended by latest graduating class:** The school's first eighth grade class will graduate in June 2006.

Faculty

Ethnicity: 74% Caucasian (non-Latino), 12% Latino, 8% Asian, 3% African-American, 3% multi-racial. **Percentage of teachers with graduate degrees:** 57%. **Percentage with current California credential:** 36% (43% with out-of-state credentials). **Faculty selection/training:** Bachelor's degree and teaching experience required, master's degree and teaching credential preferred. **Teacher/student ratio:** 1:8. **Special subject teachers:** Spanish, art, music, PE, drama, environmental education. **Average teacher tenure:** N/P.

Middle School

Description: "Our middle school (G5-8) emphasizes academic preparation for high school while continuing to instill in students a passion for learning. Such an emphasis provides students with the tools necessary for critical thinking, academic proficiency and intellectual development. Collaborative work and independent study remain constants as students learn to reason in greater depth about increasingly abstract concepts. All middle school students participate in an advisory group twice a week. Classes are subject-specific and taught by a math/science teacher and a humanities teacher." **Teacher/student ratio:** 1:10. **Elective courses offered:** Yes. (Classes N/P.) **Achievement tracking in:** N/A. **Student social events:** A variety of social events are organized by parents and teachers.

Student Support Services

No. of Licensed Counselors on staff: None. **Counselor/student ratio:** N/A. **Learning specialists on staff:** None. **Learning differences/ disabilities support:** "At CDS, we know that all children learn differently. We have as many different kinds of learners as we have students, and we teach accordingly. An effective parent-teacher partnership is critical for a child's success, and at CDS teachers and parents meet regularly to monitor each child's education. Where there is a particular concern we keep in touch even more frequently, making sure that we are all doing what we need to do to insure success. We know that we cannot be effective with all children, but our experience has shown that we can be effective if children are taking responsibility for their own education, and the adults are properly organized to support this effort in ever-increasing degrees of complexity. Our admission process is designed to identify children and families with whom we think we can work effectively." **High school placement support:** High school placement counseling.

Student Conduct and Health

Code of conduct: "Our students honor three important guidelines for conduct: 1) take responsibility for yourself, as well as the social and physical environment, 2) be respectful at all times, no matter what, 3) use difficult situations to learn and grow. Limit-setting at CDS is the process of teaching and reminding what it takes to be a respectful and respected member of a group." **Prevention education and awareness addressed in:** Health and human sexuality begins in G2. Alcohol and drug education begins in middle school (G5).

Athletics

Sports offered: "Our PE and athletics program focuses on the whole person—body and mind—and emphasizes participation, cooperation and teamwork." **Team play begins:** (Intermural) In G5 in the Private School Athletic League with coed volleyball, boys and girls soccer, coed track and field, and coed futsal. Students are also encouraged to join Viking soccer teams and Little League, for which many parents are volunteer coaches.

Campus/Campus Life

Campus description: "Located across from historic Mission Dolores in San Francisco and nestled safely in the middle of the block behind Notre Dame Plaza, our campus has one of the largest outdoor schoolyard spaces in San Francisco. Bordered by palm trees, our sunny campus features an organic garden and farm, which is home to chickens and sheep. Equipped with swings, a climbing structure and sandbox, bikes and a basketball court, our campus gives children a safe place to play freely, be themselves and explore the natural environment. The stately, Spanish-colonial style architecture of our school building offers large, airy classrooms for students in grades K-8, art studio, the David Minus Science Center and a library. The preschool, located in three bungalow classrooms adjacent to the farm and garden, has easy access to the large, sunny playground." **Library:** "Our new library opened summer 2004." **Sports facilities:** The school uses the gymnasium at the neighboring Columbia Park Boys & Girls Club. **Theater/Arts facilities:** None. **Computer lab:** Computers are in all the classrooms. **Science lab:** Yes. **Lunch program:** Children bring own lunch daily. **Bus service:** Public. The school is on and near major MUNI lines and BART. **Uniforms/dress code:** None. **Opportunities for community service:** "Service learning at CDS is education in action, combining experiential learning with community service. Guided by teachers and community members, our students address real community needs—both within and outside our own school community—by planning and executing service projects that are carefully tied to curricula. All projects are developmentally appropriate for the age groups involved."

Extended Day

Morning care: Begins at 7:30 a.m. **After-school care:** Until 6 p.m. **Grade levels:** All. **Cost:** Ranges from $6.45-$8.75/hour. **Drop-in care available:** Yes. **Coverage over major holidays:** "Some." **Homework help:** Yes. **Snacks:** Provided. **Staff/student ratio:** 1:10. **After-school classes:** "An integral component of our school community and open to all students in the Bay Area, our extended day program provides a comfortable, fun place for children to spend time after school. Taking full advantage of our protected acre of land, experienced teachers create a dynamic environment that is fun and engaging, and provides ample time for play. Children may choose from a wide variety of organized, age-appropriate activities including enrichment classes taught by CDS teachers, community teachers and instructors from accredited local organizations (*i.e.* chess, movie-making, gymnastics, science, art, yoga, etc.)." Cost: N/P.

Summer Programs

Open to all students in the Bay Area, the school offers four summer camps in two-week sessions for children in PS-G8 Each session has a different theme. Each session included outdoor activities and field trips. Cost: N/P.

Parent Involvement

Parent/teacher communication: Two scheduled parent-teacher conferences/year, weekly all-school and classroom newsletters, regular e-mail, telephone and in-person communication. **Participation requirements:** "Parents are encouraged, but not required, to participate in the CDS community in some capacity during the school year. By getting involved, parents have the opportunity to develop deeper relationships with other parents and families, with their child's teachers' and with the CDS staff. Plus, it's fun." **Parent education programs offered?:** Yes.

What Sets the School Apart From Others

"Preparing young people academically is the central function of all schools. At CDS, we believe that academic performance is not education itself, but the result of education, and that education is a process of leading each child's unique genius out into the world in ever widening circles of personal challenge and social complexity. We have established a culture of diversity in which children spend less time and energy trying to 'measure up' and instead–with our guidance–focus on discovering their own gifts, passions and unique genius. It is our goal at CDS to guide each child's unique genius out into the world. It is also our goal that in so doing, all of our students will: love learning; take responsibility for themselves, their community and the environment around them; think critically and creatively; show respect for themselves and others; and be academically prepared."

How Parents/Students Characterize School

Parent comment(s): "CDS instills an excitement and enthusiasm for learning simply by making it so much fun. I love that my daughter loves to go to school and feels such pride in the school." • "The teachers are great–knowledgeable, warm and caring professionals."
Student comment(s): N/P.

CHINESE AMERICAN INTERNATIONAL SCHOOL
150 Oak Street (between Gough and Franklin Sts.) (Hayes Valley)
San Francisco, CA 94102
(415) 865-6000
www.cais.org

Andrew W. Corcoran, Head of School
John Leiner, Director of Admission, j_leiner@cais.org

General

Co-ed PreK-8 day school. Founded in 1981. Independent. Non-sectarian. Nonprofit. **Member:** NAIS, CAIS, BADA. **Enrollment:** Approx. 385. **Average class size:** 18 in K, 16 in G1-5, 18 in G6. **Accreditation:** WASC (term N/P). **Endowment:** N/P. **School year:** Sept.-June. **Instructional days:** 177. **School day:** 8:30 a.m. to 3:30 p.m. for K, 8 a.m. to 3 p.m. for G1-5, and 8 a.m. to 3:30 p.m. for G6-8.

Student Body

Ethnicity: 53% Asian/Asian American, 24% multi-racial/ethnic, 17% Caucasian (non-Latino/a), 4% Hispanic/Latino(a), 2% African-American.

Admission

Applications due: Early Jan. (call for date). **Application fee:** $75. **Application process:** Tour/info. session, application, screening and evaluation of applicants. **No. of applications:** N/P. **Percentage of class made up of school's preschool class:** N/P. **Admission evaluation requirements for K:** Screening and current school/teacher recommendations. **Other grades:** Two-day visit, evaluation, current school/teacher recommendations. **Preferences:** Siblings. **What sort of student do you best serve?** "CAIS welcomes all families interested in providing their children with a bilingual and multicultural learning experience."

Costs

Latest tuition: $16,050 for PreK-K, $16,850 for G1-5, $17,000 for G6-8. **Sibling discount:** None. **Tuition includes:** Lunch: No; Transportation: No; Laptop computers for school use; Other: Morning extended care. **Tuition increases:** Annually. **Other costs:** None. **Percentage of students receiving financial aid:** Approx. 23%. **Financial aid application deadline:** Mid-Jan. (call for date). Financial aid is based on need. **Average grant:** $7,400. **Percentage of grants of half-tuition or more:** N/P. **Donations:** N/P.

School's Mission Statement

"Our mission at Chinese American International School is to educate students for academic excellence, moral character, and international perspective through immersion in American and Chinese culture and language."

Academic Program

Philosophy: "The CAIS program prepares students to be bilingual, biliterate and bicultural when they graduate; demonstrate intellectual curiosity that inspires a lifelong love of learning; act with civility and compassion, and respect diverse beliefs and cultures; contribute to society, family, and peers out of a sincere desire to be of service, and exhibit diligence, resiliency, integrity and self respect; be committed to preserving the global environment and improving the human condition." **Foreign languages:** Mandarin and after-school enrichment classes in French. **Computer training:** Yes. **No. of computers available for students:** "Computers and laptops are available in each class." **No. of hours weekly of:** Art- 1; Drama- 1; Music- 1; Computers- 1; Foreign language- students spend half of the day with an English-speaking teacher and the other half with a native, Mandarin Chinese-speaking teacher; PE- 2. **Outdoor education:** Yes. **Grading:** Letter grades begin in G6. **Average nightly homework:** N/P. Posted on the Internet: Yes. **Percentage of students participating Johns Hopkins Center for Talented Youth Program:** "A large number of our students qualify." **Other indicators of academic success:** "Our students have placed first numerous times in MATHCOUNTS competitions, science fairs, and Chinese speech contests." **High schools attended by latest graduating class:** "University, Lick, Cate, Lowell, Bentley, among others."

Faculty

Ethnicity: 57% Asian/Asian American, 42% Caucasian (non-Latino), 1% multi-racial/ethnic. **Percentage of faculty with graduate degrees:** N/P. **Percentage of with current California credential:** N/P. **Faculty selection/training:** N/P. **Teacher/student ratio:** 1:8 in PreK-K, 1:5 in G1-5, 1:13 in G6-8. **Special subject teachers:** Art, music and movement, science, computer technology, Chinese brush painting. **Average teacher tenure:** N/P.

Middle School

Description: In middle school (G6-8), students attend two classes in Mandarin each day—in language arts and social studies. The remaining core subjects—English, mathematics, and science, as well as world, Chinese, and U.S. history—are taught in English. Students also attend classes in computer technology, art, music, and PE. **Teacher/student ratio:** 1:13. **Elective courses offered:** Art, brush painting, music, computer technology in G7-8, and an annual Student Exchange Program for G7 in which CAIS students live with their Chinese host families for two weeks and host their Chinese "buddies" who stay with them in

San Francisco. **Achievement tracking in:** N/P. **Student social events:** Monthly and annual dances, celebrations of cultural events, and community service with French American International School (FAIS) students.

Student Support Services

No. of Licensed Counselors on staff: One full-time. **Learning specialists on staff:** A Reading Specialist and a Learning Specialist. **Learning differences/disabilities support:** "The Students Services department ensures that all children are fully supported. Students requiring special accommodations to the program will have a Student Services Plan to ensure that the child receives consistent support from his/her teachers and parents. The school's program ensures that children who are able to manage their personal learning styles thrive best at CAIS." **High school placement support:** "The CAIS High School Placement Office provides information about local and national high schools; guides students and parents towards appropriate school choices; facilitates attendance to local fairs and events; acts as a liaison between parents, students and high school personnel; and ultimately advocates for students."

Student Conduct and Health

Code of conduct: "CAIS students are taught to appreciate differences, respect diversity, be honest, be kind, be respectful, and be safe." **Prevention education and awareness addressed in:** The school has a middle school advisory class with a small group environment where pre-teen topics can be discussed openly with the guidance of an advisor.

Athletics

Sports offered: Volleyball, basketball, handball, softball, soccer, swimming, cross-country, triathlon, futsal. **Team play begins in:** K (intramural).

Campus/Campus Life

Campus description: The International Schools Campus is located at the corner of Oak and Franklin Streets. Home to Chinese American International School, French-American International School, and

International High School. **Library:** Staffed with a Library Specialist and Media Specialists. Contains 11,564 volumes, 2,100 of which are Mandarin Chinese titles, including 100 videotapes and 46 DVDs. Additionally, Chinese Jr. Great Books are offered. 120 computers. **Sports facilities:** Gymnasium, off-site fields, and swimming pool. **Theater/Arts facilities:** Art Studios (2) and a Performing Art Studio. **Computer lab:** Yes. **Science lab:** 2. **Lunch program:** Yes, vendor provided. **Bus service:** No. **Uniforms/dress code:** No. **Opportunities for community service:** "The main goal of the CAIS community service program is to establish a tradition of giving back to one's community. The program is facilitated through advisory classes and curriculum projects in middle school. Students are encouraged to initiate their own community service activities. Emphasis is placed on serving the local Chinese-speaking community. Joint community service projects with French-American International School; for example, tsunami relief efforts for Southeast Asia."

Extended Day
Morning care: Begins at 7:30 a.m. **After-school care:** Until 6 p.m. **Grade levels:** PreK-8. **Cost:** $250/month, $80/week, $20/day. **Drop-in care available:** Yes. **Coverage over major holidays:** No. **Homework help:** Yes. **Snacks:** Provided for PreK and K. **Staff/student ratio:** 1:10. **After-school classes:** Chinese and Western cultural classes, visual and performing arts, chess, math games, martial arts, and French and Spanish language classes. **Cost:** Approx. $250/month.

Summer Programs
"Exploration Camp balances academic classroom work in core English subjects with fun weekly field trips, where kids can exercise both body and mind. Mandarin Immersion Camp gives students an opportunity to develop and utilize their Mandarin-speaking abilities through immersion-based activities such as singing, Chinese calligraphy, dance, arts and crafts, martial arts, cooking, and everyday conversation. Students with little or no Mandarin skills are welcome. Sanctuary Explorers Camp encompasses field trips, lessons, and activities that are carefully selected to engage children in the importance of habitat conservation." **Cost:** $1,000 for the full day, $700 for a half day.

Parent Involvement

Parent/teacher communication: Two Parent/Teacher conferences are available per year and as needed. Ongoing communication is encouraged between parents, faculty, administration and staff. Parents and staff receive *Thursday Flash*, a semimonthly newsletter sent via e-mail. **Participation requirements:** Each parent is expected to contribute a minimum of 20 volunteer hours per student each academic year, and to contribute financially to the annual fund. **Parent education programs offered?:** Yes.

What Sets the School Apart From Others

"CAIS offers a unique, bilingual immersion education in American and Chinese culture and language. Our student body consists of many different types of children from varied racial and ethnic groups and cultural backgrounds. Family diversity is important to our community and is highly valued. CAIS is comprised of the following racial and ethnic backgrounds: Asian/Asian American, Caucasian, multiracial/Asian, Hispanic, Latino/a, and African American. The varied backgrounds include: Japanese, Filipino, Arab, Burmese, Chinese Thai, German, Scottish, Vietnamese, Norwegian, Irish, Dutch, Greek, Lebanese, African American/Black, Polish, Russian, and Korean. Additionally, we have many adoptive families, single-parent families, gay and lesbian families, and grandparents within our inclusive community. CAIS is the nation's leader in pre-collegiate Mandarin Chinese and English language immersion education. In 1987 the United States Department of Education described CAIS as the national prototype for Chinese language education in elementary schools."

How Parents/Students Characterize School

Parent comment(s): "We moved from Calexico, California to San Francisco so our three children could attend CAIS. There is no other school like it, and we wanted our children to be exposed to the potential it presents." ◆ "Every time I come into the school, the environment is very happy, healthy, and positive."

Student comment(s): "I'm learning a lot from being around different kids at my school. There's a kid from China and he speaks Tibetan, and there's a girl form China who speaks Hebrew." ◆ "The teachers are patient, and they help you learn difficult things easily. My friends are so excited to hear me talk in Chinese."

CONVENT OF THE SACRED HEART ELEMENTARY SCHOOL
2222 Broadway (at Webster) (Pacific Heights)
San Francisco, CA 94115
(415) 563-2900 *fax (415) 929-6928* (Admissions)
www.sacredsf.org

Ann Wachter, RSCJ, Head of School, wachter@sacredsf.org
Pamela Thorp, Director of Admission, thorp@sacredsf.org

General

Girls K-8 day school. Founded in 1887. Catholic (53%). Convent Elementary School along with Stuart Hall for Boys, Convent of the Sacred Heart High School and Stuart Hall High School, is one of the four Schools of the Sacred Heart in San Francisco. Independent. Nonprofit. **Member:** CAIS, Network of Sacred Heart Schools, NAIS, NCGS, NCEA, ERB, CASE, BADA. **Enrollment:** 324. **Average class size:** 15-20. **Accreditation:** CAIS/WASC (6-year term: 2005-11), Network of Sacred Heart Schools. **Endowment:** $9 million. **School year:** Sept.-June. **Instructional days:** N/P. **School day:** Begins at 8:15 a.m. Dismissal is 2:45 p.m. Monday-Thursday for K. Dismissal for G1-8 is between 3 p.m. and 3:30 p.m. Friday dismissal for K is 1:45 p.m. and for G1-8, between 2 p.m. and 2:30 p.m.

Student Body

Ethnicity: "26% students of color."

Admission

Applications due: Mid-December for K. All other grades are due early January (call for dates). **Application fee:** $75. **Application process:** Parent tours are held two hours on a weekday morning beginning in late September. The Head of School meets with parents for a question and answer period during the tour. Parents are also invited to meet with the Head of School when their child attends play group activity. **No. of applications:** N/P. **No. of K spaces:** 40. **Percentage of K class made up of school's preschool class:** N/A. **Admission evaluation requirements for K:** Applicants must be five years old by the first of September. Assessment for readiness to begin the full day program offered by the school includes both individual screening and a play group date. Preschool evaluations are also part of each child's application. **Other grades:** Include a parent tour, teacher recommendation, previous grades and testing. **Preferences:** Siblings receive priority consideration. **What sort of student do you best serve?** "Students and families who will support the school's Mission Statement."

Costs

Latest tuition: $17,450 for K-4, $17,850 for G5-8. Tuition payable in 1, 2, or 10 installments (10 month plan carries a fee). **Sibling discount:** None. **Tuition includes:** Lunch: No; Transportation: No; Laptop computer: N/P. Other: N/P. **Tuition increases:** Approx. 7% annually. **Other costs:** Approximately $200 for K uniform including shoes. Uniforms are also available through school's thrift shop, Seconds to Go. **Percentage of students receiving financial aid:** 14%. **Financial aid application deadline:** Jan. (call for date). Financial aid is based on need. **Average grant:** N/P. **Percentage of grants of half-tuition or more:** N/P. **Donations:** Parents are solicited to participate in annual giving; participation is voluntary.

School's Mission Statement

"Founded in 1887 as an independent Catholic school, Schools of the Sacred Heart, San Francisco, carry on the educational mission of the Religious of the Sacred Heart. We share with the other members of the nationwide Network of Heart Schools five common goals and the commitment to educate to: A personal and active faith in God; A deep respect for intellectual values; A social awareness which impels to action; The building of community as a Christian value; Personal growth in an atmosphere of wise freedom. A K-12, four school complex, Schools of the Sacred Heart, San Francisco offer the unique experience of single-sex education within a coed community. Students are expected to achieve their highest level of scholarship while learning to assume leadership roles as responsible, compassionate and contributing members of society."

Academic Program

Philosophy: "Convent students are engaged in a process designed to encourage experimentation, introspection and effort. Rigorous academics in a collaborative atmosphere create an optimal learning environment. The curriculum between and within grade levels is clearly defined and articulated, enabling students to move from grade to grade experiencing continuity, growth and a sense of appreciation for and knowledge of their own individual learning styles. The emphasis is always on the student as an individual with her unique gifts and talents to explore and contribute. Learning takes place both in and out of the classroom, providing the intellectual impetus that stimulates achievement. Teachers challenge and support students and participate in the discovery process with them." **Foreign languages:** French and Spanish offered beginning in G3. Latin is mandatory in G6. **Computer training:** Beginning in K and continuing through G8. **No. of computers available for students:** Approx. 100 computers. Computers are located in the Unkefer Computer Lab, the elementary school library and stations outside the classrooms. **No. of hours weekly of** art, drama, music, computers, foreign language, PE and outdoor education: "Times vary weekly with grade of child." **Outdoor education:** N/P. **Grading:** Narrative reports in K-5. Letter grades in G6-8. **Average nightly homework:** The school's guidelines are 30-60 min. for G1-3; 60-90 min. for G4-6; 30 min. per subject for G7-8. Posted on the Internet: No. **Percentage of students participating in Johns Hopkins Center for Talented Youth Program:** N/P. **Other indicators of academic success:** "Convent Elementary School graduates are well prepared for their high school experience. They maintain high academic standards and participate in the full life of high school including sports, clubs and leadership roles in student government." **High schools attended by latest graduating class:** CSH, Lick, SI, University, SHCP, Drew, St. Paul's and The Hopkins School.

Faculty

Ethnicity: "18% are faculty of color." **Percentage of teachers with graduate degrees:** N/P. **Percentage with current California credential:** N/P. **Faculty selection/training:** Experience, college degree and/or credential. "Professional teacher development is an integral part of the school's program." **Teacher/student ratio:** 1:10 in the Lower Form; 1:15-20 in the Middle Form. **Special subject teachers:** Art, music, computers, and after-school program, which includes private instrumental music lessons in piano, flute, violin and guitar. **Average teacher tenure:** 9 years.

Middle School

Description: "The core curriculum builds on knowledge gained in the Lower Form, moving the students into increasingly comprehensive and rigorous academic study. Writing, both creative and expository, is emphasized in all subject areas. Convent students build upon their experience in a science lab and the scientific method of discovery. All students complete Algebra 1 in the eighth grade. Collaboration between the departments enhances in-depth studies. The values of citizenship continue to be stressed through the Goals and Criteria of Sacred Heart Education. A strong esprit de corps defines the atmosphere for students and faculty within each classroom and across the school. Departmentalization begins in G7." **Teacher/student ratio:** 1:15-20. **Elective courses offered:** N/P. **Achievement tracking:** None. **Student social events:** With Stuart Hall for Boys students, dances, drama club, after-school program including orchestra.

Student Support Services

No. of Licensed Counselors on staff: One full-time. **Counselor/student ratio:** N/P. **Learning specialists on staff:** One full-time and 1 part-time. **Learning differences/disabilities support:** "Educational resources as needed." **High school placement support:** The Head of School and Dean of the Middle Form counsel students and their families. Students may re-enroll to Convent of the Sacred Heart High School.

Student Conduct and Health

Code of conduct: "As articulated in the Goals and Criteria of Sacred Heart Schools." **Prevention education and awareness addressed in:** Health classes, which are mandatory in K-8. (Fitness is also included.)

Athletics

Sports offered: Volleyball, cross-country, basketball, soccer and golf. **Team play begins in:** G5 (intermural). Convent Elementary School belongs to the Independent School Athletic League (ISAL) and the Catholic Youth Organization (CYO).

Campus/Campus Life

Campus description: Convent Elementary School occupies the former Grant House and is located on the same campus as Stuart Hall for Boys and Convent of the Sacred Heart High School. Stuart Hall High School is located several blocks away at Pine and Octavia. **Library:** Houses 20,000 volumes including fiction, non-fiction and reference books, periodicals, books on tape, CD ROMs, videos and computers. **Sports facilities:** Gymnasium with basketball court and running track. **Theater/Arts facilities:** Two theaters. The newest is the Syufy Theater used for school presentations including plays, musical presentations and guest lectures. The Siboni Art and Science Center houses all the art, music and science classrooms for Convent Elementary School, Stuart Hall for Boys and Convent of the Sacred Heart High School. **Computer lab:** Yes. **Science lab:** Yes. **Lunch program:** Hot lunch daily. **Bus service:** Yes. A private bus service from St. Francis Wood/Forest Hills is available through an independent company. **Uniforms/dress code:** Uniforms. **Opportunities for community service:** "Convent Elementary School students involve themselves in community service through classroom projects, fundraisers and active on-site work. The development of social awareness and the expectation to become involved in responsible social action is an integral part of the Sacred Heart program for all students. Community service cultivates a spirit of cooperation and collaboration and fosters a comprehension of leadership today and tomorrow."

Extended Day

Morning care: Begins at 7:30 a.m. **After-school care:** Until 6 p.m. (coed). **Grade levels:** K-4. **Cost:** No charge for a.m. care. For a 5 p.m. pick up, the cost is $2,550/year; for a 6 p.m. pickup, $3,300/year. **Drop-in care available:** Yes. **Coverage over major holidays:** No. **Homework help:** Yes. **Snacks:** Provided. **Staff/student ratio:** 1:15. **After-school classes:** For students in K-8, these have included Taekwando, Spanish, robotics, fencing, art, sports, drama, chess, gymnastics, cooking, sewing, yoga and SSAT preparation and debate club. Music lessons are also available. Both extension and after-school classes are coed. **Cost:** Varies; contact school.

Summer Programs

Classes are coeducational and designed for children entering grades K-8. Two three-week sessions are offered. Extended care is available from 8 a.m. until 9 a.m. and 4 p.m. until 6 p.m. The program includes academic enrichment, basic skills, technology, cooking, drama, art, sports, counselor-in-training and community service. **Cost:** Varies; contact school.

Parent Involvement

Parent/teacher communication: Conferences are scheduled twice yearly and as needed. Special scheduling needs are accommodated. Parents also utilize e-mail, the schools' web site, Thursday Notes and Lower Form monthly grade level newsletters. **Participation requirements:** Parents are encouraged to volunteer for activities assisting with the Schools' annual fund raising activity auction/dinner and Saturday block party, creating gift items for the boutique as well as assisting with phoning and mailings. Parents also volunteer to help on class field trips and in the school library. **Parent education programs offered?:** Yes.

What Sets the School Apart From Others

"Among the oldest independent schools in California, Schools of the Sacred Heart are a part of a worldwide network of Sacred Heart Schools having their beginnings in the Society of the Sacred Heart founded in Paris in 1800. Our independent Catholic school draws on the rich tradition of Sacred Heart education worldwide, including strong intellectual challenge, faith development, social awareness and growth of the individual as a community member. Convent Elementary School offers the benefits of single sex education in a coed environment and prepares girls to assume leadership responsibilities as intelligent, compassionate, self-confident and contributing members of society."

How Parents/Students Characterize School

Parent comment: "Convent's community is very special. My daughter has thrived in her academic education and we, as a family, feel a part of a community that supports one another in so many ways."
Student comment: "I love my classes and my friends at school. My teachers are very nice."

CORPUS CHRISTI SCHOOL

75 Francis Street (at Alemany Blvd.) (Outer Mission)
San Francisco, CA 94112
(415) 587-7014 *fax (415) 587-1575*
www.corpuschristisf.org

Sister Anna Bui, Head of School, fmaccsf@aol.com

General

Coed K-8 parochial day school. Founded in 1928 under the supervision of the Salesian Fathers and the tutelage of the Sisters of St. Joseph of Orange. Since 1974 supervised by Salesian Sisters of St. John Bosco. Catholic. Nonprofit. **Member:** N/P. **Enrollment:** Approx. 300 students. **Average class size:** 30-35. **Accreditation:** WASC (6-year term: 2004-10). **Endowment:** N/P. **School year:** Aug.-June. **Instructional days:** 180. **School day:** 8 a.m. to 3 p.m.

Student Body

Ethnicity: 54% Asian, 29% Latino, 8% Caucasian (non-Latino), 7% other, 1% African-American, 1% multi-racial.

Admission

Applications due: Jan.-Aug. (call for date). **Application fee:** $30. **Application process:** Kindergarten applicants are tested on a set Sunday and on weekdays for those not able to come on the set date; G1-8 have whole day classroom visits. **No. of applications:** 50. **No. of K spaces:** 35. **Percentage of K class made up of school's preschool class:** N/A. **Admission evaluation requirements for K:** Test. **Other grades:** Test, school records and school visit. **Preferences:** Siblings. **What sort of student do you best serve?** "Students who want to learn."

Costs

Latest tuition: $3,600. **Sibling discount:** Yes (amount N/P). **Tuition includes:** Lunch: No; Transportation: No; Laptop computer: No; Other: None. **Tuition increases:** Less than 1% annually. **Other costs:** Approx. $280 for general fee and $90 for registration fee. **Percentage of students receiving financial aid:** 30%. **Financial aid application deadline:** Approx. Feb. 28 (call to check date) for Archdiocese of San Francisco and April 15 (call to check date) for the BASIC fund. Financial aid is based on need. **Average grant:** N/P. **Percentage of grants of half-tuition or more:** 50%. **Donations:** N/P.

School's Mission Statement

"Corpus Christi School follows the Catholic educational system inspired by St. John Bosco. With our students, we focus upon Reason, Religion and Loving kindness to guide in the character formation and moral development of the whole child. Service to the young is of paramount importance to our mission and furthermore, serving one's community is a crucial part of the student's experience at Corpus Christi School."

Academic Program

Philosophy: "At Corpus Christi School, we draw enlightenment and inspiration from the life example and educational method of St. John Bosco, upon which the Salesian charism is founded. Our philosophy finds its deepest roots in this educational system, which focuses upon reason, religion and loving kindness. All of our staff are spiritual and educational facilitators who role model Christian values. Our goal is to guide in the formation of each student's total development. Each of our students is encouraged to reach his/her full potential and to become an active and responsible citizen. In order to achieve these goals, we strive to offer each student a rigorous academic curriculum designed to stimulate lifelong love of learning. As our parents are regarded as the primary educators of each child, the faculty and staff collaborate with them by following the spiritual leadership of our Salesian fathers and the Daughters of Mary Help of Christians (known as Salesian Sisters). Together, we offer service to the young people of today and strive to build a community of faith, which upholds the Salesian model of family spirit, optimism, and joy." **Foreign languages:** None. **Computer training:** Staff development training for teachers and training for parents. **No. of computers available for students:** 80 laptops for the use of the students from K-8. There are 15 laptops for the use of each teacher and 35 desktops with updated software programs. **No. of hours weekly of:** Art- 40 min.; Drama- N/A; Music- 40 min.; Computers- varies, with classes having access to computer lab and 4 mobile laptop classroom labs each with 20 computers; Foreign language- N/A; PE- 1. **Outdoor education:** None. **Grading:** A-F, beginning in K. **Average nightly homework:** 1-2 hrs. and more for G6-8. Posted on the Internet: For G4-8. **Percentage of students participating in Johns Hopkins Center for Talented Youth Program:** None. **Other indicators of academic success:** "1) To use and incorporate technological resources into the curriculum to enhance and improve education and communication; 2) to recognize and utilize the Schoolwide Learning Expectations into the students; daily lives; 3) to encourage the students to become more critical, analytical, and comprehensive readers." **High schools attended by latest graduating class:** SI, SHCP, Riordan, Mercy-SF, ICA, Notre Dame, Westmoor, Lowell, El Camino, Burton, Gateway.

Faculty

Ethnicity: 60% Caucasian (non-Latino), 30% Asian, 10% Latino. **Percentage of teachers with graduate degrees:** 95%. **Percentage with current California credential:** 90%. **Faculty selection/training:** "Degree." **Teacher/student ratio:** 1:21. **Special subject teachers:** 5 (subjects N/P). **Average teacher tenure:** N/P.

Middle School

Description: G6-8, departmentalized. **Teacher/student ratio:** 1:30. **Elective courses offered:** N/P. **Achievement tracking in:** Accelerated math and reading; online Alex Math program. **Student social events:** "5 each year."

Student Support Services

No. of Licensed Counselors on staff: None. **Counselor/student ratio:** N/A. **Learning specialists on staff:** One. **Learning differences/disabilities support:** N/P. **High school placement support:** N/P. Other: "The teachers are always available for the students in terms of educational learning. Study Hall Services for G5-8 is free for homework help. Newspaper club meeting and instruction are set for students to develop their writing skills. Informal instruction for guitar and drum lessons are offered for interested students."

Student Conduct and Health

Code of conduct: "Written in the Family and Student Handbooks." **Prevention education and awareness programs:** Taught informally by the homeroom teachers.

Athletics

Sports offered: Basketball, volleyball, baseball, soccer. **Team play begins in:** G3 (intramural).

Campus/Campus Life

Campus description: The school is a two floor building with 9 spacious classrooms, 2 computer labs, a library, and 3 yards. **Library:** Yes, computerized with scanning system. **Sports facilities:** The school has 3 yards. The upper yard has 3 basketball courts with a removable volleyball court, the middle yard has 2 basketball courts with a removable volleyball court, and the lower yard has 4 basketball courts. **Theater/Arts facilities:** N/P. **Computer lab:** Two. **Science lab:** Yes. **Lunch program:** Yes, $3/lunch. **Bus service:** Public transportation. **Uniforms/dress code:** Uniforms. **Opportunities for community service:** "We offer a variety of opportunities or projects for community service."

Extended Day

Morning care: No formal program. **After-school care:** Until 6 p.m. **Grade levels:** K-8. **Cost:** $5 flat fee from 3-6 p.m. and $10 flat fee from 1-6 p.m. **Drop-in care available:** Yes. **Coverage over major holidays:** No. **Homework help:** K-4 help supervised by a Salesian Sister and a lay teacher; G5-8 help in Study Hall supervised by a G8 teacher. **Snacks:** Provided. **Staff/student ratio:** N/P. **After-school classes:** Math and reading. **Cost:** N/P.

Summer Programs

The school offers a summer program with math and language arts classes. **Cost:** $340 for 4½ weeks.

Parent Involvement

Parent/teacher communication: Conferences, website, e-mail, newsletter. **Participation requirements:** Parents and guardians are required to participate in the parent-teacher conferences held twice a year. **Parent education programs:** Parent education and technology programs are offered during monthly parent meetings.

What Sets the School Apart From Others: N/P.

How Parents/Students Characterize School

Parent comment(s): "Great family spirit reigns."
Student comment(s): "Everyone knows everybody."

THE DISCOVERY CENTER SCHOOL
65 Ocean Avenue (at Alemany)(Outer Mission District)
San Francisco, CA 94112
(415) 333-6609 *fax* (415) 333-5477
www.dcssf.com

Janet Wherry, Head of School, JAWherry@WherryAcademy.com
Tina Niesl, Director of Admission, JAWherry@WherryAcademy.com

General

Coed K-8 day school. Founded in 1970. Independent. For profit. **Member:** NCAA. **Enrollment:** Approx. 160. **Average class size:** 12. **Accreditation:** NIPSA (1-year term: 2004-05). **Endowment:** N/P. **School year:** N/P. **Instructional days:** 188. **School day:** 8:30 a.m. to 3:30 p.m.

Student Body

Ethnicity: 40% Caucasian (non-Latino), 10% Asian, 10% Latino, 10% African-American, 10%, multi-racial; 20% other.

Admission

Applications due: Aug. (call for date). **Application fee:** $75. **Application process:** Please call for specifics. **No. of applications:** 30. **No. of K spaces:** 24. **Percentage of K class made up of school's preschool class:** N/A. **Admission evaluation requirements for K:** Visit and screening. **Other grades:** Grades, tests, class visit. **Preferences:** None. **What sort of student do you best serve?** "We are looking for bright, motivated students."

Costs

Latest tuition: $9,000. **Sibling discount:** 15%. **Tuition includes:** Lunch: No; Transportation: No; Laptop computer: No; Other: No. **Tuition increases:** Approx. 0% annually. **Other costs:** Approx. $200 for books, $400 other fees. **Percentage of students receiving financial aid:** 10%. **Financial aid application deadline:** Aug. (call for date). Financial aid is based on need. **Average grant:** $4,000. **Percentage of grants of half-tuition or more:** None. **Donations:** Voluntary.

School's Mission Statement

"The Discovery Center School provides a positive learning environment while preparing each student for college."

Academic Program

Philosophy: "Each student is an individual with unique talents, achievements, and capabilities. With that in mind, a full traditional comprehensive program is offered. Each student is given the maximum chance for success." **Foreign languages:** Spanish. **Computer training:** Yes. **No. of computers available for students:** 18. **No. of hours weekly of:** Art- 5; Drama- 2; Music- 3; Computers- 5; Foreign language- 5; PE- 5. **Outdoor education:** N/P. **Grading:** A-F, beginning in K. **Average nightly homework:** 1 hour. **Posted on the Internet:** No. **Percentage of students participating in Johns Hopkins Center for Talented Youth Program:** N/P. **Other indicators of academic success:** N/P. **High schools attended by latest graduating class:** "Serra, Drew, Wherry, Lick, Lowell, and more."

Faculty

Ethnicity: 25% Caucasian (non-Latino), 25% Asian, 25% Latino, 10% African-American, 10% multiracial, 5% other. **Percentage of teachers with graduate degrees:** 50%. **Percentage with current California credential:** 100%. **Faculty selection/training:** "Credential, experience, in-house." **Teacher/student ratio:** 1:12. **Special subject teachers:** 3 (subjects N/P) **Average teacher tenure:** 6 years.

Middle School

Description: "G6-8, comprehensive program, college preparatory." **Teacher/student ratio:** 1:12. **Elective courses offered:** Private music lessons. **Achievement tracking in:** All subject areas. **Student social events:** Ranch activities, parties, performances.

Student Support Services

No. of Licensed Counselors on staff: One full-time. Counselor/student **ratio:** 1:160. **Learning specialists on staff:** None. **Learning differences/disabilities support:** None. **High school placement support:** "Students are placed in the best high schools."

Student Conduct and Health

Code of conduct: "We expect respect shown to students, teacher, and themselves." **Prevention education and awareness programs:** "We encourage abstinence in drugs, sex, etc., while informing students in all areas."

Athletics

Sports offered: Basketball, baseball, tennis, horseback riding. **Team play begins in:** G5 (intramural).

Campus/Campus Life

Campus description: "The campus is large with an outdoor play area." **Library:** N/P. **Sports facilities:** Outdoor basketball courts. **Theater/ Arts facilities:** The school uses the main building for theater performances as well as an amphitheater. **Computer lab:** Yes. **Science lab:** Yes. **Lunch program:** No. **Bus service:** No. **Uniforms/dress code:** "No uniforms. Dress sensibly, covered and safe." **Opportunities for community service:** Work on campus or at school ranch.

Extended Day

Morning care: Begins at 7 a.m. **After-school care:** Until 6 p.m. **Grade levels:** All. **Cost:** $400/year. **Drop-in care available:** Yes. **Coverage over major holidays:** Yes. **Homework help:** Yes. **Snacks:** Provided. **Staff/student ratio:** 1:12. **After-school classes:** Art, music, etc. **Cost:** Varies; contact school.

Summer Programs

Summer Odyssey runs from mid-June to mid-August. It includes a combination of academics and activities including a field trip once a week. **Cost:** $200/week.

Parent Involvement

Parent/teacher communication: Conferences, website, e-mail, newsletter. **Participation requirements:** None. **Parent education programs offered?:** None.

What Sets the School Apart From Others

"The school accomplishes the arduous task of preparing each student for college. The atmosphere is positive and supportive. The result is a happy, well-educated individual. We have small class sizes and caring teachers. The rules harken back to the 50's where students led a more simple life and kids could be kids."

How Parents/Students Characterize School

Parent comment(s): "The best!"

Student comment(s): "This is our home."

FRENCH–AMERICAN INTERNATIONAL SCHOOL

150 Oak Street (between Gough and Franklin)(Hayes Valley)
San Francisco, CA 94102
(415) 558-2080 *fax (415) 558-2065*
www.fais-ihs.org

Jane Camblin, Head of School, janec@fais-ihs.org
Andrew Brown, Director of Admission,
andrewb@fais-ihs.org

General

Coed PreK-12 day school. Founded in 1962. Independent. Nonprofit. **Member:** The College Board, The Council of International Schools in the Americas (CIStA), The National Association of Independent Schools (NAIS), The European Council of International Schools (ECIS). **Enrollment:** Approx. 600 (PreK-8). **Average class size:** 16. **Accreditation:** L'Agence pour l'Enseigement Français à l'Etranger (AEFE), The Council of International Schools (CIS), The International Baccalaurate Organization (IBO), WASC and CAIS. (Terms: N/P) **Endowment:** $1.5 million. **School year:** Sept.-June. **Instructional days:** 172. **School day:** 8:20 a.m. to 3:15 p.m.

Student Body

Ethnicity: 64% Caucasian (non-Latino), 15% multi-racial, 9% Asian, 8% African-American, 3% Latino, 1% other.

Admission

Applications due: Jan. (call for date). **Application fee:** $100. **Application process:** Campus visit, appointment with Admission Director, and completed application. **No. of applications:** Varies. **No. of K spaces:**

More than 20. **Percentage of K class made up of school's preschool class: 75%. Admission evaluation requirements for K:** General readiness screening, confidential recommendation and letter of motivation. **Other grades:** After first grade, French competence is necessary. Applicants must provide report cards or dossiers and test scores if appropriate. Applicants to grades above K take part in a day-long evaluation and class visit. **Preferences:** "Diversity is a key element in the mission of the French-American International School. Our younger children are being immersed—psychologically and emotionally—in diversity just as they are being immersed in language. It is a point of pride that a FAIS education is international, multilingual and open to the world. We actively recruit families representing a multiplicity of nationalities who are native speakers of languages from all around the globe. We actively seek students from racially, culturally and socio-economically diverse families. Our family configurations are multifarious too. We welcome single parent, gay and lesbian, divorced and separated, as well as adoptive and foster families. From the very beginning our students rub shoulders with others who reflect an astonishing variety of attitudes, religions and political persuasions. We think they learn more because of this, and gain a profound understanding of the richness of the human experience." **What sort of student do you best serve?** "Bright, social children from diverse backgrounds whose parents are very supportive of bilingualism, strong academics and a global outlook."

Costs

Latest tuition: $16,570 for PreK-5, $17,880 for G6-8. Sibling discount: None. **Tuition includes:** Lunch: No; Transportation: No; Laptop computer: No; Other: Text books, and most field trips. **Tuition increases:** Approx. 4-8% annually. **Other costs:** Less than $1,000 in other fees for overnight trips, book clubs, supplies and the like. **Percentage of students receiving financial aid: 28%. Financial aid application deadline:** Dec. (call for date). Financial aid is based on need. **Average grant:** N/P. **Percentage of grants of half-tuition or more:** N/P. **Donations:** "Our advancement department is very active soliciting voluntary donations for the annual fund, capital campaign, auctions, etc."

School's Mission Statement

"Guided by the principles of academic rigor and diversity, the French-American International School offers programs of study in French and English to prepare its graduates for a world in which the ability to think critically and to communicate across cultures is of paramount importance."

Academic Program

Philosophy: "Our curriculum is based on the core of program of the French Ministry of Education. In PreK-2 the program is taught by immersion, 80% in French and 20% in English. In G3-5 we emphasize balanced bilingualism and a transfer of competencies between the two languages. The ratio changes to 50% French and 50% English. Most children enter PreK and K without previous knowledge of French." **Foreign languages:** French, Spanish, Chinese, Italian, German and Latin. **Computer training:** Weekly classes PreK-9. **No. of computers available for students:** Approx. 150. **No. of hours weekly of:** Art- 1 or more; Drama- 1 or more; Music- 1 or more; Computers- 1 or more; Foreign language- varies; PE- 3 or more. **Outdoor education:** Field trips and overnights only. **Grading:** A-F (converted from the French 1-20 system). Letter grades begin in middle school. **Average nightly homework:** Varies. Posted on the Internet: Currently being developed. **Percentage of students participating in Johns Hopkins Center for Talented Youth Program:** N/P. **Other indicators of academic success:** "Year after year, at the end of G4 our global ERB scores hover several points above the independent school norms in all criteria. This is empirical evidence that a bilingual program does not sabotage learning in English program. Our French standardized tests far exceed national averages in France." **High schools attended by latest graduating class:** IHS, Lick, University, Urban, Lowell, Andover, and Exeter.

Faculty

Ethnicity: 80% Caucasian (non-Latino), 6% Asian, 4% African-American, 4% multi-racial, 4% other, 2% Latino. **Percentage of teachers with graduate degrees:** 90%. **Percentage with current California credential:** 30% (more than 60% are credited by the French Ministry of Education). **Faculty selection/training:** "In general we seek experienced international educators with at least 3 years experience. We have a generous professional development budget." **Teacher/student ratio:** Approx. 1:16. **Special subject teachers:** Art, music, theatre, computers, PE, third languages. **Average teacher tenure:** Approx. 5 years.

Middle School

Description: "The Middle School offers a bilingual course of study in French and English from 6th through 8th grade. Our curriculum encourages personal growth enriched by academic rigor, the ability to listen and to understand, and an awareness and openness towards the outside world. Students entering the Middle school must have a high level of literacy in French." **Teacher/student ratio:** 1:18. **Elective courses offered:** Art, music, theatre, computers, PE, Chinese, Spanish, Italian, and German. **Achievement tracking in:** All subjects. **Student social events:** Exchange visits, regular dances, concerts, performances and community service celebrations.

Student Support Services

No. of Licensed Counselors on staff: Four. **Counselor/student ratio:** 1:30. **Learning specialists on staff:** Two. **Learning differences/disabilities support:** Strategies are developed as a result of external diagnostic testing and are handled in-house. **High school placement support:** "85% of Middle School graduates continue on to our own International High School. Full and active support for applications to 'rival' high schools is in place."

Student Conduct and Health

Code of conduct: "The Middle School is a peaceful and studious academic community where each individual shows respect for and is respected by others. There is a Code of Conduct for both the Middle and Lower Schools." **Prevention education and awareness programs:** The school's counselors provide health, social (and parenting) education school-wide, most often featuring outside experts.

Athletics

Sports offered: Basketball, soccer, volleyball, cross-country and baseball. **Team play begins:** "We are a fully fledged participant in the Bay Counties League."

Campus/Campus Life

Campus description: "Expansive 6 floor campus occupying an entire city block in the heart of San Francisco's civic and cultural corridor." **Library:** Two libraries containing print, video and DVD selections in 3 languages—English, French and Chinese. There is a reference section, periodicals and computer stations for on-line research. **Sports facilities:** "One of the best gymnasiums in the city adjacent to large outside spaces. Sports fields, tennis courts and pool are contracted offsite." **Theater/Arts facilities:** The entire 6th floor, and much of the basement, is devoted space for visual and performing arts. **Computer labs:** 3. **Science labs:** 5. **Lunch program:** Voluntary at extra cost. **Bus service:** No. **Uniforms/dress code:** "There is no school uniform, but students are expected to dress appropriately for the school day. In the upper grades there is zero tolerance for slogans or messages contrary to the mission of the school." **Opportunities for community service:** A wide range of opportunities are available beginning in G2.

Extended Day

Morning care: Begins at 7:30 a.m. **After-school care:** Until 6 p.m. **Grade levels:** All. **Cost:** Varies; contact school. **Drop-in care available:** Yes. **Coverage over major holidays:** Yes, but not the winter vacation. **Homework help:** Available in two languages. **Snacks:** Provided. **Staff/student ratio:** 1:8. **After-school classes:** A variety of classes including fencing, music, photography, and art. **Cost:** $120+ per class.

Summer Programs

"We are a premier location for both fun and rigorous bilingual summer programs. Our programs offer students PreK through 8th grade the unique opportunity to learn, enhance and expand their language skills in a fun, creative atmosphere. Our mission is to develop self-confidence in written and verbal language skills and to foster an awareness of the cultural diversity within our international community." **Cost:** N/P.

Parent Involvement

Parent/teacher communication: Regular parent-teacher conferences, website, e-mail, newsletters. "Very active" Parent Associations and room parent network. **Participation requirements:** "12 hours is the minimum requested volunteer commitment by the school. Many parents do much more. Whole-hearted, parental involvement is key to supporting the immersion process." **Parent education programs offered?:** Yes.

What Sets the School Apart From Others

"The French-American International School offers world-class bilingual education in the heart of San Francisco. At FAIS we offer the better of two educational worlds—we are both the largest PreK-12 independent school in the Bay Area and a fully-accredited, French public school. Our own International High School experience culminates in a two-year baccalaureate program. We are one of very few schools in the world offering both the International Baccalaureate and the French Baccalaureate."

How Parents/Students Characterize School

Parent comment: "If you want your child to be completely bilingual by age eight, to rub shoulders with people of widely varying national and socioeconomic backgrounds, and to become immersed in a sophisticated and content-rich academic environment, then this is the place for you. The kids work hard, the pace is intense, but they seem to have a great time and their horizons are wider than those of many others their age."

Student comment: "The acquisition of facts is not the priority, knowledge is not the issue, but understanding is, and understanding goes beyond just dates, and laws, and formulas. This reminds me of a Calvin and Hobbes strip, in which Calvin complains that, in school, 'for some reason they'd rather teach us stuff that any fool can look up in a book.' Fortunately, the experience at IHS is different; the things we learn are not self sufficient, but they depend on the thought that is put behind them, the idea that drives them. As Calvin knew, any fool can look up facts in a book. Our teachers know this as well, which is why with each fact we learn, we are not assimilating, but reacting, understanding, and thinking."

The Hamlin School
2120 Broadway St. (btwn. Webster and Buchanan) (Pacific Heights)
San Francisco, CA 94115
(415) 922-0300 *fax (415) 674-5409*
www.hamlin.org

Coreen Ruiz Hester, Head of School, hester@hamlin.org
Lisa Lau Aquino '81, Director of Admission, aquino@hamlin.org

General
All girls K-8 day school. Founded in 1863. Independent. Nonprofit. **Member:** NAIS, CAIS, NCGS. **Enrollment:** Approx. 400. **Average class size:** 16 for K, 22 for G1-8. **Accreditation:** CAIS (6-year term: 2000-06). **Endowment:** $8.4 million. **School year:** Sept.-June. **Instructional days:** 175. **School day:** 8:25 a.m. to 2 p.m. for K, 8:25 a.m. to 3:15 p.m. for G1-8.

Student Body:
Ethnicity: "32% students of color."

Admission
Applications due: March (call for date). **Application fee:** $75. **Application process:** A completed application, parent interview, student

visit, and a nonrefundable $75 application fee are required elements of the admission process. "Hamlin encourages families to visit our school, discuss our program, and tour our buildings." **No. of applications: 200+. No. of K spaces: 46. Percentage of K class made up of school's preschool class: N/A. Admission evaluation requirements for K:** Student screening, preschool teacher evaluation, parent interview. **Other grades:** Student visit, school records, teacher recommendations, ISEE exam for G5-8, parent interview. **Preferences:** Sibling. **What sort of student do you best serve?** "The Hamlin School best serves girls who are motivated, hardworking and eager to learn. We offer a challenging academic program in an environment of encouragement and support."

Costs

Latest tuition: $19,275. **Sibling discount:** None. **Tuition includes:** Lunch: No; Transportation: No; Laptop computer: No; Other: Textbooks, field trips, outdoor education programs, yearbook. **Tuition increases:** Approx. 7% annually. **Other costs:** Approx. $30-$150 uniforms. **Percentage of students receiving financial aid:** 15%. **Financial aid application deadline:** Jan./Feb. (call for date). Financial aid is based on need. **Average grant:** $12,000. **Percentage of grants of half-tuition or more:** 65%. **Donations:** Voluntary. Include time, annual fund, capital campaign, parent association events.

School's Mission Statement

"For well over a century, the mission of The Hamlin School has been 'to educate girls and young women to meet the challenges of their time.' The program at Hamlin aims to develop the intellect, the character, and the citizenship of each girl to prepare her to face the future with courage and confidence. ♦ Hamlin offers a challenging academic program in an environment of encouragement and support. Students master the skills that provide a foundation for life-long learning as well as the habits of speculation, inquiry, and critical thinking. Our methods are both experiential and collaborative, promoting engagement and creativity. Hamlin students graduate knowing how to learn, appreciating the value of industry, and possessing a love of knowledge. ♦ Hamlin is committed to be an inclusive community where diversity is a component of excellence and all members of the community are respected. We welcome and benefit from the perspectives that emerge from a diversity of ethnicity, culture, religion, socioeconomic status, learning style, sexual orientation, and family structure. The participation of all is important to the health of the community. ◆ Hamlin cultivates leadership skills in every young woman and promotes the importance of service to others, both within and beyond our community. Through mutual respect, honesty, and kindness, we impress upon our students the importance of personal integrity and ethical decision-making.◆ In the tradition of Sarah Dix Hamlin, we inspire girls to find the best in themselves and to contribute with energy and distinction to the world around them."

Academic Program

Philosophy: See Mission Statement. **Foreign languages:** French and Spanish. **Computer training:** Yes. **No. of computers available for students:** 72 plus 25 wireless laptops. **No. of hours weekly of:** Art- 1.5-2.5 in K-4, 3-4 in G5-8; Drama- K-4 after-school program, 3-4 in G5-8th (elective); Music- 1.5-2.5 in K-4, 1.5-3 in G5-8; Computers- 45 min.-1.5 hrs. in K-8; Foreign language- 45 min.-2.5 hrs. in K-4, 3-4 in G5-8; PE- 1.5-2.5 in K-4; 3-4 in G5-8. **Outdoor education:** Fieldtrips in every grade. Overnight trips begin in G4. **Grading:** A-F, beginning in G5. **Average nightly homework:** Varies. Posted on the Internet: No. **Percentage of students participating in Johns Hopkins Center for Talented Youth Program:** N/P. **Other indicators of academic success:** N/P. **High schools attended by latest graduating class:** Bay School, Branson, CSH, Creekview High School, Drew, IHS, Lick, Limon, Lowell, MA, Mercy-SF, Mills, Andover, Redwood, San Domenico, University, and Urban.

Faculty

Ethnicity: "18% of color." **Percentage of teachers with graduate degrees:** 42%. **Percentage with current California credential:** N/P. **Faculty selection/training:** Graduate degree preferred; minimum 3 years head teaching experience. **Teacher/student ratio:** 1:7. **Special subject teachers:** Art, music, dance, drama, French, Spanish, technology, library, PE. **Average teacher tenure:** 15 years.

Middle School

Description: The middle school spans G5-8. The program is entirely departmentalized with all academic classes meeting 5 days weekly in 45-minute sessions. PE and electives also meet daily. **Teacher/student ratio:** 1:7. **Elective courses offered:** Drama, dance, yearbook, computer, music. **Achievement tracking in:** French, math. **Student social events:** Culture club, debate club, community service, literary magazine, student government.

Student Support Services

No. of Licensed Counselors on staff: Two part-time. **Counselor/student ratio:** 1:200. **Learning specialists on staff:** Three. **Learning differences/disabilities support:** Individual and group support for mild to moderate learning differences. **High school placement support:** High school placement counselor. **Other:** Weekly advising program.

Student Conduct and Health

Code of conduct: "The Hamlin Creed, written by Hamlin students, embodies the values of the entire community. The Creed guides the interactions among students, faculty, and family. Be respectful; Be responsible; Be caring; Be honest; Be positive." **Prevention education and awareness programs:** The school's program covers drug and alcohol awareness, smoking, health and human sexuality education, body image, media literacy, self-defense, and harassment.

Athletics

Sports offered: Volleyball, basketball, soccer, cross-country, running club, softball, and futsal. **Team play begins in:** G5 (intermural).

Campus/Campus Life

Campus description: "Urban." **Library:** 13,000 volumes, 9 computers. **Sports facilities:** Gymnasium and rooftop. **Theater/Arts facilities:** Gymnasium/theater. **Computer lab:** Yes. **Science lab:** Yes. **Lunch program:** Yes. **Bus service:** No. **Uniforms/dress code:** Uniforms. **Opportunities for community service:** Multiple opportunities through the Lend-A-Hand program for families and students; Middle School community service program.

Extended Day

Morning care: Begins 7 a.m. **After-school care:** Until 6 p.m. **Grade levels:** K-8. **Cost:** $6.66/hour. **Drop-in care available:** Yes. **Coverage over major holidays:** Yes. **Homework help:** Yes. **Snacks:** Provided. **Staff/student ratio:** 1/8. **After-school classes:** The school's After School Academy includes a variety of non-academic classes such as creative dance, theater, circus arts, yoga, carpentry, Mandarin, Tree Frog Treks, fencing and more. Cost: Approx. $225 per term.

Summer Programs

"Hamlin Summer Camp brings the wilderness, sleep-away camp community into the heart of San Francisco. Campers participate in various camp activities such as Climbing Wall, Sports & Games, and Arts & Crafts. They also explore the city on adventurous field trips to Golden Gate Park, Yerba Buena and the city's National Parks. Hamlin Summer Camp creates an environment where children can strengthen their social skills and build relationships with children of all ages and leaders as well. Hamlin offers summer camps for girls and boys entering G1-9. Also, for our Hamlin incoming Kindergarten girls we have Cubs Club which is filled with arts and crafts, drama, games, imaginative play and more." **Cost:** N/P.

Parent Involvement

Parent/teacher communication: Conferences, phone, e-mail, newsletter, weekly folder. **Participation requirements:** "Parents are an integral part of the school, and we encourage all of our parents to become involved with the Hamlin community. Through the Parents Association, parents are on campus helping in the lunchroom and the library, preparing for numerous Hamlin community events, organizing community service projects, or helping with school fundraisers. You can also find parents reading stories in the classrooms, driving on fieldtrips, sharing a particular expertise as a guest speaker in the classroom, and so much more." **Parent education programs offered?:** Yes.

What Sets the School Apart From Others: N/P.

How Parents/Students Characterize School

Parent comment(s): "Academic, nurturing, inclusive, visionary."
Student comment(s): "Engaging, caring, community, responsibility."

HOLY NAME OF JESUS SCHOOL

1560 40th Avenue (at Lawton) (Outer Sunset District)
San Francisco, CA 94122
(415) 731-4077 fax (415) 731-3328
www.holynamesf.com

Mrs. Noreen Murphy, Principal, principal@holynamesf.com
Director of Admission, admissions@holynamesf.com

General

Co-ed K-8 parochial day school. Founded in 1941. Catholic. Non-profit. **Member:** NCEA. **Enrollment:** Approx. 420. **Average class size:** 25. **Accreditation:** WASC (6-year term: 2003-09). **Endowment:** N/P. **School year:** Aug.-June. **Instructional days:** 180. **School day:** 8 a.m. to 3 p.m.

Student Body

Ethnicity: 54% Asian, 19% multi-racial, 15% Caucasian (non-Latino), 10% other, 1% Latino, 1% African-American.

Admission

Applications due: Jan. (call for date). **Application fee:** $50. **Application process:** Applications are available from the school office beginning in October. Submit the application, a small photo of the child, the application fee, a copy of the birth certificate, a copy of the baptismal certificate (if applicable), and a copy of his/her immunization records to the school office either in person or by mail. Applicants for G1-8 must also submit copies of current report cards and standardized test scores. A Preschool Evaluation Form will be sent to preschools of kindergarten applicants. Once all paperwork has been submitted, the child will be scheduled for a test/evaluation. Parents are usually notified within 1 week of testing as to whether their child is accepted. **No. of applications:** Varies. **No. of K spaces:** 50. **Percentage of K class made up of school's preschool class:** N/A. **Admission evaluation requirements for K:** Preschool evaluation form, screening and school visit. **Other grades:** Prior report card, test scores, evaluation test. **Preferences:** Siblings, Catholic parishioners, other qualified children. **What sort of student do you best serve?** "Holy Name welcomes enthusiastic children who want a culturally diverse environment to learn and grow academically, socially, physically and emotionally."

Costs

Latest tuition: $4,200 for parish and service hour contributors, $5,100 for non-supporting families. **Sibling discount:** Yes (amount N/P). **Tuition includes:** Lunch: No; Transportation: No; Laptop computer: No Other: N/P. **Tuition increases:** Approx. 5% annually. **Other costs:** $100 for uniforms, $20 for yearbooks, $270 for G7 outdoor education. **Percentage of students receiving financial aid:** 8%. Financial aid is based on need. Provided through the Archdiocese of San Francisco and the BASIC Fund. **Financial aid application deadline:** Feb. (call for date). **Average grant:** N/P. **Percentage of grants of half-tuition or more:** N/P. **Donations:** 25 service hours per family.

School's Mission Statement

"Holy Name Parish School is a Catholic school committed to offering its students a strong spiritual foundation and a solid academic education. Each student is expected to achieve his or her highest level of scholarship while learning values to help them become compassionate, contributing and responsible members of society."

Academic Program

Philosophy: "We, the faculty of Holy Name Parish School, are committed to providing a quality Catholic education for each student. We believe that this education is vital to the formation of a responsible, maturing Christian child. We strive: 1) To form a Catholic community; 2) To form a Christian community; 3) To teach and demonstrate Christian values emphasizing respect for the rights and dignity of every person; 4) To support and supplement the family as the educators of their children; 5) To show concern for the well-being, the progress and the individual needs of each child; 6) To develop the whole child spiritually, intellectually, physically, socially, culturally and emotionally; 7) To develop each child's potential and creativity." **Foreign languages:** "Cantonese and beginning Mandarin classes are offered after school three days a week. Spanish and Gaelic language classes are also offered after school." **Computer training:** "Students have computer class in the computer lab with a computer teacher each week. Students also have access to and use computers in their classrooms." **No. of computers available for students:** Three in each classroom, 18 in the computer lab and 6 laptops available for PowerPoint presentations. **No. of hours weekly of:** Art- 1; Drama-("annual musical production of G8 by a professional director who is also a classroom teacher at Holy Name"); Music- 1; Computers- 1: Foreign language- (optional and after-school); PE- 1. **Outdoor education:** One week in G7. **Grading:** A-E, beginning in G3. **Average nightly homework:** 25 min. for G1-2; 45 min. for G3-4; 60-90 min. for G5-6; 90-120 min. for G7-8. Homework posted on the Internet: No. **Percentage of students participating in Johns Hopkins Center for Talented Youth Program:** 10%. **Other indicators of academic success:** Participation in the Bay Area Academic Decathlon and the large percentage of students accepted to schools of their choice. **High schools attended by latest graduating class:** SHCP, SI, Lowell, Mercy-SF, Riordan, CSH, Mercy-Burlingame.

Faculty

Ethnicity: 75% Caucasian (non-Latino), 13% Asian, 8% Filipino, 4% Latino. **Percentage of teachers with graduate degrees:** 35%. **Percentage with current California credential:** 90%. **Faculty selection/training:** N/P. **Teacher/student ratio:** 1:22. **Special subject teachers:** Music, computers, PE. **Average teacher tenure:** 12 years.

Middle School

Description: G7-8. Departmentalized. Junior high students rotate between classrooms and are taught by 8 different teachers for various subjects. **Teacher/student ratio:** 1:30. **Elective courses offered:** High School Entrance Exam preparation classes are offered to 8th grade students. **Student social events:** N/P.

Student Support Services

No. of Licensed Counselors on staff: One full-time. Counselor/student ratio: 1:400. **Learning specialists on staff:** One part-time. **Learning differences/disabilities support:** Learning specialist and work modifications accompanied by a modified report card. **High school placement support:** "The junior high teachers, counselor and principal all offer guidance on choosing the best high school for each student."

Student Conduct and Health

Code of conduct: "A code of conduct and disciplinary measures are clearly stated in the Holy Name School Parent Handbook". **Prevention education and awareness addressed in:** Youth Aware Life Skills, a drug/alcohol/tobacco awareness program is presented by the National Council on Alcoholism and Other Drug Addictions – Bay Area to students in G4-6. Sex, health and harassment are covered in the curriculum provided by the Archdiocese of San Francisco.

Athletics

Sports offered: Boys basketball, soccer, and baseball; girls volleyball and basketball. **Team play begins in:** G3 (intermural).

Campus/Campus Life

Campus description: "A multi-faceted facility." **Library:** A computerized library with 5,000 volumes. **Sports facilities:** A large gymnasium. **Theater/Arts facilities:** The school uses with gymnasium, which has a large stage, audio system and stage lighting. **Computer lab:** Yes. **Science lab:** No. **Lunch program:** Optional lunches are provided on Fridays. **Bus service:** No. **Uniforms/dress code:** Uniforms. **Opportunities for community service:** Junior high students are required to perform 10 hours of community service.

Extended Day

Morning care: Begins at 7 a.m. **After-school care:** Until 6 p.m. **Grade levels:** All grades. **Cost:** $180/mo. **Drop-in care available:** Yes. **Homework help:** Yes. **Snacks:** Provided. **Staff/student ratio:** 1:10.

After-school classes: Chinese language, Art of Self-Discipline, piano, chess, Irish language, Irish music (Tin Whistle). Cost: N/P.

Summer Programs

Summer school is offered to students registered with Holy Name School in Kindergarten entering G1-8. **Cost:** For the Academic Program (8 a.m.-11 a.m.), $350 for 5 weeks (not available on a weekly basis); for Summer Camp (11 a.m.-2 p.m.), $ 75/week or $300 for 5 weeks; for Recreation Camp (2 a.m.-6 p.m.), $75/week or $300 for 5 weeks; entire program (all 3 programs) (8 a.m.-6 p.m.) $800 for 5 weeks.

Parent Involvement

Parent/teacher communication: Parent-teacher conferences, website, Tuesday Parent Bulletin. **Participation requirements:** Families are required to give 25 service hours, participate in the scrip program, and support the school' fundraisers. **Parent education programs offered?** Yes.

What Sets the School Apart From Others

"Holy Name School has a warm, nurturing staff who genuinely care for their students. Holy Name provides a culturally diverse environment in which students learn and grow academically, socially, physically and emotionally."

KATHERINE DELMAR BURKE SCHOOL
7070 California Street (32nd Avenue) (Sea Cliff)
San Francisco, CA 94121
(415) 751-0177 fax (415) 666-0535
www.kdbs.org

Jessie-Lea Abbott, Head of School, Jessie-lea@kdbs.org
Renee Thompson, renee@kdbs.org
Mary Jizmagian, Associate Director of Admissions, mary.j@kdbs.org

General

Girls K-8 day school. Founded in 1908, Independent, Nonprofit. **Member:** NAIS, CAIS, NCGS, NBOA, ISBOA, ERB, BADA. **Enrollment:** Approx. 400. **Average class size:** N/P. **Accreditation:** CAIS (6-year term: 2000-06). **Endowment:** $7 million. **School year:** Aug.-June. **Instructional day:** 183. **School day:** For K-4, begins at 8:30 a.m. with dismissal from 2:15 p.m. to 3:20 p.m.; for G5-8 8:15 a.m. to 3:30 p.m.

Student Body

Ethnicity: 71% Caucasian (non-Latino), 16% Asian, 5% Latino, 4% African-American, 4% multi-racial.

Admission

Applications due: Dec. (call for date). **Application fee:** $75. **Application process:** "The thorough application process begins in September and continues through the fall and winter; responses are mailed to applying families in mid-March. Families begin to get to know the school by attending the Admissions Preview (open house) and a tour. KDBS gets to know each applicant through her visit to campus, teacher and school recommendations, transcripts, and age/grade-appropriate admissions testing." **No. of applications:** Approximately 170. **No. of K spaces:** 44. **Percentage of K class made up of school's preschool class:** N/A. **Admission evaluation requirements for K:** Group visit, individual screening, teacher and pre-school director recommendations, parent tour, parent interview; **Other grades:** Admissions test (ISEE) for applicants to G5-8, student visit, teacher recommendations, transcript, parent tour, parent interview. **Preferences:** Siblings and children of alumnae. **What sort of student do you best serve?** "We serve a wide range of students who have the common characteristic of being ready and eager to learn."

Costs

Latest tuition: $18,805 for K-5; $19,460 for G7-8. **Sibling discount:** N/A. **Tuition includes:** Lunch: No; Transportation: No; Laptop computer: No; Other: Books, fees, and outdoor education. **Tuition**

increases: Approx. 7% annually. **Other costs:** Uniforms cost $123 in the Lower School and $136 in the Upper School. **Percentage of students receiving financial aid:** Approximately 20%. **Financial aid application deadline:** Jan. (call for date.) Financial aid is based on need. **Average grant:** $9,700. **Percentage of grants of half tuition or more:** 79%. **Donations:** Voluntary. Donations last year totaled $1.03 million for the annual fund, capital campaign, auctions.

School's Mission Statement
"Educate, Encourage, and Empower Girls."

Academic Program
Philosophy: "We provide our rigorous academic program in an environment that cherishes each girl for who she is. Our students excel because we treasure and promote learning through the joys and explorations of childhood. Our skillful and dedicated teachers and staff create a cooperative, collaborative environment that fosters independence, responsibility and respect for self and others." **Foreign languages:** French, Spanish, and Mandarin. **Computer training:** Beginning in K. **No. of computers available for students:** 133. **No. of hours weekly of:** Art- 1.5; Drama- .75; Music- 1.5; Computers- 1.5; Foreign language- 2-3 beginning G5; PE- 3. **Outdoor education:** Yes, begins in G3. **Grading:** A-F, beginning in G5 in addition to qualitative feedback. **Average nightly homework:** Formal homework begins in G2 when students are expected to spend approximately thirty minutes a night on this work. The amount of homework increases incrementally each year and eighth graders complete approximately two to three hours of homework each night. Posted on the Internet: No. **Percentage of students participating in Johns Hopkins Center for Talented Youth Program:** 9%. **Other indicators of academic success:** "Performance as reported by high schools." **High schools attended by latest graduating class:** Bay School, Colorado Rocky Mountain School, CSH, Drew, Gateway, Groton, IHS, Lick, Lowell, MA, Middlesex, Phillips Academy, SHCP, University, St. Andrew's, SI, St. Paul's, Stevenson, Tamalpais, Thacher, Urban.

Faculty

Ethnicity: 77% Caucasian (non-Latino), 10% Asian, 5% Latino, 3% African-American, 5% other. **Percentage of teachers with graduate degrees:** 40%. **Percentage with current California credential:** 80%. **Faculty selection/training:** The school seeks candidates with relevant teaching experience and at least a BA degree. **Teacher/student ratio:** 1:8. **Special subject teachers:** Art, community service and service learning, drama, library, music, science, PE and athletics, and technology. **Average teacher tenure:** 10 years.

Middle School

Description: KDBS Upper School begins in G5. **Teacher/student ratio:** 1:8. **Elective courses offered:** Art, drama, chorus, journalism, photography, newspaper, cooking, sewing, calligraphy, needlepoint, and yearbook. **Achievement tracking in:** Math, beginning in G7. **Student social events:** Eighth Grade independent school dances.

Student Support Services

No. of Licensed Counselors on staff: One part-time. **Counselor/student ratio:** N/P. **Learning specialists on staff:** 1.5 FTE. **Learning differences/disabilities support:** N/P. **High school placement support:** The school has a half-time High School Guidance Counselor. **Other:** A Reading Specialist (at 80% time).

Student Conduct and Health

Code of conduct: "The school works in partnership with its families. Parents and school share responsibility for helping students learn how to behave individually and in communities. In addition, the school holds the responsibility for creating a positive school climate in which respect for self and community helps us all be equally free to grow, learn, and to develop as individuals. At Burke's, we emphasize the importance of respecting the differences in others. Deliberate unkindness has no place at Burke's or anywhere else. The school strives to maintain a climate of honesty and trust." (An expanded and detailed description of "conditions of enrollment" is contained in the KDBS Handbook and is provided to every school family.) **Prevention education and**

awareness addressed in: "These areas are covered in virtually every grade with a special emphasis in the G8 Science curriculum. Girls study reproductive health which includes anatomy, sexually transmitted infections, sexual decision-making, and birth control. Seventh and Eighth graders meet with a visiting drug and alcohol abuse prevention educator."

Athletics

Sports offered: Volleyball, cross-country, basketball, soccer, and softball (G7-8). **Team play begins in:** (Club) G5, and Varsity and Junior Varsity in G7.

Campus/Campus Life

Campus description: "Burke's is a city school with a country campus. The school sits on a three and one-half acre campus in Sea Cliff. The spacious campus beckons students and encourages both physical and intellectual exploration." **Library:** The library contains nearly 30,000 volumes, and eight computers. **Sports facilities:** Gymnasium, sports field, and ground-level greentop. **Theater/Arts facilities:** Two art studios, and two performance spaces. **Computer lab:** Two desktop labs and two laptop "virtual" labs. **Science lab:** Yes. **Lunch program:** Yes. **Bus service:** No. **Uniforms/dress code:** Uniforms. **Opportunities for community service:** "Burke's girls at every grade level participate in age-appropriate community service activities that are embedded in classroom learning and help prepare them for 'life in community.' Through service-learning students learn to understand the ways in which they can make a difference both within and beyond their own communities. Students engage in activities that emerge from their own interests or relate to community interests. Examples of our partner organizations/projects are Haight-Ashbury Food Program, SPCA, campus recycling, Breast Cancer Awareness, disaster-relief, local schools, and senior centers."

Extended Day

Morning care: Begins at: 7:30 a.m. **After-school care:** Until 6 p.m. **Grade levels:** K-8. **Cost:** No charge for a.m. care; p.m. care is $7/hour.

Drop-in care available: Yes. **Coverage over major holidays:** No. **Homework help:** Available informally in G3-4. Study Hall is available for girls in G5-8 and the supervisor is available to answer questions. **Snacks:** Provided at 3:15 p.m. and 5 p.m. **Staff/student ratio:** Approx. 1:12. **After-school classes:** A variety of classes such as chess, debate, karate, dance, technology, art exploration, ceramics, violin, piano, singing, drama, painting, and knitting. Cost: $20/hour.

Summer Programs
Burke's offers a summer camp for children entering K-G1. The camp offers a variety of activities in one-week modules from mid-June through late July. Activities offered include art, sports, cooking, sewing, and hands-on science projects. **Cost:** N/P.

Parent Involvement
Parent/teacher communication: "Because girls learn and thrive when families and schools work together, Burke's provides both formal and informal opportunities for parents to support their daughter's education. In addition to regular written progress reports and parent-teacher conferences, there are scheduled parent education meetings throughout the year. The school also publishes a weekly newsletter called *Tuesday Notes*. Information is also posted on the KDBS website and school-wide e-mail messages are sent as needed and appropriate." **Participation requirements:** "Burke's expects our parents to participate in parent-teacher conferences. Parents are also encouraged to become active in the Parents' Association by volunteering to help with projects on or off campus or from their homes." **Parent education programs offered?:** Yes.

What Sets the School Apart From Others
"KDBS offers a rigorous academic program in a school culture that fosters individual growth and learning through the exploration of childhood."

How Parents/Students Characterize School
Parent comment(s): "Burke's is a strong and caring community. The combination of excellent academics, creative arts, athletics, service to

community, and character development is outstanding. We are proud of our daughter's academic achievements and equally happy with the fine young woman that she is becoming."

Student comment(s): "Burke's is a school that appreciates me for who I am and a place that challenges me to grow, contribute, and improve. I like knowing that I matter and that it's okay to struggle and make mistakes."

KITTREDGE SCHOOL

2355 Lake Street (at 25th Avenue) (Richmond District)
San Francisco, CA 94121
(415) 750-8390 *fax (415) 751-2011*
www.kittredge.org

Peter Lavaroni Head of School, lavaroni@kittredge.org

General

Coed K-8 day school. Founded in 1944. Independent/Proprietary. **Member:** NIPSA. **Enrollment:** Approx. 85. **Average class size:** 14. **Accreditation:** National Independent Private School Association (NIPSA) (7-year term: 2004-11). **Endowment:** N/A. **School year:** Aug. 30-June 9. **Instructional days:** 175. **School day:** 8:30/8:40 a.m. to 3 p.m.

Student Body
Ethnicity: N/P.

Admission
Applications due: Approx. Jan. 10 (call for date). **Application fee:** $50. **Application process:** Parents/guardians must attend an open house or tour the school before submitting an application. The completed application with the application fee must be returned to the school. Current school records and recommendations must be completed by the prior school and sent to Kittredge before a visit for the child is arranged. Children applying for K will be evaluated during a play date/screen-

ing arranged by the school in January. Children applying for G1-8 will spend a full school day at Kittredge in their current grade. Decisions will be mailed early March. Parents will be expected to respond within a week's time by returning the completed contract with deposit. **No. of applications:** Approx. 45. **No. of K spaces:** 7. **Percentage of K class made up of school's preschool class:** N/A. **Admission evaluation requirements for K:** Recommendations from the child's preschool are required and a play date/screening must be attended. Students must be 5 years old by the first day of school. **Other grades:** Parents must have the child's current school complete and return the student recommendation forms and record release form. Selected students will spend a full school day at Kittredge where they will be assessed for appropriate fit. The principal will administer a short achievement test during the student's visit day. **Preferences:** Siblings may be evaluated and accepted early. **What sort of student do you best serve?** "Children that will thrive in a small environment that is both academically challenging and nurturing."

Costs

Latest tuition: $11,300 for K-5, $11,900 for G6-8. **Sibling discount:** 10% for youngest sibling. **Tuition includes:** Lunch: No; Transportation: No; Laptop computer: School use only; Other: Books and most supplies. **Tuition increases:** Approx. 5% annually. **Other costs:** Up to approximately $300 in fees for outdoor education, yearbook, some sports teams, drama club, and chess club. **Percentage of students receiving financial aid:** 5%. **Financial aid application deadline:** Call for date. Financial aid is based on need and/or merit. **Average grant:** 5-20%. **Percentage of grants of half-tuition or more:** None. **Donations:** N/A.

School's Mission Statement

Kittredge School's mission is to offer its students "challenging academics in a warm and nurturing environment."

Academic Program

Philosophy: "Kittredge School is structured, friendly and productive. We believe in recognizing the worth and dignity of students and faculty alike while creating an atmosphere where strong academic goals are combined with supportive human interaction. Kittredge School recognizes the need for educating the whole child. Students receive weekly instruction in fine arts, music and drama as well as Spanish three times a week. The school also provides a daily formal physical education program. Kittredge School recognizes the necessity of self-discipline in order for a student to progress to his/her maximum potential. The goal is to help each student recognize his/her obligations to appropriate citizenship. Through published standards and effective modeling by concerned teachers, students learn the balance between freedom and responsibility. Kittredge School expects and requires students to exercise appropriate self-discipline and to respect people and property, providing a safe environment for each student to develop his/her individuality." **Foreign languages:** Spanish. **Computer training:** N/P. **No. of computers available for students:** 17. **No. of hours weekly of:** Art- 1; Drama- 1; Music- 1; Computers- 1-3; Foreign language- 2-3; PE- 2.5. **Outdoor education:** Varies by grade with G7 and G8 having an annual week-long trip to Yosemite Institute. **Grading:** A-F, beginning in G4. **Average nightly homework:** Varies from 15-20 min. in K to 60-120 min. in G8. Posted on the Internet: No. **Percentage of students participating in Johns Hopkins Center for Talented Youth Program:** 28% in upper grades. **Other indicators of academic success:** Test scores and school placements. **High schools attended by latest graduating class:** Bay School, CSH, Drew, Gateway, Lowell, Stuart Hall.

Faculty

Ethnicity: 60% Caucasian (non-Latino), 10% Asian, 10% multi-racial, 20% other. **Percentage of teachers with graduate degrees:** 50%. **Percentage with current California credential:** 83%. **Faculty selection/training:** "Kittredge hires classroom teachers that hold teaching credentials, usually from California. Experience and advanced degrees are a plus. Kittredge School searches for teachers that want to work in the environment as described in our philosophy." **Teacher/student ratio:** Approx. 1:14. **Special subject teachers:** Art, music, Spanish, drama, PE. **Average teacher tenure:** 10.1 years.

Middle School

Description: Comprised of G6-8. Classes are team-taught by several core teachers. **Teacher/student ratio:** 1:15 maximum. **Elective courses offered:** N/P. **Achievement tracking in:** Math with algebra or pre-algebra. **Student social events:** The school participates in all independent school dances.

Student Support Services

No. of Licensed Counselors on staff: None. **Counselor/student ratio:** N/A. **Learning specialists on staff:** None. **Learning differences/disabilities support:** "Kittredge School's small classes allow its teachers to support children with learning differences by working with them, their parents and the specialists secured by the families from outside of school. Teachers are made aware of the recommendations for the students with identified differences and implement as many as possible. Though Kittredge School is not designed specifically for students with learning differences, many such students have thrived because of the concern and care offered by the teachers, the staff and the other students, and by the diligence of the teachers to challenge each student appropriately." **High school placement support:** A high school counselor with 25 years experience with local high schools.

Student Conduct and Health

Code of conduct: "Kittredge School places a high priority on students assuming responsibility for their behavior and treating others with respect. Students are expected to be courteous, cooperative, honest, well mannered and considerate. Behavior that conflicts with these values is not condoned and will be subject to counseling and possible disciplinary action." **Prevention education and awareness addressed in:** "Kittredge students are exposed to prevention education and awareness in grade appropriate curriculum."

Athletics

Sports offered: Cross-country, volleyball, basketball, futsal, softball and track. **Team play begins:** G6 (intermural). Team sports, and the necessary individual skills are taught in all of the daily PE classes. Sportsmanship is emphasized in all athletic events.

Campus/Campus Life

Campus description: Kittredge School's entire campus is situated in a converted three-story house in the Richmond District of San Francisco. **Library:** Each classroom has its own library of grade-appropriate books. **Sports facilities:** The school uses city playgrounds and rents local gyms for sport events. **Theater/Arts facilities:** The school rents local theaters for shows. **Computer lab:** Yes. **Science lab:** No. **Lunch program:** No. **Bus service:** No. **Uniforms/dress code:** "Kittredge School does not use uniforms, but a balanced dress code is enforced." **Opportunities for community service:** The Kittredge School Parent Association offers opportunities for students and their families to participate voluntarily throughout the community. Kittredge School holds special community service days for the whole school and for individual classes.

Extended Day

Morning care: Begins at 7:45 a.m. **After-school care:** Until 6 p.m. **Grade levels:** "All, but most appropriate for K-6." **Cost:** $270 a month. **Drop-in care available:** Yes. **Coverage over major holidays:** Yes. **Homework help:** Yes. **Snacks:** Provided. **Staff/student ratio:** 1:8. **After-school classes:** Varies each semester. Cost: N/P.

Summer Programs

"The Kittredge School Summer Program emphasizes the basic skills of mathematics, reading and all forms of English language arts. Our small class size (15 students max.) allows each teacher to engage the students in a variety of activities designed to enrich their academic foundation and keep them involved and interested in learning. Extended Day is available where supervised study, recreational and educational activities are provided in conjunction with the morning academic program." **Cost:** The morning program (9 a.m.-1 p.m.) costs $1,025 without extended care or, with extended care (7:45 a.m. to 6 p.m.), $1,475.

Parent Involvement

Parent/teacher communication: "Communication between parents and teachers is important at Kittredge. Day-to-day informal communication is made easier by the student/teacher ratio and relatively small size of the school. Formal communication includes three scheduled parent-teacher conferences. A back-to-school night is held one evening each September. The administration publishes a weekly newsletter to keep parents informed of the happenings around the school. The Parents' Association meets once a month and produces its own monthly newsletter. Report cards are issued four times a year, at the end of the quarter and semester periods." **Participation requirements:** "Though there are no formal requirements, parents are expected to conduct themselves in a responsible manner with their interactions with the school. They are to reinforce the school rules with their children and take an active role in their child's personal development." **Parent education programs offered?:** "The school and the parent association offers multiple yearly opportunities for parents to meet specialists and members of the Kittredge School faculty and staff to share information."

What Sets the School Apart From Others
"Small size and intimacy."

How Parents/Students Characterize School
Parent comment(s): "Recently, I was asked about what we think about Kittredge. As I went on and on listing the virtues of the school, I realized something I had not noticed before, that there are no bullies at the school. I don't know how you do it—I suspect by establishing a kind and courteous environment with clear expectations for student behavior—but you do!" • "Kittredge has been a hugely positive element in my daughter's life. The small family-like environment has supported her (and her family as well) in her formative years. My daughter has become a self-confident and contributive student who cares about her classmates, teachers and studies. The challenging academics have continued to shape her strong work ethic."
Student comment(s): "This is a school where it is cool to be nice." "Kittredge is a very good school. The best part of the 'Kittredge experience' is the teachers. The teachers are animated and seem to like their job a lot, probably because of the small class sizes. The teachers try their hardest to make the kids in this school want to learn."

KROUZIAN–ZEKARIAN–VASBOURAGAN ARMENIAN SCHOOL

825 Brotherhood Way (btwn. Lake Merced & 19th Av.) (Lakeshore)
San Francisco, CA 94132
(415) 586-8686 *fax (415) 586-8689*
www.kzv.org

Mrs. Ollia Yenikomshian, Head of School, kzvprincipal@yahoo.com

General

Coed PreK-8 day school. Founded in 1980. Religious. Nonprofit. **Member:** N/P. **Enrollment:** Approx. 150. **Average class size:** 16. **Accreditation:** WASC (6-year term: 2003-09). **Endowment:** $1.5 million. **School year:** Sept.-June. **Instructional days:** 182. **School day:** 8:20 a.m. to 3:30 p.m.

Student Body

Ethnicity: 90% Caucasian (non-Latino), 5% Latino, 5% other.

Admission

Applications due: April (call for date). **Application fee:** $250. **Application process:** Interview. **No. of applications:** N/P. **No. of K spaces:** 22. **Percentage of K class made up of school's preschool class:** 80%. **Admission evaluation requirements for K:** Screening. **Other grades:** N/P. **Preferences:** N/P. **What student do you best serve?** N/P.

Costs

Latest tuition: $6,000. **Sibling discount:** Yes (amount N/P). **Tuition includes:** Lunch: No; Transportation: No; Laptop computer: No; Other: None. **Tuition increases:** Approx. 10% annually. **Other costs:** Approx. $1,000 for books, $150 uniforms, $100 other fees. **Percentage of students receiving financial aid:** 30%. **Financial aid application deadline:** April (call for date). Financial aid is based on need. **Average grant:** $1,000. **Percentage of grants of half-tuition or more:** None. **Donations:** Each family is required to make a cash donation of $400 per year for the annual fund.

School's Mission Statement

"KZV aims to provide a high-quality educational environment in which students are educated, through a bilingual curriculum, to become Armenian-Americans confident in their identity and heritage, fluent in both English and Armenian, appreciative of their cultures and well-prepared as members of the American society. High academic standards are coupled with a commitment to develop the whole child in a Christian and family-like atmosphere."

Academic Program

Philosophy: N/P. **Foreign languages:** Armenian. **Computer training:** N/P. **No. of computers available for students:** 20. **No. of hours weekly of:** Art- 1; Drama- 1; Music- 1; Computers- 1; Foreign language- 10; PE- 2. **Outdoor education:** Yes. **Grading:** A-F, beginning in G1. **Average nightly homework:** 2.5 hours. Posted on the Internet: Yes. **Percentage of students participating in Johns Hopkins Center for Talented Youth Program:** None. **Other indicators of academic success:** N/P. **High schools attended by latest graduating class:** Lowell, SI, Mercy-SF, Mercy-Burlingame, Riordan.

Faculty

Ethnicity: 90% Caucasian (non-Latino), 5% Asian, 5% other. **Percentage of teachers with graduate degrees:** 15%. **Percentage with current California credential:** 50%. **Faculty selection/training:** Experience and degree. **Teacher/student ratio:** 1:12. **Special subject teachers:** Art, music, computers. **Average teacher tenure:** 7 years.

Middle School

Description: G6-8, departmentalized. **Teacher/student ratio:** 1:14. **Elective courses offered:** None. **Achievement tracking in:** Beginning G6. **Student social events:** "Some."

Student Support Services

No. of Licensed Counselors on staff: One part-time. **Counselor/student ratio:** N/P. **Learning specialists on staff:** No. **Learning differences/disabilities support:** No. **High school placement support:** "Yes."

Student Conduct and Health
Code of conduct: "Behavior policy." **Prevention education and awareness addressed in:** Health class.

Athletics
Sports offered: N/P. **Team play begins in:** G3 (intramural).

Campus/Campus Life
Campus description: N/P. **Library:** Yes. **Sports facilities:** Sports fields. **Theater/Arts facilities:** Yes, with stage. **Computer lab:** Yes. **Science lab:** No. **Lunch program:** Yes. **Bus service:** No. **Uniforms/dress code:** Yes. **Opportunities for community service:** Yes.

Extended Day
Morning care: Begins at 7:30 a.m. **After-school care:** Until 6 p.m. **Grade levels:** PreK-8. **Cost:** $5/hour. **Drop-in care available:** Yes. **Coverage over major holidays:** No. **Homework help:** Yes. **Snacks:** Not provided. **Staff/student ratio:** 1:10. **After-school classes:** Chess, yearbook, traditional dance, team sports. **Cost:** N/P.

Summer Programs
The school offers "Hye Em Yes" Bay Area Summer Day Camp for children ages 6-14 years and Nabasdag (The Rabbit) Play Camp for children ages 2 ½-5 years. **Cost:** $150 per session, $250 for both sessions. $125 discount for the second child, and $100 for a third child.

Parent Involvement
Parent/teacher communication: Conferences, websites, e-mail, newsletter. **Participation requirements:** "Yes, Bingo." **Parent education programs:** None.

What Sets the School Apart From Others
"Bilingualism."

How Parents/Students Characterize School
Parent comment(s): "Family oriented."
Student comment(s): "Dynamic."

The Laurel School

350 9th Avenue (Clement and Geary) (Inner Richmond District)
San Francisco, CA 94118
(415) 752-3567 fax (415) 752-6870
www.thelaurelschool.com

Andrea Montes, Head of School, amontes@thelaurelschool.com

General

Coed PreK-8 day school. Founded in 1969. Independent. Nonprofit. **Member:** N/P. **Enrollment:** Approx. 85. **Average class size:** 9. **Accreditation:** N/P. **Endowment:** N/A. **School year:** Sept. to June. **Instructional days:** 180. **School day:** 8:30 a.m. to 3 p.m. Monday through Thursday, 8:30 a.m. to 1:30 p.m. Friday.

Student Body

Ethnicity: N/P.

Admission

Applications due: Call for date. **Application fee:** $100. **Application process:** Contact the school. **No. of applications:** N/P. **No. of K spaces:** 9. **Percentage of K class made up of school's preschool class:** N/A. **Admission evaluation requirements for K:** School visit. **Other grades:** School visit, grades, test scores, recommendations. **Preferences:** N/P. **What sort of student do you best serve?** "Laurel School's best fits are: 1) Children who are shy and benefit from a small, nurturing learning environment; 2) Children whose strengths lie in their learning, but have difficulty fitting in socially; 3) Typically developing children who benefit from small class sizes and have a chance to develop leadership skills; 4) Children who struggle with their learning, but do not qualify for Special Education services through their school districts; 5) Children who need extra time to find their voices and whose voices will be heard at Laurel; 6) Children who need an individualized learning program due to diagnoses of Language Based Learning Disabilities, Non-Verbal Learning Disabilities, Sensory Integration Dysfunction, ADD/ADHD, or other related conditions."

Costs

Latest tuition: $15,400 plus a $500 supply fee. **Sibling discount:** 10%. **Tuition includes:** Lunch: No; Transportation: No; Laptop computer: No; Other: N/P. **Tuition increases:** Approx. 10% annually. **Other costs:** Approx. $100 for uniforms, $100 for other fees. **Percentage of students receiving financial aid:** 20%. **Financial aid application deadline:** Call for date. Financial aid is based on need. **Average grant:** N/P. **Percentage of grants of half-tuition or more:** N/P. **Donations:** "Annual fund, auctions."

School's Mission Statement

"The Laurel School is dedicated to cultivating the individual potential of each child in a community that practices mutual respect, embraces diversity, and inspires a life-long love of learning."

Academic Program

Philosophy: "The key to unlocking your child's academic, emotional, and social growth is understanding who he/she is and how he/she learns. The Laurel School's individualized teaching approach recognizes the whole child. We focus on the unique abilities and learning style of each child and develop specific strategies for learning and personal achievement." **Foreign languages:** None. **Computer training:** "Macintosh." **No. of computers available for students:** 40. **No. of hours weekly of:** Art 1- Drama- 1; Music- 1; Computers- daily; Foreign language- N/A; PE- 2. **Outdoor education:** N/P. **Grading:** A-F, beginning in G6. **Average nightly homework:** Individualized for each student. Posted on the Internet: No. **Percentage of students participating in Johns Hopkins Center for Talented Youth Program:** N/P. **Other indicators of academic success:** N/P. **High schools attended by latest graduating class:** Drew, SHCP, Riordan, Stuart Hall, Sterne School, Gateway.

Faculty

Ethnicity: N/P. **Percentage of teachers with graduate degrees:** N/P. **Percentage with current California credential:** N/P. **Faculty selection/training:** N/P. **Teacher/student ratio:** 1:9. **Special subject**

teachers: Art, music, science, drama, movement/dance, PE. **Average teacher tenure:** 8 years.

Middle School

Description: "Middle school is from G6-8. The program follows a traditional middle school model with students transitioning to a variety of classrooms for each subject area. The emphasis is on individualizing academic programs." **Teacher/student ratio:** 1:9. **Elective courses offered:** Study skills, Spanish, keyboarding, high school preparation. **Achievement tracking in:** N/P. **Student social events:** 4 dances per year.

Student Support Services

No. of Licensed Counselors on staff: N/P. **Counselor/student ratio:** N/P. **Learning specialists on staff:** N/P. **Learning differences/disabilities support:** "The majority of our teachers have Special Education training and backgrounds." **High school placement support:** "The middle school teachers work closely with every family to identify prospective high school placements for every child." Other: Speech and language therapy available.

Student Conduct and Health

Code of conduct: "Students are expected to conduct themselves in an appropriate manner at all times. They should show courtesy to all faculty, staff, and other students. Each teacher has his/her own classroom rules which the administration supports." **Prevention education and awareness addressed in:** N/P.

Athletics

Sports offered: N/P. **Team play begins:** G3 through Catholic Youth Organization (CYO) team.

Campus/Campus Life

Campus description: "A safe and secure urban setting with many neighborhood resources just out our front doors." **Library:** The school uses the Richmond branch of the San Francisco Public Library, across the street from the school. **Sports facilities:** Gymnasium. **Theater/Arts facilities:** Auditorium. **Computer lab:** Yes. **Science lab:** Yes. **Lunch program:** Yes. **Bus service:** Yes. **Uniforms/dress code:** Uniforms. **Opportunities for community service:** Graduation requirements include 30 hours of community service.

Extended Day

Morning care: Begins at 7:45. **After-school care:** Until 6 p.m. **Grade levels:** All. **Cost:** $6.50/hour. **Drop-in care available:** Yes. **Coverage over major holidays:** No. **Homework help:** Yes. **Snacks:** Provided. **Staff/student ratio:** 1:15. **After-school classes:** N/P.

Summer Programs

The school offers a four-week summer program with academic emphasis on reading, language arts, and math. **Cost:** Approx. $650.

Parent Involvement

Parent/teacher communication: Conferences, e-mail, and newsletter. **Participation requirements:** Thirty hours for two parent families and 20 hours for single parent families are required. **Parent education programs offered?:** Yes.

What Sets the School Apart From Others

"Top 10 Reasons Why Laurel School is Unique: 1) Small class size and a low student to teacher ratio allow each teacher the time to understand and best teach each child; 2) Each student's diverse gifts, talents, and challenges are celebrated in a positive way; 3) Families and educators work together to create an inclusive school community where each student truly feels a sense of belonging; 4) The needs of each student are met through the small class size and individualized curriculum; 5) At Laurel every teacher knows every child; 6) Each student is a full and participating member of the Laurel School community; 7) Teachers confer and collaborate to meet each child's educational physical, and social needs; 8) The entire class benefits from the collaboration of the classroom teachers and outside specialists because all children have different learning styles; 9) Laurel has a flexible curriculum. Programs are adapted and accommodations take place seamlessly throughout the school as needed; 10) Laurel School is a small school where positive changes can quickly happen. New programs are embraced and introduced. There is no bureaucracy to slow program implementation."

How Parents/Students Characterize School

Parent comment(s): "Our child was caught between the cracks of the public school system. We found the Laurel School. Now he loves school, works extremely hard, and has made tremendous progress."
Student comment(s): "The Laurel School is like a second home—a big family. There's acceptance of each other's differences."

LISA KAMPNER HEBREW ACADEMY
645 14th Avenue (at Balboa) (Richmond District)
San Francisco, CA 94118
(415) 752-7333 *fax (415) 752-5851*
www.hebrewacademy.com

Rabbi Pinchas Lipner, Head of School, info@hebrewacademy.com
Mimi Real, Ph.D., Director of Admission, info@hebrewacademy.com

General
Coed Jewish PS-8 day school. Founded in 1969. Independent. Jewish. Nonprofit. **Member:** Torah Umesorah. **Enrollment:** Approx. 100. **Average class size:** 12. **Accreditation:** None. **Endowment:** N/P. **School year:** Sept.-June. **Instructional days:** 173. **School day:** 8:30 a.m. to 3:36 p.m.

Student Body
Ethnicity: 96% Caucasian (non-Latino), 2% Asian, 2% African American.

Admission
Applications due: Rolling. **Application fee:** $50. **Application process:** School visit and interview, application form, references, testing

administered at school. **No. of applications:** N/P. **No. of K spaces:** N/P. **Percentage of K class made up of school's preschool class:** 75%. **Admission evaluation requirements for K:** School visit, interview with Preschool Director. **Other grades:** Same. **Preferences:** Jewish by Jewish law or by acceptable conversion. **What sort of student do you best serve?** "We want students who want to be active in and contribute to a learning community that has high intellectual and moral standards. We value a positive attitude towards learning, personal creativity, kindness and moral strength. We value students who want to contribute to their families, their community and the Jewish people."

Costs

Latest tuition: "Varies by grade." **Sibling discount:** "On case by-case basis." **Tuition includes:** Lunch for K only; Transportation: No; Laptop computer: No; Other: N/P. **Tuition increases:** Do not occur annually. **Other costs:** Approx. $250 for books, $600 other fees (building fund). **Percentage of students receiving financial aid:** 88%. **Financial aid application deadline:** None. Financial aid is based on need. **Average grant:** N/P. **Percentage of grants of half-tuition or more:** N/P. **Donations:** N/P.

School's Mission Statement

"Our campus is a place for a learning partnership with the strong and simple family values of love and respect for one another. In a world of increasing turbulence, the Hebrew Academy is a safe place. Every student is valued for his or her own potential. We provide a morally structured but accepting environment. Our success rate is high: our students enter universities, Yeshivas and careers of their choice. Educating a child is a responsibility best shared between the home and school. The Hebrew Academy is a Jewish day school, which strives to provide an excellent academic and Jewish education. We endeavor to expose our children to an intensive appreciation of their religious and ethical responsibilities. The creation of the State of Israel is one of the seminal events in Jewish history. Recognizing the significance of the State and its national institutions, we seek to instill in our students an attachment to the State of Israel and its people as well as a sense of responsibility for their welfare. Our goal is to develop knowledgeable, independent, proud Jews who will contribute to their Jewish and general communities. We are guided by the Biblical injunction: 'Train up a child in the way he should go and when he is old he will not depart from it.' (Proverbs 22:6)."

Academic Program

Philosophy: See Mission Statement. **Foreign languages:** Hebrew. **Computer training:** None. **No. of computers available for students:** None. **No. of hours weekly of:** Art- N/P; Drama- N/P; Music- N/P; Computers- none; Foreign language- 3.3; PE- 1.5. **Outdoor education:** N/P. **Grading:** VG-U, A-F, beginning in G6. **Average nightly homework:** Varies by grade. Posted on the Internet: No. **Percentage of students participating in Johns Hopkins Center for Talented Youth Program:** None. **Other indicators of academic success:** "Our students perform exceptionally well on standardized tests. Our curriculum is one grade level above that in public schools" **High schools attended by latest graduating class:** Lisa Kampner Hebrew Academy High School (98% of school's 8th graders continue at Hebrew Academy), Lowell, JCHS.

Faculty

Ethnicity: 100% Caucasian. **Percentage of teachers with graduate degrees:** 75%. **Percentage with current California credential:** 75%. **Faculty selection/training:** BA or BS required plus further study; experience required. **Teacher/student ratio:** 1:10. **Special subject teachers:** Hebrew, Judaic studies. **Average teacher tenure:** 14 years.

Middle School

Description: G7-8, departmentalized. **Teacher/student ratio:** 1:12. **Elective courses offered:** None. **Achievement tracking in:** Reading, language skills, math, social studies, science. **Student social events:** "Varied."

Student Support Services

No. of Licensed Counselors on staff: One part-time; **Counselor/student ratio:** N/P. **Learning specialists on staff:** None. **Learning differences/disabilities support:** Reading specialist, G1-4. **High school placement support:** "Most students remain at Lisa Kampner Hebrew Academy."

Student Conduct and Health

Code of conduct: "Spelled out in Parent/Student Handbook." **Prevention education and awareness addressed in:** Included in curriculum.

Athletics

Sports offered: No organized sports teams at this time.

Campus/Campus Life

Campus description: "A modern stucco building in a quiet park-like residential neighborhood close to Golden Gate Park." **Library:** "Spacious and airy, with approximately 7,000 volumes that include secular and Judaic works in both English and Hebrew." **Sports facilities:** Full-sized gymnasium/multi-purpose room, outdoor basketball area. **Theater/Arts facilities:** The school has a stage where middle and high school students put on annual productions. **Computer lab:** No. **Science lab:** Yes. **Lunch program:** Partial. **Bus service:** No. **Uniforms/dress code:** Boys' dress code is shirts with collars, neat pants, no shorts, yarmulke and tzitzit required. Girls wear modest attire-skirt below the knee with no slits; top must have sleeves and must not expose midriff or collarbone. **Opportunities for community service:** Not required until high school.

Extended Day

Morning care:: Not available. **After-school care:** Until 6 p.m. **Grade levels:** K-6. **Cost:** Varies; contact school. **Drop-in care available:** No. **Coverage over major holidays:** No. **Homework help:** Yes. **Snacks:** Provided in K only. **Staff/student ratio:** 1:4. **After-school classes:** None until high school.

Summer Programs: None.

Parent Involvement

Parent/teacher communication: Conferences, newsletters. **Participation requirements:** Attendance at school functions and plays. **Parent education programs:** None.

What Sets the School Apart From Others

"The Lisa Kampner Hebrew Academy is a remarkable school with exceptional students. We provide a morally structured but accepting environment. Our success rate is high: our students enter universities, Yeshivas and careers of their choice. Our standards are high, and we look for students with the ability to reach their personal and academic goals. The relationships between faculty and students are unique in their depth, friendship and mutual respect. The Lisa Kampner Hebrew Academy is a school where academic, creative and personal potential are fulfilled and lifetime relationships are forged. Each student is part of a close knit and outstanding whole whose well-being is the focus of our highly trained and caring faculty."

How Parents/Students Characterize School

Parent comment(s): "Academically rigorous and outstanding. My children couldn't get a better education. And I know my children are safe and are learning good moral values and learning to be good Jews. Also, everyone knows the reputation of the school for getting its students into good universities."

Student comment(s): "Hebrew Academy is like a family; you feel the warmth and closeness the minute you walk through the front door." ◆ "I wish I could stay at the Hebrew Academy forever."

Live Oak School

1555 Mariposa Street (across from Jackson Park) (Potrero Hill)
San Francisco, CA 94107
(415) 861-8840 *fax (415) 861-7153*
www.liveoaksf.org

Holly Horton, Head of School, holly_horton@liveoaksf.org

General

Coed K-8 day school. Founded in 1971. Independent. Nonprofit.
Member: CAIS, BADA. **Enrollment:** 225. **Average class size:** 22 in
lower school, 18 in middle school. **Accreditation:** Some years, Toddler
camps and language camps are offered. (term N/P). **Endowment:**
None. **School year:** Sept.-June (trimesters). **Instructional Days:** 175.
School day: 8:30 a.m. to 3:15 p.m.

Student Body

Ethnicity: 74% Caucasian, 10% multi-racial, 5% Latino, 5% African
American, 3% Asian, 3% other.

Admission

Applications due: Jan. (call for date). **Application fee:** $75. **Application Process:** Tour, application, student visit/screening, parent interview. **No. of applications:** 170. **No. of K spaces:** 22. **Percentage of
K class made up of school's preschool class:** N/A. **Admission requirements for K:** School visit and screening and current school recommendation/evaluation. **Other grades:** Another entry point for the
school is G6, where the school normally has 15 middle school spaces
open. Students applying for G6 engage in a school visit and screening,
and submit current school recommendation, evaluation and records.
Spaces are available in other grades by attrition and applicants to those
grades should schedule a student visit, screening/assessment, and submit school records and school recommendation/evaluation. **Preferences:** Siblings. **What sort of student do you best serve?** "Live Oak
serves a diversity of students in a creative and academically challenging
environment that invites students to stretch themselves. With a focus
on differentiated instruction, and on preparing students to be power-

ful learners, we serve a wide range of students well, though we are not equipped to serve students with severe learning or emotional needs."

Costs

Latest tuition: $16,100 for lower school, $16,950 for middle school. **Sibling discount:** None. **Tuition includes:** Lunch: No; Transportation: Van service; Laptop computer: No; Other: field trips, annual camping trip, books. **Tuition increases:** 5%-10% annually. **Other costs:** $500 work assessment fee and $1,000 capital deposit fee for first 3 years; $700 for G8 trip to Washington D.C. **Percentage of students receiving financial aid:** 27%. **Financial aid application deadline:** Jan. (call for date). Financial aid is based on financial need. **Average grant:** 48%. **Percentage of grants of half-tuition or more:** N/P. **Donations:** Annual Fund, Capital Campaign, Auction.

School's Mission Statement

"Live Oak School supports the potential and promise of each student. We provide a strong academic foundation, develop personal confidence and the ability to collaborate with others, inspire students to act with compassion and integrity, and nurture a passion for learning to last a lifetime."

Academic Program

Philosophy: "Live Oak School is a strong community of students, staff and families. Together, we work to create a compelling and challenging learning environment inspired by progressive thought and grounded in shared values. Our school community educates children through a respectful partnership between school and home. Families participate actively in the life of the school. We create and nurture a diverse K-8 community. We embrace our similarities and differences and encourage the sharing and valuing of our unique backgrounds. We understand that childhood is a time to explore, to try new things, to open doors, and to learn about learning. We place a balanced emphasis on art, music, drama, physical education, the humanities and sciences, promoting integration and connectedness within the curriculum. Our students learn by making connections. They integrate new information with existing knowledge to construct meaning. They work cooperatively with their peers, communicate what they know, ask questions, learn others' perspectives, and negotiate solutions to solve problems. ✦ Students engage actively in the learning process, and benefit from direct experience, exploration and hands-on learning. Our teachers are themselves, life-long learners. They know our students well and differentiate instruction, capitalizing on student strengths and interests in order to foster success in meeting academic goals." **Foreign languages:** Spanish. **Computer training:** Yes. **No. of computers available to students:** 22 in computer lab; 20 in classrooms and library. **No. of hours weekly of:** Art- 1; Drama- 1 (G6-8); Music- 1; Computers- determined by curriculum needs; Foreign language- 3 (G4-8); PE- 2. **Outdoor education:** Yes (G4-8). **Grading:** K-6 narratives, comments. Letter grades begin in G7. **Average nightly homework:** 1-2 hours depending on grade level and student. Posted on the Internet: Yes. **Percentage of students participating in Johns Hopkins Center for Talented Youth Program:** 15%. **High schools attended by latest graduating class:** CAT, Drew, Mercy-SF, Urban, Lick, Lowell, SHCP, University, SOTA.

Faculty

Ethnicity: 78% Caucasian, 12% Latino, 8% Asian, 2% African-American. **Percentage of teachers with graduate degrees:** 35% ("teachers and staff"). **Percentage with current California credential:** 65%. **Faculty selection/training:** Experience, degree, training. **Teacher/student ratio:** 1:11 in the lower school, 1:18 in the middle school. **Special subject teachers:** "Art, music, computers, etc." **Average teacher tenure:** 7 years.

Middle School

Description: Departmentalized program begins in G6 with two sections of approximately 17 students in each section for G6-8. **Teacher/student ratio:** 1:17. **Elective courses offered:** Courses vary each trimester and have included drama, athletics, debate, public speaking, cooking, Student Council, yearbook, photography, writing, independent reading, and advanced Spanish. **Achievement tracking in:** Spanish. **Student social events:** Dances, school events.

Student Support Services

No. of Licensed Counselors on staff: None. **Counselor/student ratio:** N/A. **Learning specialists on staff:** One full-time. **Learning differences/disabilities support:** "Learning Specialist, well-trained faculty." **High school placement support:** High School Placement Counselor.

Student Conduct and Health

Code of conduct: "Live Oak has high expectations for student behavior." **Prevention education and awareness programs:** Drug education, sex education, advisory.

Athletics

Sports offered: Volleyball, cross-country, basketball, futsal. **Team play begins in:** G6.

Campus/Campus Life

Campus description: Newly renovated, three story, urban campus. **Library:** "Beautiful library that houses 8,000 volumes." **Sports facilities:** Courtyard playground, public park across the street from the school. **Theater/Arts Facilities:** Grand Hall with stage, Music Room, Art Studio. **Computer lab:** Yes, 22 workstations + computers in classrooms. **Science lab:** Yes. **Lunch program:** Hot lunch on Wednesdays, pizza lunch on Mondays, bag lunch program on other days. **Bus service:** Morning bus service. **Uniforms:** No. **Opportunities for community service:** "Yes, integrated into program."

Extended Day

Morning care: Begins at 7:30 a.m. **After-school care:** Until 6 p.m. **Grade levels:** K- 8. **Cost:** $6/hour. **Drop-in care available:** Yes. **Coverage over major holidays:** Yes. **Homework help:** Yes. **Snacks:** Provided. **Staff/student ratio:** Approx. 1:8. **After-school classes:** "Wide variety including Aikido, ceramics, science, music, and chess." **Cost:** N/P.

Summer Programs

The school's 8-week summer program, Summer Oaks, provides a theme based program for children in K-2, which includes swimming, and a wide variety of course offerings for children in G3-8. **Cost:** $200/week.

Parent Involvement

Parent/teacher communication: Conferences, e-mail, phone, and newsletter. **Participation requirements:** Parents of students in the Lower School are required to donate 60 hours per year; Middle School parents donate 30 hours per year. **Parent education programs offered?:** Yes.

What Sets the School Apart From Others

"We nurture a small, strong community where students are known well by many. An inclusive, diverse environment that embraces differences. Live Oak is a school that truly strives to meet the needs of its students and puts students at the center of all we do. We have a challenging, rich, integrated, differentiated and balanced program."

LYCÉE FRANÇAIS LA PÉROUSE, THE INTERNATIONAL FRENCH SCHOOL
San Francisco campus (PreK-G12):
755 Ashbury Street (at Frederick) (Haight/Ashbury)
San Francisco, CA 94117
(415) 661-5232 *fax (415) 661-0945*
www.lelycee.org

Marin County campus (PreK-G5)
330 Golden Hind Passage
Corte Madera, CA 94925
(415) 924-1737 *fax (415) 924-2849*

Michèle Gragnola, Head of School, mgragnola@lelycee.org
Isabelle Desmole, Director of Admission, idesmole@lelycee.org

General

Co-ed Preschool-G12 French day school (with all subjects taught in French and extensive English). Founded in 1967. Independent. Non-sectarian. Nonprofit. **Member:** CAIS/BADA. The San Francisco campus includes a lower school which is Preschool (beginning at age 3) through G12; the Corte Madera (Marin County) campus includes preschool (beginning at age 2.5) through G5. **Enrollment:** Approx. 655. **Average class size:** 15-20. **Accreditation:** WASC/CAIS/French Ministry of Education (term N/P). **Endowment:** None. **School year:** Sept.-June. **Instructional days:** N/P. **School day:** 8:15 a.m. to 3:15 p.m.

Student Body

Ethnicity: "The school has 31 nationalities represented. 60% are French (26% French, 30% French-U.S., 4% French-other) plus 34% Americans and 6% other nationalities."

Admission

Applications due: Jan. (call for date). **Application fee:** $100 per child. **Application process:** Visits by appointment and open houses held throughout the year. (Call our open house message center at 415-661-5401 ext. 135 for dates and details.) Students coming from other French schools or the French system are automatically admitted to grade level based on their report cards. Non-French speaking students are welcome to apply up to the first grade. **No. of applications:** N/P. **No. of K spaces:** 85. **Percentage of K class made up of school's pre-school class:** 75%. **Admission evaluation requirements for K:** None, open enrollment. **Other grades:** Two+ years of grade reports, recommendations, and a student/parent meeting. **Preferences:** French citizens, siblings, alumni from a Lycée Français. **What sort of student do you best serve?** "Internationally minded, academically oriented, future contributing citizen of the world."

Costs

Latest tuition: $12,930 (K1-K3), $8,600 (K1 part-time), $13,550 (G1-5), $14,375 (G6-9). **Sibling discount:** 10% (2nd), 20% (3rd), 30% (4th) child. **Tuition includes:** Lunch: No; Transportation; No;

Laptop computer: 20 wireless laptops available to all students. **Tuition increases:** Approx. 4% annually. **Other costs:** None. **Percentage of students receiving financial aid:** Approx. 25%, including full-tuition and half-tuition grants. French citizens are eligible for grants from the French government. **Average grant:** $2,000. **Percentage of grants half-tuition or more:** 60%. Fifty-five percent of French government grants to French nationals, 5% of Lycée grants. **Financial aid application deadline:** March (call for date). Financial aid is based on need. **Donations:** Parents are asked to participate in the annual giving campaign and several fundraisers. $300,000 is raised annually.

School's Mission Statement

"The Lycée Français La Pérouse provides international-minded families of the greater Bay Area an academically-rigorous curriculum in a French/English fully bilingual environment. Based on the French national education system, the Preschool-12 innovative program prepares students for completion of the educational requirements of both France and the United States and provides an excellent preparation for both European and North American colleges and universities. The diverse and international nature of the student body and faculty fosters a spirit of community and prepares students to be contributing citizens of the world."

Academic Program

Philosophy: "The Lycée Français La Pérouse is a French International school, with classes from the 'petite section de maternelle' (two years before Kindergarten) through 12th grade. The Lycée is accredited by the French Government, as well as by the California Association of Independent Schools and the Western Association of Schools and Colleges. Students receive an academically rigorous education, learning all the subjects of a French school, complemented by the English education commensurate with their year in school. The Lycée is a full immersion school, where students learn all their subjects in French, except for English and U.S. history." **Foreign languages:** French, English, 3rd language in G6, 4th in G8. **Computer training:** "The SF campus is equipped with both a computer lab and a teaching center dedicated to teaching on the Internet and taking advantage of the many French educational programs available through the Internet." **No. of computers available for students:** Two computer labs and 20 wireless classroom laptops. **No. of hours weekly of:** Art- 1; Drama- 1; Music- 1; Computers- 1; Foreign language- 6; PE- 2. **Outdoor education:** N/P. **Grading:** "The Lycée uses the French system of grading on a scale of 0 to 20, complemented by written evaluations. The French system is more rigorous than American grading and is known and respected by American colleges and universities." **Average nightly homework:** ½-1 hour in G1-5; 1-1.5 hours in G6-9. Posted on the Internet: Yes. **Percentage of students participating in Johns Hopkins Center for Talented Youth Program:** N/P. **Other indicators of academic success:** N/P. **High schools attended by latest graduating class:** Lycée Français La Pérouse.

Faculty

Ethnicity: 95% Caucasian (non-Latino), 1% Asian, 1% Latino, 1% African-American, 1% multi-racial 1% other. **Percentage of teachers with graduate degrees:** "The French Ministry of Education sends certified teachers from France for 1-4 years, while other French teachers are hired locally. Yearly evaluations are held by French officials. English and U.S. history teachers hold California teaching credentials. In-service days are held on an on-going basis as well as continuing education." **Percentage with current California credential:** 100% of English teachers. **Faculty selection/training:** See above. **Teacher/student ratio:** 1:5. **Special subject teachers:** Art, music, computer science, American math, ESL, FSL (French as a Second language). **Average teacher tenure:** N/P.

Middle School

Description: Beginning in G6 each subject is taught by a specialist, Spanish and German are added to the curriculum. Science is expanded to include biology, geology, chemistry, and physics. Students also study English literature, U.S. and World history and geography in English. At the conclusion of G9 students take the "Brevet des Colleges" examination in French, mathematics and history. **Teacher/student ratio:** 1:9. **Elective courses offered:** Theater, drawing, music, sports. **Achievement tracking in:** N/P. **Student social events:** "Various."

Student Support Services

No. of Licensed Counselors on staff: Two. **Counselor/student ratio:** N/P. **Learning specialists on staff:** Two. **Learning differences/disabilities support:** N/P. **High school placement support:** N/P.

Student Conduct and Health

Code of conduct: Disciplinary policy for drug/alcohol use, improper language and sexual/racial harassment in school regulations. **Prevention education and awareness addressed in:** "Civic education from G6-10; sex education through biology class; support systems specific to middle school students." A psychologist is on site 3 hours per week.

Athletics

Sports offered: Basketball, volleyball, cross-country, soccer, softball. **Team play begins in:** G6.

Campus/Campus Life

Campus description: In 1996, Lycée moved into a 42,000 sq. ft. building at the site of the former St. Agnes School. The building has been extensively remodeled to include three floors of classrooms, computer, physics and biology labs, a music room, an extensive library with a rooftop terrace (open only to the upper grades), and a greenhouse. **Library:** N/P. **Sports facilities:** N/P. **Theater/Arts facilities:** N/P. **Computer lab:** Yes. **Science lab:** Yes. **Lunch program:** Yes. **Bus service:** From the Peninsula, $1,650/year for the round trip, and from the North Bay, $1,500/year round trip. **Uniforms/dress code:** No uniforms. (dress code: N/P.) **Opportunities for community service:** Yes.

Extended Day

Morning care: Available on a need basis. **After-school care:** Until 6 p.m. **Grade levels:** All. **Cost:** $7/hour. **Drop-in care available:** Yes. **Coverage over major holidays:** No. **Homework help:** Yes, four days a week. **Snacks:** Provided. **Staff/student ratio:** N/P. **After-school classes:** The school offers after-school classes, changing on a trimester basis. Cost: N/P.

Summer Programs

"The Lycée Français La Pérouse offers a unique and exciting four-week summer camp for children from the ages of 5 to 13. The summer camp, which focuses on bilingualism and theater takes place under the sun in Corte Madera. The various programs have been designed to address the creative and playful side of children, all in an educational environment. Participants are filmed during their activities and field trips. A DVD capturing every moment of discovery and emotional occasion is offered at the end of the summer camp. Transportation from San Francisco is provided for a fee. Activities vary depending on age, but include picnics on Angel Island, rock climbing, and days at the beach. The camp is from 9 a.m. to 3 p.m. with extended care from 8 a.m. and to 6 p.m." **Cost:** $300/session with extended care costing $5/hour.

Parent Involvement

Parent/teacher communication: Parent/teacher conferences three times a year. **Participation requirements:** Parents are expected to participate in fundraising by contributing financially to the Annual Appeal and volunteering 10 hours a year, by assisting in organizing the annual auction, gardening, painting, or by lodging or sponsoring a student. Parents are encouraged to serve on committees of the Board of Directors and to seek election to the Board or School Council. Other volunteer opportunities are available including a French market in June at the Marin campus, translating, library help, and newsletter publication. **Parent/teacher communication:** Students receive five report cards a year. Two conferences between parents and teachers are held on a one-on-one basis. One class council per trimester is held with all teachers, student delegates, parent delegates, and the administration. **Parent education programs:** Cross-cultural workshops; U.S. college panel discussions with alumni; a French educational system counselor from France available annually; lectures/discussions on bilingualism, communication, safety and other issues.

What Sets the School Apart From Others

"The Lycée belongs to a network of over 400 French schools worldwide and receives financial support from the French government. Founded in 1967 by parents, the Lycée is an academic institution accredited by the French Ministry of Education. The Lycée's students have access to any other French school at their own grade level. As a result of the high quality English curriculum, students are also qualified to enter an American school at or above their grade level and are fully prepared to enter European or North American colleges and universities."

How Parents/Students Characterize School

Parent comment(s): "I believe that the Lycée is educating tomorrow's world leaders. Who else can be better prepared to face this international world than our own children, who at age eight can already tell us how a French person's approach is different from an American's and that neither one is better, they are just different?" ✦ "The environment is so positive. It's obvious that the instructors have a vision. They are well prepared to carry out their mission, and they are secure in their role. I like the fact that my son's teachers have such excellent morale."
Student comment(s): N/P.

MARIN CHRISTIAN ACADEMY

1370 S. Novato Boulevard
Novato, CA 94947
(415) 892-5713
www.visitmca.org

Christopher R. Mychajluk, Head of School, cmychajluk@cls.clcnet.org
Erin Bischel, Director of Admission, ebischel@cls.clcnet.org

General

Coed PS-8 day school. Founded in 1979. Christian. Nonprofit. **Member:** Association of Christian Schools International (ACSI). **Enrollment:** Approx. 200. **Average class size:** 17. **Accreditation:** ACSI (N/P term). **Endowment:** N/P. **School year:** Sept.-June. **Instructional days:** 175. **School day:** 8:30 a.m. to 3 p.m.

Student Body

Ethnicity: N/P.

Admission

Applications due: Admission is rolling. **Application fee:** $250. **Application process:** Forms, testing, interview, report cards, and test scores. **No. of applications:** N/P. **No. of K spaces:** 18. **Percentage of K class made up of school's preschool class:** 85%. **Admission evaluation requirements for K:** Testing and interviewing. **Other grades:** N/P. **Preferences:** Sibling. **What sort of student do you best serve?** "MCA best serves the student that excels in an environment that is challenging, structured, and safe."

Costs

Latest tuition: $4,210-$4,820. **Sibling discount:** 7%. **Tuition includes:** Lunch: No; Transportation: No; Laptop computer: No; Other: None. **Tuition increases:** Approx. 7% annually. **Other costs:** Approx. $187 for books, $30-160 other fees. **Percentage of students receiving financial aid:** 10%. **Financial aid application deadline:** "1st round April 15th then based on fund availability." Financial aid is based on need. **Average grant:** $2,500. **Percentage of grants of half-tuition or more:** 90%. **Donations:** Voluntary.

School's Mission Statement

"Marin Christian Academy is dedicated to high spiritual and academic standards that address the development of the whole child—spiritual, mental, social, physical and emotional."

Academic Program

Philosophy: "Christian." **Foreign languages:** Spanish. **Computer training:** Yes. **No. of computers available for students:** 45. **No. of hours weekly of:** Art- 1; Drama- seasonal, KinderDance; Music- 1 (seasonal); Computers- 1.5; Foreign language- 1.5; PE- 1.5. **Outdoor education:** Camp. **Grading:** A-F, beginning in G1. **Average nightly homework:** .5 hr. in K-3; .75 hr. in G4-5; 1-2 hrs. in G6-8. Posted on the Internet: No. **Percentage of students participating in Johns Hopkins Center for Talented Youth Program:** N/P. **Other indicators of academic success:** "SAT scores/well-balanced students." **High schools attended by latest graduating class:** MC, Novato High School, San Marin High.

Faculty

Ethnicity: 100% Caucasian (non-Latino). **Percentage of teachers with graduate degrees:** 25%. **Percentage with current California credential:** 98%. **Faculty selection/training:** Degree and experience. **Teacher/student ratio:** 1:17. **Special subject teachers:** English, math, science, art, computers, choir. **Average teacher tenure:** 8.5 years.

Middle School

Description: G6-8. **Teacher/student ratio:** 1:16. **Elective courses offered:** Drama, computers, home economics, Spanish. **Achievement tracking in:** All subject areas. **Student social events:** N/P.

Student Support Services

No. of Licensed Counselors on staff: None. **Counselor/student ratio:** N/P. **Learning specialists on staff:** None. **Learning differences/disabilities support:** Powerline Reading Program. **High school placement support:** Letters of recommendation provided. **Other:** "Pastors and Youth Ministers are available for student/parent counseling."

Student Conduct and Health

Code of conduct: The has a code of conduct designed to promote peace and maintain order and mutual respect. **Prevention education and awareness addressed in:** Abstinence education and awareness programs.

Athletics

Sports offered: Call school for details. **Team play begins in:** G6 (intramural).

Campus/Campus Life

Campus description: "Internet, video, and TV installed in each room. Conveniently located right off the highway. Facilities enable the full development of a child." **Library:** "Accredited with 2,800 volumes." **Sports facilities:** Multi-purpose room, sports fields. **Theater/Arts facilities:** Theater. **Computer lab:** Yes. **Science lab:** Yes. **Lunch program:** Yes. **Bus service:** No. **Uniforms/dress code:** Dress code. **Opportunities for community service:** None.

Extended Day

Morning care: Begins at 6:30 a.m. **After-school care:** Until 6 p.m. **Grade levels:** All. **Cost:** N/P. **Drop-in care available:** Yes. **Coverage over major holidays:** PreK only. **Homework help:** Yes. **Snacks:** Provided. **Staff/student ratio:** 1:20. **After-school classes:** Piano/band. Cost: N/P.

Summer Programs

"MCA Summer Day Camp provides and exciting and fun time that will include games, crafts, field trips, and Bible devotions times in a warm, healthy, Christian environment." Lego Robotics classes available. Cost: N/P.

Parent Involvement

Parent/teacher communication: Conferences, e-mail, weekly newsletter, website. **Participation requirements:** None. **Parent education programs offered?** Yes.

What Sets the School Apart From Others

"Only fully accredited Christian School in Northern Marin. We provide a safe environment that challenges each student to develop fully in areas of mind, body, and spirit."

How Parents/Students Characterize School

Parent comment(s): "My daughter is a graduate of UC-Berkeley. Recently she told me how thankful she was that I sent her to Marin Christian Academy because the study habits, learning skills and academics she learned were very important to her success in college."
Student comment(s): "MCA was an excellent foundation for the rest of my academic career. Not only did teachers instruct me about history, math, and English, but also they taught me life skills and values that are still a part of who I am today. It was where I learned how to learn."

Marin Country Day School
5221 Paradise Drive
Corte Madera, CA 94925-2107
(415) 927-5900 fax (415) 924-1082
www.mcds.org

Lucinda Lee Katz, Head of School, llkatz@mcds.org
Jeff Escabar and Ann Borden, Directors of Admission,
  jescabar@mcds.org, aborden@mcds.org

General
Coed K-8 day school. Founded in 1956. Independent. Nonprofit. Member: NAIS, CAIS, ASCD, ESHA, CASE, GLSEN, NAPSG, POCIS, ABADO, BADA, ISBOA. **Enrollment:** Approx. 540. **Average class size:** 18. **Accreditation:** CAIS/WASC (6-year term: 2004-10). **Endowment:** $10.3 million. **School year:** Sept.-June. **Instructional days:** 170. **School day:** 8:20 a.m. to 3 p.m. (dismissal for K is 2 p.m.).

Student Body
Ethnicity: 74% Caucasian (non-Latino), 9% Asian, 8% multi-racial, 5% African-American, 3% Latino, 1% other.

Admission
Applications due: Jan. (call for date). **Application fee:** $100. **Application process:** Applicant families should contact the admission office beginning in October of the year prior to the date the student would enter school, to request an application and schedule a Community Visiting tour. After submitting the application, both a parent appointment and an evaluation date will be scheduled by the admission office. For grades other than K, the evaluation date will be the first Saturday in February. Applicants to G6-8 will spend a day visiting campus. Main entry points are K and G6; admission to other grades is by attrition only. **No. of applications:** 200+. **No. of K spaces:** 54. **Percentage of K class made up of school's preschool class:** N/A. **Admission evaluation requirements for K:** Screening/school visit, preschool recom-

mendations. **Other grades:** School transcript, teacher recommendations, testing, school visit. **Preferences:** Siblings, children of employees and alumni. **What sort of student do you best serve?** "Students who demonstrate the capacity and motivation to affirm the school's core values and to find success in a comprehensive and challenging program."

Costs

Latest tuition: $18,825 for K-2, $19,480 for G3-5, $21,800 for G6-8. **Sibling discount:** None. **Tuition includes:** Lunch: Yes; Transportation: No; Laptop computer No; Other: Books and educational materials, outdoor education, field trips, laboratory fees, yearbooks, athletic uniforms. **Tuition increases:** Approx. 5% annually. **Other costs:** None. **Percentage of students receiving financial aid:** 23%. **Financial aid application deadline:** Jan. (call for date). Financial aid is based on need. **Average grant:** $12,200. **Percentage of grants of half-tuition or more:** 68%. **Donations:** "The school raises annually $1.6 million (Annual Giving). The school relies on voluntary giving to support the operating budget. We strive for 100% participation from families currently in school and gifts of any size are appreciated. The school also solicits donations for capital projects and the endowment."

School's Mission Statement

"Our school is a community that inspires children to develop a love of learning, thoughtful perspectives and a diversity of skills; nurtures in each of them a deep sense of respect, responsibility and compassion; and challenges them to envision and work toward a better world."

Academic Program

Philosophy: "Through a broad, balanced and personally challenging curriculum that values the arts, music, physical education and experience in the outdoors in addition to traditional academic disciplines, a skilled and caring faculty seeks to develop every student's potential. Such basic skills as thinking, communicating, creating and collaborating are reinforced in every aspect of a child's experience. Because of the school's low student-teacher ratios, teachers know students and their parents well. The close relationship among teachers and students nurtures self-esteem, respect for differences, a willingness to take risks, and pride in the school community. The school is organized around core values of respect, responsibility and compassion. An MCDS education is active and engaging; teachers employ many strategies and methods to accommodate a variety of learning needs and styles, with close collaboration among teachers to build bridges among disciplines." **Foreign languages:** Spanish. **Computer training:** Yes. **No. of computers available for students:** 150. **No. of hours weekly of:** Art- 2 periods (80 min.); Drama- 1 period G6-8 (40 min.); Music- 2 periods (80 min.); Computers- as needed; Foreign language- 2 periods G3-4, 3 periods G5, 5 periods G6-8; PE- 4 periods. **Outdoor education:** Yes. **Grading:** Progress reports K-5, letter grades in G6-8. **Average nightly homework:** Varies by grade—occasional and topical in G1-2; 20-60 min. plus reading in G3-6; 20-30 min. per subject for 5 academic subjects in G6; 30-45 min. per subject in G7-8. **Posted on the Internet:** Yes. **Percentage of students participating in Johns Hopkins Center for Talented Youth Program:** N/P. **Other indicators of academic success:** "Quality of student work, GPA's, success of our alums in high school." **High schools attended by latest graduating class:** Bay School, Branson, Cate, Deerfield, Drew, Exeter, Galileo, Lick, MA, Redwood, SI, Stevenson, Tamalpais, Thacher, University, and Urban.

Faculty

Ethnicity: 85% Caucasian (non-Latino), 5% Latino, 3% African-American, 3% Asian, 2% multi-racial, 2% other. **Percentage of teachers with graduate degrees:** 53%. **Percentage with current California credential:** N/P. **Faculty selection/training:** Experience, degree; continuing professional development. **Teacher/student ratio:** 1:8. **Special subject teachers:** Spanish, art, music/drama, technology, PE, library. **Average teacher tenure:** 10 years.

Middle School

Description: "MCDS Upper School (G6-8) is an engaging environment in which hard work and caring, responsible behavior are the norm. The program allows students to further discover who they are; acquire fundamental, lifetime learning skills and attitudes; become critical and creative thinkers; explore various interests and talents—intellectual, artistic and physical—and grow and develop into empowered young people eager to contribute to making the world a better place, now and in the future. In sixth grade, the school admits new students to expand the size of the class so that returning students can make new friends and the school can broaden its course offerings. Upper School students begin the day in grade-level homerooms supervised by a faculty advisor, who also serves as liaison with parents. Upper School is departmentalized and students travel between classes to study English, social studies, math, science, Spanish, visual and performing arts, and physical education. Tutorials and activity periods are provided. Many students stay at school after dismissal to play on athletic teams or to participate in drama, music, supervised study hall or other elective activities." **Teacher/student ratio:** N/P. **Elective courses offered:** N/P. Achievement tracking: N/P. **Student social events:** N/P.

Student Support Services
No. of Licensed Counselors on staff: One (80% time). **Counselor/student ratio:** 1:540. **Learning specialists on staff:** Seven. **Learning differences/disabilities support:** Student Support Service members work with parents and teachers to develop strategies to best support students' learning, and directly with students, individually and in small groups. The Upper School uses the Transitions Program. **High school placement support:** Secondary School Placement Counselor, Upper School Division Head, eighth grade faculty.

Student Conduct and Health
Code of conduct: "The guiding principle for all behavior begins with our core values: respect, responsibility and compassion. We believe that honoring these values creates a safe, purposeful environment where the important work of teaching, learning and growing can take place. School rules are designed to provide a healthy, safe and friendly learning environment for all children. Clear expectations and developmentally appropriate consequences when expectations are not honored help ensure that standards of behavior and performance are reasonable, consistent and enforced fairly. An appropriate consequence is one that helps the student contribute something positive to the community

in return. In Middle and Upper School, a system of 'checks' (G3-5) or 'marks' (G6-8) helps monitor behavior. It is the responsibility of all MCDS teachers and staff to model and to be aware of appropriate behavior—to praise, support and reward student behavior when it is consistent with our core values, and to identify it and assign the appropriate consequence when it is not. Very serious behavior violations require an individual approach, beginning with a full discussion with the student and a careful investigation of the incident. Parents and/or guardians are involved in the process. In extremely serious cases, the Division Head will work with the Head of School in determining the appropriate course of action. In extreme situations, suspension and even expulsion may be considered. The school and parents must work together to ensure that MCDS is a safe and caring environment for all children." **Prevention education and awareness addressed in:** "Drug/alcohol education is provided through workshops. The sixth grade curriculum incorporates a body image/eating disorders program, which allows students to receive the information at an age when it is most likely to be meaningful, but timely enough to be primarily preventative. Sixth grade also takes part in a series of workshops designed to help them develop the tools to deal with the challenges and stresses of academic and social life typical of the age group. Small groups meet for activities and discussions aimed at broadening their understanding of the human brain, natural reactions to stress, and ways to cope. In seventh grade, students study body image, sexuality and AIDS awareness in the context of human biology. AIDS education is also part of the eighth grade curriculum. Parent education opportunities are also offered in these areas."

Athletics

Sports offered: Soccer, basketball, volleyball, baseball, softball and cross-country. **Team play begins in:** G6 (intermural).

Campus/Campus Life

Campus description: "MCDS is located on 35 naturally beautiful acres which begin at the Bay and run up the hills of Ring Mountain, where the school property abuts the Marin County Open Space District. Low, simple frame buildings fit naturally into their setting. The athletic fields, playgrounds, gardens, informal study areas and marine science dock all invite interaction with the outdoors. The structures accommodate classrooms, a library, science laboratories, a computer laboratory, separate music and art buildings, a performing arts auditorium, gymnasium, multipurpose room and offices." **Library:** 28,000 volumes, 80 periodicals, on-line catalog, electronic database subscriptions, eight computer stations. **Sports facilities:** Gymnasium, two sports fields. **Theater/Arts facilities:** Performing Arts Building, stage in gymnasium, music and art rooms, ceramics room. **Computer lab:** Yes, and 4 mobile labs. **Science lab:** Yes. **Lunch program:** Yes. **Bus service:** Yes. **Uniforms/dress code:** Dress code based on clothing that is comfortable and appropriate for a school setting. **Opportunities for community service:** Service Learning curriculum in K-8; Community Service Club in G6-8; 8th grade Community Service Week; family community service program.

Extended Day

Morning care: Begins at 8 a.m. **After-school care:** Until 6:15 p.m. **Grade levels:** K-5; study hall/after-school activities in G6-8. **Cost:** Up to $15/day (indexed at rate of tuition). **Drop-in care available:** Yes. **Coverage over major holidays:** No. **Homework help:** Yes. **Snacks:** Provided. **Staff/student ratio:** Varies by attendance; average 1:13. **After-school classes:** The school's after-school activities program (ASAP) varies by semester. Classes may include cooking, martial arts, sports, chess, arts and crafts, and nature adventure. Individual and group music instruction is also available (Forte). **Cost:** N/P.

Summer Programs

"Beyond Borders is a multicultural leadership program for a diverse group of 4th-6th graders from Marin and San Francisco. The program combines an interactive curriculum focused on cross-cultural exploration and self-discovery, field trips and a performing arts project developing original plays. The program begins with a five-week summer session followed by a series of Saturday workshops and outings throughout the school year. Cultural resources in the Bay Area are utilized through weekly field trips, guest performers, storytellers and/or oral historians. Beyond Borders is unique among Bay Area enrichment programs in its focus on the 'global village,' breaking down stereotypes and fostering respect, collaboration and creativity. Beyond Borders creates a safe environment in which children share their backgrounds, strengths and weaknesses and develop and discover their individual talents." **Costs:** Based on a sliding scale from $15 to $1,200. Bus transportation is provided. ✦ Turtle Rock Institute (www.turtlerockinstitute.org.) is a K-8 summer enrichment program with a focus on creativity, excitement and fun. Kids exercise their imaginations as they explore morning classes such as filmmaking, art, music, rock climbing, theater, computer animation, mountain biking, web design, cooking and more. Afternoons at TRI feature recreational summer fun such as squirting hoses, making lanyards, building sand castles, hiking on Ring Mountain, turning cartwheels in the grass and eating popsicles in the sunshine." **Costs:** $315 for 1 week, $610 for 2 weeks, $810 for 3 weeks, $1,100 for 4 weeks, and $1,300 for 5 weeks.

Parent Involvement

Parent/teacher communication: Conferences, progress reports, meetings, roundtables, website, e-mail, telephone, on-line newsletter. **Participation requirements:** "MCDS expects that families will support the school as actively as individual circumstances permit. The school offers a wide variety of volunteer opportunities with differing time commitments and locations." **Parent education programs offered?** Yes.

What Sets the School Apart From Others

"Marin Country Day School is a warm, inclusive community guided by core values of respect, responsibility and compassion. The school is dedicated to helping children become excellent learners and good people, motivated to make a difference in the world. Service learning and character education are integral elements of the program. MCDS is committed to the principles and practices of diversity throughout the school community. The curriculum is broad-based and personally rigorous, including a thorough grounding in the traditional academic disciplines as well as art, athletics, drama, music and outdoor education. Teachers work collaboratively in developing an active program that encourages students to question, to reason and to make connections. The classroom atmosphere is highly participatory, with teachers acting as coaches and mentors who encourage students' exploration, discovery and reflection. Perhaps the school's most enduring characteristic is its vibrant spirit—of students, families, teachers and staff engaged in working together to make Marin Country Day School a good place for children."

How Parents/Students Characterize School

Parent comment(s): N/P.
Student comment(s): N/P.

MARIN HORIZON SCHOOL

305 Montford Avenue
Mill Valley, CA 94941
(415) 388-8408 *fax (415) 388-7831*
www.marinhorizon.org

Rosalind Hamar, Head of School, rhamar@marinhorizon.org
Kathy J. Williams, Director of Admission, admissions@marinhorizon.org

General

Coed PreK–8 day school. Founded in 1977. Independent. Nonprofit. **Member:** NAIS, CAIS, IMC, BADA, BAMA. **Enrollment:** Approx. 250. **Average class size:** 20. **Accreditation:** CAIS (6-year term 2003-09) and State of California preschool license. **Endowment:** $208,000. **School year:** Sept.-June. **Instructional days:** 175. **School day:** 8:20 a.m. to 3 p.m. for G1-8, 8:40 a.m. to 2 p.m. for PreK and K.

Student Body

Ethnicity: 77% Caucasian (non-Latino), 10% multi-raical, 7% African-American, 5% Asian, 1% Latino.

Admission

Applications due: Early to mid-Jan. (call for date). **Application fee:** $50. **Application process:** Interested families should contact the admissions office in September or early October to request a tour and application packet for the following academic year. After attending a tour or open house and submitting an application, a parent appointment and student visit date will be scheduled. **No. of applications for K:** 30. **No. of K spaces:** 10-15. **Percentage of K class made up of school's preschool class:** 67%. **Admission evaluation requirements for K:** Screening, school visit, teacher recommendations, parent questionnaire about student. **Other grades:** Screening, previous report cards/grades, standardized test scores, school visit, teacher recommendations, parent questionnaire about student. **Preferences:** N/P. **What sort of student do you best serve?** "Students who have the ability to support the school's mission, can work independently and cooperatively in the classroom and have the desire to be successful in a challenging program."

Costs

Latest tuition: $10,720-$18,000 depending on grade level. **Sibling discount:** None. **Tuition includes:** Lunch: No; Transportation: No; Laptop computer: No; Other: Field trips and outdoor education camp. **Tuition increases:** Approx. 7% annually. **Other costs:** Annual capital deposit of $1,000 per child is required for PreK-7. The maximum accrued deposit is $10,000 per child or $15,000 per family whichever is the lesser amount. The principal is returned to the family the September following the graduation or permanent withdrawal of their child from school. **Percentage of students receiving financial aid:** 18%. **Financial aid application deadline:** Jan. (call for date). Financial aid is based on need. **Average grant:** $9,500. **Percentage of grants of half-tuition or more:** 65%. **Donations:** "Voluntary giving is critical to support the operating budget. For over 6 years, MHS has achieved 100% participation by trustees, faculty, administration and parents in the annual fund. Thus far, $2.17 million in pledges has been made for the Cornerstone Campaign to enhance teaching facilities and build a new 12,800 square foot building for the 4th-8th grade classrooms."

School's Mission Statement

"Our mission is to challenge students to be self-reliant thinkers and lifelong learners. We inspire academic excellence, nurture students' natural love of learning, and encourage them to be confident individuals who are responsible to each other, the community, and the world."

Academic Program

Philosophy: "MHS offers a rich and challenging academic program that is respectful of children's individual and developmental needs. This is accomplished through small classes and multi-grade classrooms, a solid mastery of the fundamentals, an emphasis on independent, critical thinking, the development of leadership and strong communication and social skills, and a focus on the community and the earth. Inspired by Montessori's philosophy, our program nurtures and cultivates children's innate curiosity and love of learning while guiding them in the development of their basic reading, writing, math and computer skills. MHS has modified the multi-age classroom model to create a combination that meets the social and developmental needs of today's children. Our primary classes include 3-, 4- and 5- year old (in their Kindergarten year) students. There is one 1st grade classroom that is grade specific, and there are two 2nd/3rd and two 4th/5th grade classrooms. The multi-age classroom allows students to progress in areas where they have a strong aptitude and get support in areas of challenge while offering more opportunities for leadership and responsibility. It also strengthens the teacher/student/parent relationships. The MHS curriculum is interdisciplinary and experiential, with critical thinking skills and the arts integrated into the curriculum at all levels. Field trips and outdoor education camp/experiences enhance the program and provide opportunities to extend the classroom into the community." **Foreign languages:** Spanish in K-8. **Computer training:** Yes. **No. of computers available for students:** 56. **No. of hours weekly of:** Depends on grade level. In general, Art- 1-2; Drama- 0-1; Music- 1-2; Computers- integrated into the curriculum: Foreign language- 1-4: PE- 1-2. **Outdoor education:** One week for elementary and middle school students on an environmental studies trip. **Grading:** Matrix progress reports with narratives. No letter grades. Percentage grading begins in G6. **Average nightly homework:** Ranges by grade level from 20 min. to 2 hours. Posted on the Internet: No. **Percentage of students participating in Johns Hopkins Center for Talented Youth Program:** N/P. **Other indicators of academic success:** "High school acceptances, individual work/achievements of students, individual progress reports." **High schools attended by latest graduating class:** Bay School, Branson, CSH, Drew, Tamalpais, MA, SHCP, San Domenico, SI, Stuart Hall, and Urban.

Faculty

Ethnicity: 96% Caucasian (non-Latino), 2% Asian, 1% Latino, 1% African-American. **Percentage of teachers with graduate degrees:** N/P. **Percentage with current California credential:** "All head teachers and co-teachers hold Montessori and/or state elementary teaching credentials." **Faculty selection/training:** Experience, education and philosophical fit. **Teacher/student ratio:** 1:9. **Special subject teachers:** Art, Spanish, music, computer technology, PE, library sciences. **Average teacher tenure:** 7 years.

Middle School

Description: "Our middle school, which includes G6-8, provides a bridge between the academic foundation of the elementary years and the increased challenges students will encounter in high school and beyond. It is intentionally small—not more than 72 students—because of the value of a small community for early adolescents. MHS provides an educational environment where students are well known personally and academically by their teachers, and can receive the kind of guidance they need at this time of vulnerability and great change in their lives. The middle school is departmentalized. The three-year interdisciplinary rotations—U.S. history and government, Europe and Africa in the Middle Ages, and Japan and the Pacific Rim—include language arts, humanities, geography and fine arts. In addition, each year there is a middle school simulation that synthesizes and deepens each student's understanding of what they have learned. These simulations include a 7-scene murder mystery presentation of Murder in Londinium entwining Celtic and Pax Romana cultures, a mock trial trying Harry S. Truman for crimes against humanity in Hiroshima and Nagasaki, or team creations of Rube Goldberg machines and the spirit of innovation that led to the U.S. Industrial Revolution. Science and math are also integrated into these major projects. Mathematics includes mastery of computation, problem solving, introductory algebra, and geometry. Science includes biology, physical science, chemistry, and physics. Other offerings include computer technology (PowerPoint presentations), Spanish, health, and PE." **Teacher/student ratio:** 1:12. **Elective courses offered:** Electives change every year and may include metal arts, ceramics, drama, calligraphy, photography, dance or journalism. **Achievement tracking in:** N/P. **Student social events:** Limited social events.

Student Support Services

No. of Licensed Counselors on staff: Two part-time. **Counselor/student ratio:** N/P. **Learning specialists on staff:** One full-time, 2 part-time. **Learning differences/disabilities support:** MHS provides a Learning Support Program to support the success of students who need additional academic support. This program includes regular direct support from a LSP teacher, classroom observations, and regular communication between parents, teachers, and outside specialists retained by the family. Parents of students who are placed in this program by the school are assessed an additional fee while the student is in the program. **High school placement support:** During the fall semester, the high school preparation course is taught to support students and their families in the skills and strategies helpful in the application and decision making process. The course includes SSAT preparation, assessment skills to determine appropriate "matches" between student and school and interviewing techniques. **Other:** One part-time occupational therapist on staff. A sensory motor program is conducted for Kindergarten and followed through 1st grade if appropriate.

Student Conduct and Health

Code of conduct: The school has behavioral guidelines that are universal and each class establishes class rules. In addition there are accountability policies for both the elementary grades and middle school. To avoid behavioral problems, the schools offers conflict resolution training and instruction through Advisory Group meetings. **Prevention education and awareness addressed in:** Drug, alcohol, and sex education is addressed through weekly health classes. There is a no tolerance disciplinary policy for drug/alcohol use, improper language and sexual/racial harassment. Support systems specific to middle school students include counseling by teachers and guidance counselor, individually and through advisory groups.

Athletics

Sports offered/team play begins in: Intramural sports include soccer, basketball and flag football. Intermural sports begin in G3 with invitational cross-country meets, and in G4-8 for cross country meets, basketball, track and field, flag football and soccer.

Campus/Campus Life

Campus description: MHS is situated in the Homestead Valley neighborhood of Mill Valley on 2.5 acres with access to Marin County fields and open space. **Library:** On campus, 5,000 volume library and adjacent computer lab, staffed by a full-time librarian. **Sports facilities:** Playground and adjacent grass field. **Theater/Arts facilities:** Outdoor amphitheater. Theatrical productions are held at nearby theaters. **Computer lab:** Yes. **Science lab:** Yes. **Lunch program:** Yes. Organic hot lunch offered for nominal fee. **Bus service:** None. Carpooling is strongly encouraged. **Uniforms/dress code:** No uniforms. Dress should be comfortable and appropriate for school. **Opportunities for community service:** "MHS's community service program is widely recognized. Our students of all ages, their parents, and teachers work together on various community service projects and directly contribute to more than 20 different non-profit and community service organization throughout the year. Students have collected and delivered over 30,000 pounds of food in the last 10 years to the Marin Community Food Bank, worked on projects with the seniors at The Redwoods, and participated in neighborhood and local clean-up days."

Extended Day

Morning care: Begins at 7:30 a.m. at the Horizon Center, the school's before- and after-school program. **After-school care:** Until 6 p.m. **Grade levels:** Primary-G8. **Cost:** Varies depending on usage; approx. $7/hour. **Drop-in care available:** Yes. **Coverage over major holidays:**

Yes. **Homework help:** Yes. A study hall for G4-8 is part of the program. Organic snacks are provided. **Staff/student ratio:** 1:12 or fewer. **After-school classes:** Available for students in Primary through G8 the classes frequently include cooking, chess, Irish step dancing, capoeira, drama, guitar, gymnastics, yoga, baseball and soccer. **Cost:** N/P.

Summer Programs

Summer Camp sessions run approximately 8 consecutive weeks usually in mid-June through early August. The camp offers programs for 3- to 9-year-olds with a counselor to camper ratio of 1:8. Activities include cooking, swimming, gardening, magic, theatre and art with field trips every Friday. Swimming and gymnastics are offered for ages 4 and up. **Cost:** Varies depending on the number of days per week and number of weeks per summer enrolled. Extended care is also provided from 8-9 a.m. and 3-5:30 p.m. for a per hour fee.

Parent Involvement

Parent/teacher communication: Parent/teacher conferences and written progress reports twice a year; class notes; e-mail communications; weekly school newsletter; website. **Participation requirements:** Parents are strongly encouraged to participate in many aspects of the MHS community including but not limited to trustees, board committees, Parent Board officers, class parents, special programs, field trips, and chaperones. **Parent education programs offered?:** Throughout the year, speakers are invited to discuss issues involved in parenting with the MHS community and the broader community. Topics such as adoption perspectives, earthquake preparedness and adolescence are presented.

What Sets the School Apart From Others

"MHS offers a Montessori-inspired curriculum with strong curricular focus on multiculturalism, the environment, and community service. In addition to basic skill development, academic preparation emphasizes research, writing, and presentation skills across the curriculum. Teachers are 'facilitators of learning' more than 'dispensers of knowledge.' Different learning styles are acknowledged via a mix of teaching/learning strategies ranging from hands-on projects to seminars and presentations."

How Parents/Students Characterize School

Parent comment(s): "What's special about Marin Horizon? Well, first, I love that the curriculum is holistic and explores the natural connections between disciplines. I was also struck by how energized and engaged the students and faculty are, and that the school fosters independent and critical thinking."

Student comment(s): "It's uncommon that one school can produce so many brilliant minds but MHS does so by teaching children how to teach themselves at a young age. Being equipped at six to structure work and apply focus and tenacity to a task, helped me to establish strong study habits at nine and further maturing those skills throughout middle school, educationally preparing myself for the high school work load. I truly cannot thank the MHS community enough. But I try, in any endeavor I involve myself, knowing it is truly a reflection of those who helped me get where I am now. To some MHS is just a school, for others their home away from home, but for me it will always be the community that truly helped prepare me for life."

Marin Montessori School

5200 Paradise Drive
Corte Madera, CA 94925
(415) 924-5388   fax (415) 924-5305
www.marinmontessori.org

Elizabeth Larose Dunn, Head of School, elarose@marinmontessori.org
Golnar Casey, Director of Admission, gcasey@marinmontessori.org

General

Coed PS-6 day school. Founded in 1963. Independent. Nonprofit. **Member:** N/P. **Enrollment:** Approx. 207. **Average class size:** 30 in Primary (2½-3 to 6 yrs.), 25 in Elementary (6-12 yrs). **Accreditation:** Association Montessori Internationale (AMI)(1-year term: 2004-05).

Endowment: N/P. **School year:** Sept.-June. **Instructional days:** 176. **School day:** 8:30 a.m. to 11:35 a.m. for Toddler/Primary Half Day; 8:30 a.m. to 2:55 p.m. for Toddler/Primary Full Day; 8:30 a.m. to 3 p.m. for Elementary.

Student Body
Ethnicity: 86% Caucasian (non-Latino), 4% Asian, 4% multi-racial, 3% other, 2% African-American, 1% Latino.

Admission
Applications due: Jan. (call for date). **Application fee:** $75. **Application process:** Attend an open house scheduled on a Saturday in October and January and a tour scheduled between October and February. Family visits/classroom visits are by invitation. **No. of applications:** 130. **No. of K spaces:** 4-5. **Percentage of K class made up of school's preschool class:** 30% of students in Primary (3-6) are from the Toddler class. **Admission evaluation requirements for K:** "The kindergarten year being the final year of the primary cycle, the family must be certain they are continuing on to our elementary program. We review past school records and the classroom visit." **Other grades:** School records, current teacher recommendations, classroom visit, and screening in some cases. **Preferences:** Siblings. **What sort of student do you best serve?** "Any child is suited to the Montessori environment, which nurtures the whole being of the child: socially, emotionally and academically. They thrive the most when their parents are wholeheartedly committed to the Montessori philosophy and way of learning, and all that it offers."

Costs
Latest tuition: $10,830 for Primary Half Day, $14,780 for Primary Full Day, $14,990 for Elementary. **Sibling discount:** None. **Tuition includes:** Lunch: No; Transportation: No; Laptop computer: No; Other: No. **Tuition increases:** Approx. 7% annually. **Other costs:** None. **Percentage of students receiving financial aid:** 14%. **Financial aid application deadline:** Feb. (call for date). Financial aid is based on need. **Average grant:** $9,500. **Percentage of grants of half-tuition or more:** 66%. **Donations:** Voluntary for the annual fund and auction.

School's Mission Statement

"The mission of Marin Montessori School, in adherence to the principles of the Association Montessori Internationale (AMI) as envisioned by Dr. Maria Montessori, is to nurture the development of each child in our diverse community to his or her fullest potential – an independent, responsible, compassionate, learned individual who thinks critically and realizes clearly his or her role in the world. Thus our mission is to provide education for life."

Academic Program

Philosophy: "AMI Montessori Education as stated above." **Foreign languages:** Basic Spanish in Upper Elementary (G4-6). **Computer training:** Keyboarding, word processing, basic internet. **No. of computers available for students:** One in each elementary classroom. **No. of hours weekly of:** Art- integrated in all activities daily; Drama- full musical production each year in each elementary class, plus student initiated projects; Music- hours weekly vary; full music curriculum integrated throughout the daily classroom activities and course of lessons; Computers- varies as needed; Foreign language- varies- after-school Spanish classes offered, basic vocabulary and conversational Spanish taught in Upper Elementary (G4-6): PE- at least 1 hr./wk. **Outdoor education:** Integrated daily. **Grading:** Written evaluations, no grades. **Average nightly homework:** At least ½ hour of reading each night; other homework is only given as needed for areas of challenge. Posted on the Internet: No. **Percentage of students participating in Johns Hopkins Center for Talented Youth Program:** N/A. **Other indicators of academic success:** "We have students each year admitted to the most respected Middle School programs of Marin; students and parents often report that in Middle School, the children continue to be very self-disciplined and passionate about completing their assigned projects to their fullest potential." **High schools attended by latest graduating class:** N/A (graduates are currently in Middle School).

Faculty

Ethnicity: 75% Caucasian (non-Latino), 15% Asian, 10% Latino. **Percentage of teachers with graduate degrees:** 11%. **Percentage with current California credential:** N/A. **Faculty selection/training:**

"Rigorous AMI training and experience." **Teacher/student ratio:** 1:30 ("adult/student ratio is 1:9"). **Special subject teachers:** PE and outdoor education (gardening, etc.). **Average teacher tenure:** 14 years.

Middle School

Description: School presently goes through G6. A plan for a middle school is being formulated.

Student Support Services

No. of Licensed Counselors on staff: None. **Counselor/student ratio:** N/A. **Learning specialists on staff:** One learning specialist consultant. **Learning differences/disabilities support:** "We work with a learning specialist who observes, test, and consults with faculty to increase understanding of unique ways in which the individual child learns, enabling us to better support the child by making needed interventions and accommodations for his/her learning in the classroom. Many faculty members are trained in Mel Levine's 'Schools Attuned' work." **High school placement support:** N/A (school goes through G6). **Other:** "We provide support and information for middle school placement."

Student Conduct and Health

Code of conduct: "Grace and Courtesy—a community built on caring, respect, and consideration of others. Grace is harmony between mind and body. Courtesy is the harmony between oneself and others. Grace and courtesy are natural expressions of a community, and when they are implemented and modeled by all members of the community, a harmonious environment is created that promotes the welfare of all." **Prevention education and awareness addressed in:** "Peace education, environmental consciousness, and healthy nutrition/sound body education."

Athletics

Sports offered: "All team sports and more, through the PE class and after-school classes, such as soccer and skating." **Team play begins in:** G1 (intramural/intermural: N/P).

Campus/Campus Life

Campus description: "Five buildings, 2 of which were just completed in 2005, nestled around a beautiful marsh bordering the Bay." **Library:** "Limited libraries in the classrooms, frequent trips to the Corte Madera Library as needed." **Sports facilities:** One large field, 1 small field, 1 paved court for basketball and hockey/skating. **Theater/Arts facilities:** A multi-purpose room with stage setup. **Computer lab:** No. **Science lab:** "Extensive science equipment in all elementary classrooms." **Lunch program:** No. **Bus service:** No. **Uniforms/dress code:** "Appropriate school dress." **Opportunities for community service:** "There are many opportunities for community service, both structured and created by the children, within our own school environment, the Corte Madera and greater Bay Area communities, as well as the world at large."

Extended Day

Morning care: Begins at 7:30 a.m. **After-school care:** Until 6 p.m. **Grade levels:** Primary and Elementary (2½ years old-G6). **Cost:** $8/hour reserved; $8.50/hour drop-in. **Drop-in care available:** Yes. **Coverage over major holidays:** Yes. **Homework help:** N/A. **Snacks:** Provided. **Staff/student ratio:** a minimum of 1:12. **After-school classes:** Optional after-school classes are available for Primary and Elementary. Offerings have included: Spanish, chess, soccer, yoga/movement, art, Suzuki piano, skating, cartooning, and creative writing. **Cost:** N/P.

Summer Programs

Summer offerings vary. Most recently, a 5-week camp for Primary children included art, movement, nature, and other activities. Some years, Toddler camps and language camps are offered. **Cost:** Half-day and full-day programs are available for $145 and $275 per week respectively.

Parent Involvement

Parent/teacher communication: Two formal parent/teacher conferences are scheduled each year, fall and spring. Continual parent-teacher communication whenever needed throughout the year. Parents may schedule classroom observations at will, based on availability. Parents are encouraged to call the teacher with any concerns or questions. Classroom newsletters and the weekly school bulletin are also important sources of information. **Participation requirements:** Parents are expected to attend Back to School Night, 3 Parent Education events, 2 Parent/Teacher Conferences, and to observe their child's classroom a minimum of once a year. Parents are required to volunteer at least 20 hours per family, per year. **Parent education programs offered?** Yes.

What Sets the School Apart From Others

"The greatest gift of a Montessori Education is that each child is given the chance to build a strong sense of self, a passion for lifelong learning, the self-discipline to make good choices and a respect for the Earth and his fellow human beings. Each environment is designed to provide the balance between freedom and responsibility that allows the child to not only learn what is 'required', but to go far beyond that as s/he follows his/her interests and passions. S/he goes out into the world with all the tools necessary for leading a successful and worthwhile life that contributes to the world around him/her."

How Parents/Students Characterize School

Parent comment(s): "Marin Montessori School is not afraid to be about something deeper." "My children have just blossomed. That's why we've been at MMS so long." "We want to raise children that are very bright and very academic, but know how to be guided by their spirit first."

Student comment(s): "What I like about the school is that we have freedom that we wouldn't have at other schools, and it helps me work better." "You really learn a lot about how to respect other people and yourself." "I love the marsh; we get to see egrets and birds all the time when we're outside." "We are so lucky to have our school."

Marin Primary & Middle School
20 Magnolia Avenue
Larkspur, CA   94939
(415) 924-2608   fax (415) 924-9351
www.mpms.org

Murray E. Lopdell Lawrence, Head of School
Nicole Demaray, Director of Admission and Financial Aid,
  Ndemaray@mpms.org

General
Coed PS-8 day school. Founded in 1975. Independent. Nonprofit.
Member: CAIS, BADA. **Enrollment:** Approx. 370. **Average class size:** 15. **Accreditation:** WASC/CAIS (1-year term: 2004-05). **Endowment:** $400,000. **School year:** Sept.-June. **Instructional days:** 170. **School day:** 8:15 a.m. to 3:15 p.m.

Student Body
Ethnicity: 81% Caucasian (non-Latino), 8% Asian, 4% Latino, 4% African-American, 2%, multi-racial, 1% other.

Admission
Applications due: Approx. Jan. 14th (call for date). **Application fee:** $75. **Application process:** "Campus tour for parents, Preliminary and formal applications, transcripts (if applicable), teacher recommenda-

tions, school visit or screening, attendance at one of the four fall admission coffees. Contact Nicole Demaray for specific questions." **No. of applications:** 165. **No. of K spaces:** 26. **Percentage of K class made up of school's preschool class:** 48%. **Admission evaluation requirements for K:** In house screening, teacher recommendations, transcripts (if applicable), tour for parents. **Other grades:** N/P. **Preferences:** Sibling. **What sort of student do you best serve?** "MP&MS best serves families who are committed to and believe in the mission and philosophy of the school."

Costs

Latest tuition: $16,700 for JK-K, $16,900 for G1-4, $18,100 for G5-8. **Sibling discount:** None. **Tuition includes:** Lunch: No; Transportation: No; Laptop computer: No; Other: Tuition includes field trips and books. **Tuition increases:** Approx. 4% annually. **Other costs:** Other costs vary year by year. **Percentage of students receiving financial aid:** 15%. **Financial aid application deadline:** Approx. Jan. 14th (call for date). Financial aid is based on need. **Average grant:** $12,000. **Percentage of grants of half-tuition or more:** 68%. **Donations:** Voluntary but strongly encouraged.

School's Mission Statement

"At Marin Primary & Middle School we make education meaningful, while encouraging pride in self, respect for others, and enthusiasm for learning. • *We treasure childhood.* We honor and enjoy children's natural curiosity, competence, and exuberance. *We teach to reach children.* Using teams of teachers and educational methods tailored to how children learn best, we connect with our students, build trusting relationships, and make learning relevant, memorable and fun. *We teach children to reach.* Asking not 'how smart is the child' but 'how is the child smart,' we guide our students to see their full potential, and we equip them to pursue it with passion and purpose. • *We inspire children to make a difference.* We value academic excellence, personal integrity, and community action, and encourage our students to become informed, engaged, and ethical global citizens."

Academic Program

Philosophy: N/P. **Foreign languages:** Spanish, French. **Computer training:** Yes. **No. of computers available for students:** 40. **No. of hours weekly of:** Art- 1.5; Drama- 1; Music- 1.5; Computers, foreign language- 5x a week; PE- 45 min. sessions 4 or 5 x a week. **Outdoor education:** Curriculum guided trips to the Discovery Museum, San Francisco Symphony, Guide Dogs for the Blind, Yosemite, Washington State, Gold Country, Marin Headlands. **Grading:** A-F, beginning in G4. **Average nightly homework:** "Varies. Homework policy determined by teams of teachers." Posted on the Internet: Yes. **Percentage of students participating in Johns Hopkins Center for Talented Youth Program:** N/P. **Other indicators of academic success:** "Secondary school and college placement record." **High schools attended by latest graduating class:** Branson, MA, Stuart Hall, San Domenico, MC, Vanguard, Urban, SHCP, Marin School, University, Drew, Sonoma Academy, St. Mark's School, and Stevenson.

Faculty

Ethnicity: 88% Caucasian (non-Latino), 4% Latino, 3% other, 2% Asian, 2% multi-racial, 1% African-American. **Percentage of teachers with graduate degrees:** 40%. **Percentage with current California credential:** 65%. **Faculty selection/training:** N/P. **Teacher/student ratio:** 1:6. **Special subject teachers:** Art, music, woodworking, drama, PE, Spanish, French, technology. Extensive after-school elective program; Outdoor Education center. **Average teacher tenure:** 15 years.

Middle School

Description: Integrated subjects through G8. **Teacher/student ratio:** 1:6. **Elective courses offered:** Art, music, band, instrumental music, chorus, PE, team sports, woodworking, Outdoor education center program for all grades. After-school electives include foreign language, woodworking, technology, music, drama, homework lab, creative writing, and art. **Student social events:** Barbecues, theatrical productions, Annual Sock Hop, speaker series, Grandparents Day, Monster Mash, Harvest Festival, buddy program, Literary Day, Book Fair, extensive community service projects.

Student Support Services

No. of Licensed Counselors on staff: None. **Counselor/student ratio:** N/A. **Learning specialists on staff:** Four. **Learning differences/disabilities support:** "Yes, with certain limitations dependent on student's individual needs and the current class composition." **High school placement support:** "There is extensive support from the Eighth Grade teachers and the Administration. Aid in the secondary school admission process begins during the spring of the student's Seventh Grade year."

Student Conduct and Health

Code of conduct: "Six rules to live by: Be kind, Be respectful, Be an active listener, Be safe, Be accountable, Give your personal best." **Prevention education and awareness addressed in:** Included in life skills classes taught to all Middle School students. Special programs, assemblies and various presenters are part of this curriculum.

Athletics

Sports offered: Cross-country, track and field, soccer, basketball, flag football. **Team play begins in:** G5 (inter/intramural).

Campus/Campus Life

Campus description: "The campus includes large classrooms, a multipurpose room used for bi-weekly all-school assemblies, an expansive Library Media Center, an Outdoor Education Center, an Integrated Subjects Projects Lab, an Art room, a Music room, two fields and access to public tennis courts." **Library:** Library/media center with 13,000 volumes. **Sports facilities:** Tennis courts, baseball field, basketball court. **Theater/Arts facilities:** Multi-purpose and art room. **Computer lab:** Yes. The entire campus has wireless connection. **Science lab:** Yes. **Lunch program:** Yes. **Bus service:** No. **Uniforms/dress code:** Students in PreK-4 must abide by the dress code explained in the Family Resource Guide. Students in G5-8 wear uniforms. **Opportunities for community service:** Extensive community service opportunities on campus and in the greater area are available to students. Each middle school student is required to complete community service hours annually.

Extended Day

Morning care: Begins at 7:30 a.m. **After-school care:** Care or elective options until 6 p.m. **Grade levels:** PreK-8. **Cost:** $10 per hour. Free playground supervision before morning class time. **Drop-in care available:** No. **Coverage over major holidays:** No. **Homework help:** A homework lab for Middle School students is available at an extra cost. **Snacks:** Provided: Yes. **Staff/student ratio:** 1:6. **After-school classes:** Woodworking, art, instrumental music lessons, team sports, technology instruction, drama, martial arts, and garden club. Cost: Varies from $200-$350 per semester depending on class time and materials involved.

Summer Programs

"Summer camp is in session from mid-June to early August. Camp is for students entering PreK-7. Camp includes extensive elective opportunities including model car building, surfing, cooking, and field trips to amusement parks and sports." **Cost:** Based on number of weeks attended. Drop in attendance is available depending on space availability.

Parent Involvement

Parent/teacher communication: "Conferences, website, e-mail, Friday newsletter, extensive report cards/progress reports." **Participation requirements:** Twenty voluntary hours per year. **Parent education programs:** Speaker Series events and many other opportunities throughout the year. Parent involvement is highly important and encouraged.

What Sets the School Apart From Others

"At Marin Primary & Middle School, we believe childhood is a time to be treasured. We believe that children respond best to kindness, encouragement and mutual respect. We also recognize that relationships, relevance and high standards are critical to successful education. MP&MS students are challenged to develop a lifelong passion for learning that includes equal measures of wonder and rigorous inquiry. We teach our children to learn with and from each other, and we teach the group to respect the individual."

How Parents/Students Characterize School

Parent comment(s): "Marin Primary & Middle School truly values my child for who she is." ♦ "The teachers at MP&MS care about and understand my child." ♦ "My child loves to come to school." ♦ "MP&MS doesn't just say they educate the whole child, they really do it!"
Student comment(s): "At MP&MS, my teachers care about who I am." ♦ "I left MP&MS more than ready for high school. MP&MS gave me the gift of knowing how I learn and what my individual strengths are."

MARIN WALDORF SCHOOL

755 Idylberry Road
San Rafael, CA 94903
(415) 479-8190 *fax (415) 479-9921*
www.marinwaldorf.org

Kathryn King, Head of School, kking@marinwaldorf.org
Linda Biancaniello, Director of Admission, Linda@marinwaldorf.org

General

Coed PS-8 day school. Founded in 1972. Independent. Nonprofit. **Member:** N/P. **Enrollment:** Approx. 200. **Average class size:** 22. **Accreditation:** "Full accreditation through the Association of Waldorf Schools of North America (AWSNA), effective 05/06 school year." (Term N/P.) **Endowment:** N/P. **School year:** Sept.-June. **Instructional days:** 167. **School day:** 8:15 a.m. to 3:15 p.m.

Student Body

Ethnicity: 81% Caucasian (non-Latino), 5% Asian, 5% multi-racial, 5% other, 2% Latino, 2% African-American.

Admission

Applications due: March, rolling admissions for remainder of year. **Application fee:** $75. **Application process:** Parents are encouraged to take a tour, submit the application packet (available online at www.marinwaldorf.org), and schedule an interview with the admission director and teacher. **No. of applications:** 75+. **No. of K spaces:**

36. **Percentage of K class made up of school's preschool class: 85%.**
Admission evaluation requirements for K: Application and interview. **Other grades:** Application, teacher recommendation form, interview, class visit. **Preferences:** Sibling, prior Waldorf school attendance. **What sort of student do you best serve?** "Creative, inquisitive, enthusiastic about learning."

Costs

Latest tuition: $13,035 for elementary, $11,675 for 5-day K. In addition there is a $500 enrollment fee for all students. **Sibling discount:** 25% for second child, 40% for each additional child. **Tuition includes:** Lunch: No; Transportation: No; Laptop computer: No; Other: N/A. **Tuition increases:** Approx. 3% annually. **Other costs:** Approx. $50 musical instrument fees. **Percentage of students receiving financial aid:** 34%. **Financial aid application deadline:** Feb. (call for date). Financial aid is based on need. **Average grant:** Varies by need. **Percentage of grants of half-tuition or more:** N/A. **Donations:** Voluntary.

School's Mission Statement

"It is the mission of the Marin Waldorf School to provide an education for people that will lead them to fulfill their highest potential as free human beings and which energizes a true and life-long love of learning. Recognizing the spiritual nature of the human being, we strive to bring into practice the educational principles of Rudolf Steiner in a way that reflects their relevance for the challenges of an ever-changing and socially diverse world. It is the mission of the Marin Waldorf School to ensure that each stage of a child's development will be supported by activities that engage the mind, fire the imagination, and hone skills to serve an evolving humanity."

Academic Program

Philosophy: "We offer more than just an intellectual education, merging holistic methods that allow children to experience the connections between nature, person and society, thus learning reverence for all life." **Foreign languages:** German and Spanish. **Computer training:** None. **No. of computers available for students:** N/A. **No. of hours**

weekly of: Art- 10; Drama- 5: Music- 10; Computers- N/A; Foreign language- 5, German and Spanish; PE- 5. **Outdoor education:** G3-8. **Grading:** Written evaluations. Letter grades begin in G7. **Average nightly homework:** "G4-8 only, varies by grade." Posted on the Internet: No. **Percentage of students participating in Johns Hopkins Center for Talented Youth Program:** N/A. **Other indicators of academic success:** "N/A." **High schools attended by latest graduating class:** Tamalpais, MA, Branson, Terra Linda High, and San Domenico.

Faculty

Ethnicity: 90% Caucasian (non-Latino), 10% African-American. **Percentage of teachers with graduate degrees:** 10%. **Percentage with current California credential:** N/P. **Faculty selection/training:** Full Waldorf training, BA. **Teacher/student ratio:** 1:20. **Special subject teachers:** Art, instrumental music, PE, movement, choir, foreign language (2). **Average teacher tenure:** 8 years.

Middle School

Description: "Marin Waldorf middle school is a continuation of the early grades offering a Waldorf school curriculum rich in history, math, science, humanities, art and music." **Teacher/student ratio:** 1:20. **Elective courses offered:** N/A. **Achievement tracking in:** N/A. **Student social events:** Arranged privately.

Student Support Services

No. of Licensed Counselors on staff: None. **Counselor/student ratio:** N/A. **Learning specialists on staff:** One. **Learning differences/disabilities support:** N/A. **High school placement support:** "N/A."

Student Conduct and Health

Code of conduct: "Yes." **Prevention education and awareness addressed in:** None.

Athletics

Sports offered: Track and field, basketball, hockey, circus arts. **Team play begins in:** G7, girls basketball (intramural).

Campus/Campus Life

Campus description: "11 acres, large playing fields, school garden, large classrooms." **Library:** "3,600 volumes." **Sports facilities:** Soccer pitch field and multipurpose field. **Theater/Arts facilities:** Amphitheater. **Computer lab:** No. **Science lab:** No. **Lunch program:** Yes, organic lunch program. **Bus service:** Yes. **Uniforms/dress code:** "Dress code." **Opportunities for community service:** Yes, varies by class and age.

Extended Day

Morning care: None. **After-school care:** Until 5:30 p.m. for elementary grades and until 3:15 p.m. for K. **Grade levels:** G1-5. **Cost:** Approx. $12.50 per day for kindergarten care until 3:15 p.m.; elementary school care upon request only. **Drop-in care available:** Yes. **Coverage over major holidays:** No. **Homework help:** No. **Snacks:** Not provided. **Staff/student ratio:** 1:4. **After-school classes:** None.

Summer Programs

"Magic Forest Summer Camp, for children ages 3 years 7 months to 6 years. Crafts, gardening, traditional games, nature walks, puppetry. Camp includes two, 2-week sessions from 8:30 a.m. to 1 p.m. In addition, Circus Camp is offered for children ages 10 to 14. Contact our office for brochures." **Cost:** N/P.

Parent Involvement

Parent/teacher communication: Parent/teacher conference and two written evaluations. **Participation requirements:** Parents are asked to give 10 hours of volunteer time every year. **Parent education programs offered?** Yes.

What Sets the School Apart From Others

"MWS offers a full Waldorf curriculum taught by trained and experienced Waldorf teachers. Independent, non state supported or controlled curriculum, no mandated testing requirements. Over 900 Waldorf schools internationally."

How Parents/Students Characterize School

Parent comment(s): "I have so appreciated my son's education at Marin Waldorf School. He has had a stable and healthy environment for learning and he loves to come to school to be in his class with friends he has known for years and a teacher who knows him well."

Student comment(s): "My Waldorf education has challenged me to think creatively and to reach new heights both academically and personally. Waldorf was able to give me a nourishing relationship with my education and has ultimately given me a stronger sense of self, and the confidence to accomplish anything."

MISSION DOLORES CATHOLIC SCHOOL

3321-16th Street (at Church) (Upper Market)
San Francisco, CA 94114
(415) 861-7673   fax (415) 861-7620
www.missiondolores.org

Andreina Gualco, Head of School and Director of Admission,
 agualco@missiondolores.org

General

Coed K-8 parochial day school. Founded in 1893. Catholic. Nonprofit. **Member:** NCEA. **Enrollment:** Approx. 210. **Average class size:** 25. **Accreditation:** WASC/WCEA (6-year term: 2001-07). **Endowment:** N/P. **School year:** August-June. **Instructional days:** 180 **School day:** 8:15 a.m. to 3 p.m.

Student Body

Ethnicity: 50% Latino, 19% multi-racial, 14% Asian, 12% African-American, 4% Caucasian (non-Latino), 1% Native American.

Admission

Applications due: Rolling. **Application fee:** $30. **Application process:** "Once application is completed students are asked to come in for a screening. We administer the Brigance Readiness Test to K and G1 students." **No. of applications:** 30. **No. of K spaces:** 25. **Percentage of K class made up of school's preschool class:** N/A. **Admission evaluation requirements for K:** Pre-school recommendation; screening. **Other grades:** "Students applying for G2-8 are asked to come and spend a day at school; we also require grades, test scores, and recommendations." **Preferences:** Sibling, Catholic. **What sort of student do you best serve?** "We do not have services for children with some special needs."

Costs

Latest tuition: If a family completes 30 service hours the tuition is as follows: Catholic families $3,950 for 1st child; $2,700 for 2nd+; Non-Catholic $4,700 for 1st child; $3,220 for 2nd+. Full tuition is $5,150 per year for 1st child and $3,600 for 2nd+. All payments may be made in 10 equal installments. **Sibling discount:** See above. **Tuition includes:** Lunch: No; Transportation: No; Laptop computer: No. **Tuition increases:** Approx. 5% annually. **Other costs:** Approx. $260 for books, $150 uniforms, $90 other fees. **Percentage of students receiving financial aid:** 40%. **Financial aid application deadline:** June (call for date). Financial aid is based on need. **Average grant:** $500. **Percentage of grants of half-tuition or more:** 30%. These are grants given by the BASIC Fund or Guardsman not the school itself. **Donations:** "$120 (candy sale)."

School's Mission Statement

"We, the community of Mission Dolores School, a part of the evangelization ministry of Mission Dolores Parish, base our philosophy of education on our belief in the fundamental dignity and uniqueness of the individual as created in God's image. We acknowledge the presence of Jesus in the sacramental and ministerial life of the Church. We believe Catholic education is a process of growth that engages the student in every dimension of his/her life—spiritual, intellectual, emotional, social, cultural, and physical. Our school complements and supports the efforts of parents/guardians, who are the primary educators of their children.

It is our mission to facilitate the development of the whole person. We strive to provide a balanced curriculum in a nurturing environment where students are challenged: to integrate the Gospel values of love, peace, justice, and service in their everyday lives; ✦ to develop their abilities to think independently and to make free and responsible choices in the light of Christian values; ✦ to embrace their individual differences and cultural diversity; ✦ to appreciate all the wonders of God's creation; ✦ to value responsible stewardship for the earth and its people."

Academic Program

Philosophy: N/P. **Foreign languages:** N/P. **Computer training:** Yes. **No. of computers available for students:** "18 in lab; 2-4 in each classroom." **No. of hours weekly of:** Art- 1; Drama- None; Music- .5; Computers- 1; Foreign language- None; PE- 1-1.5. **Outdoor education:** G5. **Grading:** A-F, beginning in G3. **Average nightly homework:** "Varies by grade level." Posted on the Internet: No. **Percentage of students participating in Johns Hopkins Center for Talented Youth Program:** None. "[Students participate in various summer programs including]: Aim High at Urban; Summerbridge at University (G6-8), and at SF Day School (G4-5); Magis at SI." **Other indicators of academic success:** "90-100% of students applying to private high schools are accepted." **High schools attended by latest graduating class:** SI , Lowell, Stuart Hall, CSH, SHCP, Riordan, Mercy-Burlingame, June Jordan, Leadership, and Raul Wallenberg.

Faculty

Ethnicity: 70% Caucasian (non-Latino), 20% Asian, 10% Latino. **Percentage of teachers with graduate degrees:** 70%. **Percentage with current California credential:** 100%. **Faculty selection/training:** "Experience, degree." **Teacher/student ratio:** 1:25. **Special subject teachers:** Computers and PE. **Average teacher tenure:** 6 years.

Middle School

Description: "Commences in G5, departmentalization." **Teacher/student ratio:** 1:28. **Elective courses offered:** N/P. **Achievement tracking in:** N/P. **Student social events:** N/P.

Student Support Services

No. of Licensed Counselors on staff: One part-time. **Counselor/student ratio:** N/P. **Learning specialists on staff:** N/P. **Learning differences/disabilities support:** N/P. **High school placement support:** N/P.

Student Conduct and Health

Code of conduct: "Available in handbook." **Prevention, education and awareness programs:** N/P.

Athletics

Sports offered: For girls, volleyball and basketball; for boys, soccer and basketball. Both play in the CYO league as well as some PAL. Teams. **Team play begins in:** G3.

Campus/Campus Life

Campus description: Library, gymnasium, auditorium, computer lab. **Library:** "Yes." **Sports facilities:** Gym. **Theater/Arts facilities:** N/P. **Computer lab:** "Yes." **Science lab:** N/P. **Lunch program:** Yes. **Bus service:** No. **Uniforms/dress code:** Uniforms. **Opportunities for community service:** N/P.

Extended Day

Morning care: Begins at 7 a.m. **After-school care:** Until 6 p.m. **Grade levels:** K-8. **Cost:** $3/hour. **Drop-in care available:** Yes. **Coverage over major holidays:** No. **Homework help:** Yes. **Snacks:** Provided. **Staff/student ratio:** 1:20. **After-school classes:** Choir G2-8. **Cost:** $50 per year.

Summer Programs: N/P.

Parent Involvement

Parent/teacher communication: Conferences, website, e-mail, newsletter. **Participation requirements:** 30 hours per year. **Parent education programs:** None.

What Sets the School Apart From Others

"Mission Dolores is a truly diverse school. Our school population truly reflects the diversity of San Francisco. Not only do our students represent a United Nations of cultures, they also come from various economic classes, family situations and they have different learning styles and abilities. Our children, parents and staff do not only appreciate the differences, they celebrate and embrace the diversity that makes Mission Dolores unique!"

How Parents/Students Characterize School

Parent comment(s): "My child is receiving a quality Catholic education in a supportive family environment."

Student comment(s): "Mission Dolores School not only prepared me to succeed in the challenging academic environment at St. Ignatius College Preparatory, but it also taught me that we are citizens of the world and success is measured not only in grades but in service and outreach to all people—those like us and those who are different."—Alumna, Class of 2004

MONTESSORI DE TERRA LINDA

620 Del Ganado
San Rafael, CA 94903
(415) 479-7373   fax (415) 479-5394
www.mdtl.org

Jane Calbreath, Head of School and Director of Admission,
jane@mdtl.org

General

Coed PS-6 day school. Founded in 1970. Independent. Nonprofit. **Member:** N/P. **Enrollment:** Approx. 130. **Average class size:** 24. **Accreditation:** AMI (Association Montessori International)(1-year term: 2005-06). **Endowment:** None. **School year:** Sept.-June. **Instructional days:** Approx. 176. **School day:** 8:30 a.m. to 3 p.m.

Student Body

Ethnicity: 78.7% Caucasian (non-Latino), 13.8% multi-racial, 3.8% Asian, 2.5% Latino, 2.5% other.

Admission

Applications due: Jan. (call for date). **Application fee:** $65. **Application process:** Open house, tour/observation, child visit. **No. of applications:** 20. **No. of K spaces:** 15. **Percentage of K class made up of school's preschool class:** 75%. **Admission evaluation requirements for K:** Screening, school visit, teacher recommendations. **Other grades:** Same as for K. **Preferences:** Sibling, Montessori transfers. **What sort of student do you best serve?** "Motivated, independent learners."

Costs

Latest tuition: $10,550. **Sibling discount:** 10%. **Tuition includes:** Lunch No; Transportation: No; Laptop computer No; Other: N/A. **Tuition increases:** Approx. 6% annually. **Other costs:** Outdoor education, trips. **Percentage of students receiving financial aid:** 7%. **Financial aid application deadline:** Feb. (call for date). Financial aid is based on need. **Average grant:** $5,000. **Percentage of grants of half-tuition or more:** 90%. **Donations:** Voluntary (annual fund and auction).

School's Mission Statement

"The mission of Montessori de Terra Linda provides a unique learning environment founded on the principles developed by Dr. Maria Montessori. Our dedicated school community guides and nurtures the natural unfolding of the whole child in an atmosphere of order, beauty and harmony. Each child is actively supported in the self-directed pursuit of lifelong intellectual, emotional and spiritual growth."

Academic Program

Philosophy: "Maria Montessori's philosophy is based on the physical, academic, social and emotional developmental needs of the child and values respectful compassionate communication and relationships between children and adults." **Foreign languages:** Spanish. **Computer training:** Integrated in the curriculum. **No. of computers available for**

students: 6. **No. of hours weekly of:** Art- 5+; Drama- varies; Music- 3+; Computers- integrated in the curriculum daily; Foreign language- 3; PE- 5. **Outdoor education:** Varies. **Grading:** Annual Progress Reports begin in K. **Average nightly homework:** 30 min. Posted on the Internet: "Not at this time." **Percentage of students participating in Johns Hopkins Center for Talented Youth Program:** N/A. **Other indicators of academic success:** "SAT testing begins at G3." **High schools attended by latest graduating class:** "N/A. Montessori de Terra Linda currently goes to the 6th grade. Our students have continued to Saint Mark's School and San Domenico School."

Faculty

Ethnicity: 75% Caucasian (non-Latino), 20% Latino, 5% other. **Percentage of teachers with graduate degrees:** 10%. **Percentage with current California credential:** N/A. **Faculty selection/training:** "AMI Credential, BA, experience." **Teacher/student ratio:** 1:10. **Special subject teachers:** Music, Spanish. **Average teacher tenure:** 15 years.

Middle School

"In planning stages."

Student Support Services

No. of Licensed Counselors on staff: None. **Counselor/student ratio:** N/A. **Learning specialists on staff:** One. **Learning differences/ disabilities support:** None. **High school placement support:** N/A (school currently goes to G6).

Student Conduct and Health

Code of conduct: "Montessori philosophy which inspires respect and compassion for others. Conflict resolution curriculum is part of the Montessori philosophy which begins in preschool." **Prevention education and awareness addressed in:** Health class.

Athletics

Sports offered: Softball, volleyball, soccer, basketball, hiking, biking. **Team play begins in:** G1 (intramural).

Campus/Campus Life

Campus description: "Beautifully landscaped gardens surround the campus located within easy walking distance to grocery store, post office, restaurants, coffee shop, and bus service." **Library:** "Within the classroom." **Sports facilities:** Basketball, grassy field, sports fields walking distance, pool at recreation center one block away. **Theater/Arts facilities:** Multi-purpose building. **Computer lab:** In classroom. **Science lab:** No. **Lunch program:** No. **Bus service:** No. **Uniforms/dress code:** Dress code. No super heroes or violent themes. **Opportunities for community service:** Yes.

Extended Day

Morning care: Begins at 7:30 a.m. **After-school care:** Until 5:30 p.m. **Grade levels:** K-6. **Cost:** $7.50/hour. **Drop-in care available:** Yes. **Coverage over major holidays:** No. **Homework help:** Yes. **Snacks:** Provided. **Staff/student ratio:** 1:10 **After-school classes:** "Yes, Orff music, gymnastics, dance, and science." Costs: N/P.

Summer Programs

"Summer camp for K only."

Parent Involvement

Parent/teacher communication: Conferences, website, e-mail, newsletter. **Participation requirements:** 24 hours of volunteering per family. **Parent education programs offered?** Yes—varies each year.

What Sets the School Apart From Others

"Individualized program, warm friendly community."

How Parents/Students Characterize School

Parent comment(s): "Responsive to parents' needs."
Student comment(s): "Loving, supportive teachers."

Mount Tamalpais School

100 Harvard Avenue
Mill Valley, CA 94941
(415) 383-9434 *fax (415) 383-7519*
www.mttam.org

Dr. Kate Mecca, Head of School, kmecca@mttam.org
Sasha Mardikian, Director of Admission, smardikian@mttam.org

General

Coed K-8 day school. Founded in 1976. Independent. Nonprofit. Member: CAIS, WASC, BADA, ISBOA, NAIS. Enrollment: Approx. 240. Average class size: 12. Accreditation: CAIS/WASC (6-year term: 2005-11). Endowment: "$1.5 million +." School year: Aug.-June. Instructional days: 180. School day: 8 a.m. to 3 p.m.

Student Body

Ethnicity: 80% Caucasian (non-Latino), 5% Asian, 5% Latino, 3% African-American, 5% multi-racial, 2% other.

Admission

Applications due: Jan. (call for date). Application fee: $150. Application process: Parents must visit, go on a group tour, and meet with the Admissions Director and Head of School. Students are screened following receipt of application, which includes three reference/recommendation forms to be sent separately. Applicants to G2-8 must spend a full school day on campus during which time they are interviewed and participate in criterion-referenced testing in core subjects. No. of applications: 250+/- for K, the main entry level. No. of K spaces: 24-32. Percentage of K class made up of school's preschool class: N/A. Admission evaluation requirements for K: Screening, school visit, minimum of three recommendations (one of which must come form the child's current teacher or preschool team/director); parent interview, student interview and observation, admission test scores, copy of certified birth record, and photograph. Other grades: "Standardized test results, transcript, school visit, student interview, parent interview, at least three recommendations, one of which must come from the child's current teacher, writing sample, work portfolio, etc." **Preferences:** "Siblings and legacies do receive some preference." **What sort of student do you best serve?** "MTS seeks to enroll students who are enthusiastic, motivated learners who will thrive in a strong academic program that emphasizes individual growth, creativity, exploration, and character development, within an integrated spiraling curriculum."

Costs

Latest tuition: $18,000. **Sibling discount:** None. **Tuition includes:** Lunch: No; Transportation: No; Laptop computer: No; Other: No. **Tuition increases:** Approx. 5-7% annually. **Other costs:** Approx. $100 for specific textbooks in G6-8 only, approx. $100 for uniforms, $25-$125 other fees. **Percentage of students receiving financial aid:** 15+%. **Financial aid application deadline:** Jan. (call for date). Financial aid is based on need. **Average grant:** Varies. **Percentage of grants of half-tuition or more:** 90%. **Donations:** Annual donations are expected to the Annual Fund, Faculty Fund, as well as to the Building Fund and/or Capital Campaign or Endowment Fund when school is engaged in an active campaign. Donations of goods and/or services and attendance at the annual Auction Gala fund raising event are strongly encouraged and appreciated.

School's Mission Statement

"Mount Tamalpais School is an independent, coeducational school serving students in K-8. Mount Tamalpais School is dedicated to the active pursuit of knowledge and to integrity, community service and fairness. We want our students to embrace diversity, honoring the value of each individual's heritage, strengths, choices, feelings and ideas. We strive to celebrate the human spirit by being responsible members of our families, our school, our community and our world. We are committed to a strong interactive, multidisciplinary curriculum designed to challenge and enlighten, and to teachers who serve as guides and role models for our students. ◆ The school's program, atmosphere and overall environment have been designed to encourage the development of the whole child, with an emphasis on strong academic preparation, values, emotional growth, personal and social skills, effective thinking and problem solving capabilities, with attention to individual strengths and diversity of learning styles. Mount Tamalpais School places equal emphasis on the academic and social development of each student within a community that esteems family, the pursuit of personal excellence, the perpetuation of valued traditions, and the development of a strong moral code. Mount Tamalpais School is strongly committed to the partnership of home and school on behalf of each individual student."

Academic Program

Philosophy: "Mount Tamalpais School seeks to provide students with a solid academic foundation and to foster genuine enthusiasm for life-long learning through an intellectually stimulating and challenging program. Working with a departmentalized curriculum with teachers who are specialists in their subject areas helps to instill a love of learning and develops students who are inquisitive, thoughtful, determined, independent, intellectually curious, creative thinking and well-integrated human beings. It is our goal to include the mastery of skills and concepts at each grade level in each subject while integrating query, investigation, problem solving and higher level thinking skills. We also want students to challenge themselves, to grow in creativity, to question, to seek information, to work well independently and with others in a cooperative and collaborative manner. It is also our hope that each student will find and explore their own individual strengths and creative outlets and will be committed to contribute to the greater good." **Foreign languages:** French and Spanish in K-5, French or Spanish + Latin in G6-8, and Mandarin or Japanese in G6-8. **Computer training:** K-8. **No. of computers available for students:** 120. **No. of hours weekly of:** Art- 1.5+; Drama- 1+; Music- 1.5+; Computers- 1.5+; Foreign language- 3-5+; PE 5+. **Outdoor education:** G4-8. **Grading:** G1-3 √/_+/ -/ scale. G4-8 A-F. **Average nightly homework:** From approx. 20 min. in G1-2 to approx. 1 hour + in G8. **Posted on the Internet:** No. **Percentage of students participating in Johns Hopkins Center for Talented Youth Program:** 3-5%. **Other indicators of academic success:** "Honor Roll each trimester (B+ 90% average)." **High schools attended by latest graduating class:** Branson, University, SI, Cate, Thacher, Santa Catalina, MC, and College Prep.

Faculty

Ethnicity: 85% Caucasian (non-Latino), 6% other, 4% multi-racial, 2% Latino, 2% African-American, 1% Asian. **Percentage of teachers with graduate degrees:** 69%. **Percentage with current California credential:** 72%. **Faculty selection/training:** Degree, credential, graduate degree, experience, specialized training in subject area. **Teacher/student ratio:** 1:8. **Special subject teachers:** Art, art history, dance, drama, sewing, technology, PE, music, choral, instrumental, musical theatre, health, character development, etiquette. **Average teacher tenure:** 11 years.

Middle School

Description: G6-8, departmentalized in all grades and all subjects. **Teacher/student ratio:** 1:8; 1:12 for some classes. **Elective courses offered:** "Trimester rotation, single or double blocks depending on the course—art, dance, drama, computers and music, current events, IT, creative writing, animation, computers (all in addition to regularly scheduled classes in most of these subjects.)" **Achievement tracking in:** "Math only, according to learning style, G5-8." **Student social events:** Student Council functions and events, Spirit Days, Junior High dances (G6-8).

Student Support Services

No. of Licensed Counselors on staff: Two half-time in counseling capacity; they also teach and or serve in other roles. **Counselor/student ratio:** N/P. **Learning specialists on staff:** One full-time. **Learning differences/disabilities support:** "One full-time Learning Specialist who works with students individually and in small groups, with teachers and with parents. Students participate in differentiated instruction and receive extended time on tests. Particular students may have their schedules and/or their subject requirements modified if/when appropriate." **High school placement support:** Dean of Students/G8 Homeroom teacher/Counselor and Head of School lead the secondary school admission process for students and families in G8. This process begins in G7 with a spring meeting to help explain and organize the eighth grade year.

Student Conduct and Health

Code of conduct: "Students are expected to respect themselves, their school, the environment and others." **Prevention education and awareness addressed in:** "Our comprehensive Health Education program includes specific units on decision making, eating disorders, stereotypes, drugs, alcohol, subliminal advertising, personal choices, and sexual harassment issues."

Athletics

Sports offered: In fall, cross-country (G3-8), girls volleyball (G6-8), boys soccer (G6-8); in winter, basketball (G4-8); in spring, track and field (G3-8), lacrosse (G3-8), boys volleyball (G6-8), girls soccer (G6-8), and basketball (G2-3) **Team play begins in:** G2.

Campus/Campus Life

Campus description: "MTS is located on more than 12 acres in Mill Valley, 15 minutes north of San Francisco. We are close to the Pacific Ocean, the Bay, and Highway 101 and Shoreline Highway Route 1. The beautiful campus includes a large playing field (full soccer field overlaid by two baseball diamonds and a peripheral track), a smaller grass circle area, and a 1+ acre Cypress Grove outdoor learning area." **Library:** "The Rappoport Library Learning Center incorporates 2,500+ square feet including a small instructional classroom and individual student work stations. There is a dedicated computer minilab within the library, and our entire computer system is networked and wireless. The library houses more than 15,000 books, plus reference materials and online resources. There are 12 permanent student computer stations, two faculty/staff computer stations and unlimited laptop access within the library." **Sports facilities:** The 15,000+ sq. ft. Founder's Hall includes a full gymnasium/theatre, a dance/gymnastics room, a piano room, and a music room, in addition to two small instrumental instruction rooms and a hospitality kitchen. **Theater/Arts facilities:** See above. **Computer lab:** The main computer lab houses 20 student workstations and two faculty/staff work stations. There are several mini labs throughout the school, plus two laptop carts and one Alpha Smart cart of 16-20 each. All teachers have desktop or laptop computers at their desks; all access is wireless and networked. **Science lab:** Two dedicated science lab classrooms and a connecting shared work study/office space serve students in K-8 and the Science Department teachers. **Lunch program:** Yes. **Bus service:** Yes. **Uniforms/ dress code:** Uniforms. **Opportunities for community service:** Community service learning opportunities are woven within curriculum and explored as well through Student Council-sponsored activities. All students in G6-8 have specific community service projects each year of middle school that are done outside of school time. These assignments must be direct service with bona fide non-profit programs, especially those that serve children, the elderly, the environment, or special needs populations.

Extended Day

Morning care: Begins at 7:30 a.m. **After-school care:** Until 6 p.m. **Grade levels:** K-8. **Cost:** $5 per hour prepaid in $50 increments. **Drop-in care available:** Daily with credit card on file. **Coverage over major holidays:** No. **Homework help:** Yes. **Snacks:** Provided. **Staff/ student ratio:** 1:10 max. **After-school classes:** "Full range of classes each trimester, including dance, sewing, science adventures, computers, chess, brain games, art, rock climbing, etc. All classes are $125 for twelve sessions."

Summer Programs

The school currently offers two summer enrichment courses, each from 9 a.m. to 3 p.m. Sports camp lasts two weeks; students may sign up for one week or for both. Drama camp lasts two weeks and students sign up for both weeks, as the program culminates in a Shakespeare production. **Cost:** $375 for two weeks, including t-shirts and snacks.

Parent Involvement

Parent/teacher communication: Conferences, website, e-mail, telephone, personal interaction, newsletter. **Participation requirements:** 60 hours per year per family. **Parent education programs offered?** Yes.

What Sets the School Apart From Others

"We are a small school and we are departmentalized. Our teachers work in their main areas of interest, training and expertise. We are committed to personalized, small group instruction and to helping each student maximize his/her potential. Because students and teachers work together over a range of years (primary, middle grades, junior high) they develop close, meaningful relationships which extend beyond the classroom."

How Parents/Students Characterize School

Parent comment(s): "Parents are committed, participatory and involved. They are supportive of faculty, staff and administration, and they value the strength and closeness of the school community. Parents also appreciate the interaction with teachers and the level of care and attention given to their children."

Student comment(s): "Students love their school and love their teachers. Students enjoy the wide range of classes offered and appreciate the personal attention and interaction with faculty and staff."

Presidio Hill School

3839 Washington St. (btwn. Maple and Cherry) (Presidio Heights)
San Francisco, CA 94118
(415) 751-9318 *fax (415) 751-9334*
www.presidiohill.org

Ann Meissner, Interim Director, ameissner@presidiohill.org
Amy Pearson, Director of Admission & Financial Assistance,
  admissions@presidiohill.org or apearson@presidiohill.org

General

Coed K-8 day school. Founded in 1918. Independent. Nonprofit. **Member:** NAIS, CAIS, BADA. **Enrollment:** Approx. 186. **Average class size:** 17 in K-5, 14 in G6-8. **Accreditation:** CAIS (6-year term: 2001-07). **Endowment:** None. **School year:** Sept.-June. **Instructional days:** 180. **School day:** 9 a.m. to 3 p.m. for K-3, 8:30 a.m. to 3:25 p.m. for G4-8.

Student Body

Ethnicity: 61% Caucasian (non-Latino), 24% multi-racial, 7% Asian, 6% African-American, 2% Latino.

Admission

Applications due: Jan. (call for date). **Application fee:** $75. **Application process:** Tour or attend open house, application fee, student evaluation form, play date. **No. of applications:** 180 (K-8). **No. of K spaces:** 16-18. **Percentage of K class made up of school's preschool class:** N/A. **Admission evaluation requirements for K:** See above description of the process. **Other grades:** Parent application, student application (G6-8), student visit (G1-8), current teacher evaluation, two years of school records. **Preferences:** Sibling. **What sort of student do you best serve?** "We look for families who understand and support our school mission and core values, who will thrive in our program, and who will enrich our vibrant community through their contribution to the multicultural fabric of our school. Children who tend to thrive at Presidio Hill have a natural curiosity, find motivation from within rather than through extrinsic rewards, take an active role in learning, and enjoy a cooperative, socially interactive setting and activity-based projects."

Costs

Latest tuition: $15,900 for K-3, $16,975 for G4-8. **Sibling discount:** None. **Tuition includes:** Lunch: No; Transportation: No; Laptop computer: No; Other: Before school care beginning at 8 a.m. **Tuition increases:** "Tuition increases each year due to various rising costs and cannot be precisely predicted from year to year." **Other costs:** Approx. $250. **Percentage of students receiving financial aid:** 23%. **Financial aid application deadline:** Jan. (call for date). Financial aid is based on need. **Average grant:** $9,543. **Percentage of grants of half-tuition or more:** 62%. **Donations:** Cash donations are voluntary. The school expects parents to give their time in a capacity that best suits their family life.

School's Mission Statement

"Presidio Hill School is a co-educational independent school committed to multiculturalism and the development of our students into active and responsible participants in the world. By tradition and current emphasis, Presidio Hill encourages children to question, evaluate and think creatively and independently. Social, emotional, physical, and intellectual growth is promoted through an enriched individualized program. Basic and practical skills are taught as useful tools rather than ends in themselves. Children are encouraged in their strengths, assisted in overcoming weaknesses, and recognized for their uniqueness. Parents, staff, and students participate in decision making as a collaborative school community."

Academic Program

Philosophy: "Our child-centered curriculum encompasses the arts, sciences, and humanities. The mathematics and science programs not only build skills but also give students opportunities to use creative concepts in life situations. The language arts curriculum is literature-based throughout the grades with a school-wide emphasis on writing fluency. Critical thinking and research skills are emphasized in social studies as students learn to question information sources and develop an understanding of historical contexts. Appreciating one's responsibility in the local and global community is reinforced through service learning projects in every grade. Other curricular areas, integrated with the core subjects, include art, music, Spanish, and physical education. Presidio Hill School is committed to meeting students' individual needs in small classes with cooperative, hands-on learning. Graduates are prepared for, and attend excellent high schools throughout the Bay Area and beyond." **Foreign languages:** Spanish. **Computer training:** "Yes." **No. of computers available for students:** 35. **No. of hours weekly of:** Art- 1-2; Drama- 1-2: Music- 1-2; Computers- integrated in various subjects; Foreign language- varies according to grade level, 1-4; PE- 1-2. **Outdoor education:** Yes. **Grading:** "Evaluations in K-5 and a combination of evaluations/grades in G6-8." **Average nightly homework:** 20 min. in the lower grades and to 2-3 hrs. in middle school. Posted on the Internet: "This varies according to teacher and student interest or need." **Percentage of students participating in Johns Hopkins Center for Talented Youth Program:** N/P. **Other indicators of academic success:** "Presidio Hill School administers ERB tests yearly to all students third through eighth grade. We use these scores as well as many other methods to evaluate our students and their individual success. Students are being evaluated on a daily basis on all of their academic, social, emotional and physical skills right in the classroom. Through hands on learning the students learn not only how to take tests but also how to apply their knowledge to everyday situations. Presidio Hill School graduates get into and attend top high schools in the Bay Area and beyond. They are self-advocates and they expect and seek out relationships with their teachers." **High schools attended by latest graduating class:** Bay School, CSH, Drew, Gateway, IHS, JCHS, Lick, Lowell, MA, SHCP, SI, SOTA, University, Urban, and Washington.

Faculty

Ethnicity: 79% Caucasian (non-Latino), 6% Asian, 6% African-American, 6% multi-racial, 3% Latino. **Percentage of teachers with graduate degrees:** 40%. **Percentage with current California credential:** 61%. **Faculty selection/training:** "Minimum of a Bachelor's degree, experience, and a rigorous hiring process that involves a committee, a national search organization, telephone interviews, teaching observation and references checks." **Teacher/student ratio:** 1:13. **Special subject teachers:** Art, music, drama, PE, Spanish. **Average teacher tenure:** 8 years.

Middle School

Description: "Beginning in G6, Presidio Hill offers an entry point for a minimum of 12 new students every year. We have two sections of each grade, with 14 students per class and 28 students per grade. The middle school shares the same mission and philosophy as the younger grades and offers departmentalized classes." **Teacher/student ratio:** 1:13. **Elective courses offered:** "Art, music, drama, PE, and Self and Community are all required subjects in middle school." **Achievement tracking in:** "Is not practiced at Presidio Hill. Our middle school is small enough to meet the individualized needs of students without tracking. Spanish, however, is grouped according to achievement level." **Student social events:** School dances are regularly arranged in collaboration with partner schools in the area.

Student Support Services
No. of Licensed Counselors on staff: None. **Counselor/student ratio:** N/A. **Learning specialists on staff:** Two part-time. **Learning differences/disabilities support:** Two part-time learning specialists on staff (one for lower school and one for middle school). This staff is responsible for conducting tests, providing small group classes and individual tutoring, meeting with outside specialists or tutors, and working with the parents and staff to keep everyone informed about the student's needs. **High school placement support:** The middle school dean and 8th grade humanities teacher share the role of high school counselors by offering meetings and counseling for students and parents beginning in the spring of 7th grade. **Other:** "Presidio Hill employs a full-time multicultural dean who makes our commitment to multiculturalism tangible in the day-to-day functioning of the school in the areas of student and family support, curriculum, outreach and hiring, and programs and events."

Student Conduct and Health
Code of conduct: "Respect and responsibility are the guiding principles for the choices students must make. We teach students that their actions have consequences and guide them in making appropriate choices. Choices that diminish or violate these principles are met with consequences appropriate to the particular situation." **Prevention education and awareness addressed in:** "These programs are part of various classes and parent education evenings on a regular basis."

Athletics
Sports offered/team play begins in: Intramural sports are offered in K-5. Beginning in G6, students participate in a competitive Bay Area league, which includes sports such as cross-country, volleyball, and basketball.

Campus/Campus Life

Campus description: "The campus is over 17,000 square feet and was extensively renovated in 2001, more than doubling the facility and expanding every classroom. We have three play yards and use Julius Kahn Park in the Presidio as an extension of our own building." **Library:** Over 1,000 volumes and 4 computers. **Sports facilities:** "Rooftop yard and fields throughout the city." **Theater/Arts facilities:** Dedicated rooms for music, drama, art, and the Susan Andrews Theatre. **Computer lab:** No. **Science lab:** Yes. **Lunch program:** No. **Bus service:** No. **Uniforms/dress code:** No. **Opportunities for community service:** "Community service and service learning are deeply embedded in the history and curriculum at every grade level, guided by the principles of equity and justice."

Extended Day

Morning care: Begins at 8 a.m. **After-school care:** Until 6 p.m. **Grade levels:** All. **Cost:** Approx. $7/hour (with financial assistance available) for after-school care; morning care is free. **Drop-in care available:** $8/hr. **Coverage over major holidays:** "We offer child care during some holidays and breaks." **Homework help:** Yes. **Snacks:** Provided. **Staff/student ratio:** 1:10. **After-school classes:** "We offer after-school enrichment classes each semester. The classes and costs range each session, and a current sampling are always available through the admissions office." Cost: N/P.

Summer Programs

The school currently offers three 2-week day camp sessions called Hill Camp. Academic classes are offered in 3 morning class periods. Enrichment classes are offered in 2 afternoon sessions. Class offerings vary session to session. Extended care is also available. Campers can attend all day or just mornings or afternoons. Courses include sign language, chemistry, woodcraft, creative writing and the like. Cost: All fees for the 2-week session are $155 per individual morning academic class; $205 per afternoon enrichment; $410 for a.m. program only; $375 for p.m. program only, $750 for all day; $130 for extended care.

Parent Involvement

Parent/teacher communication: Parent-teacher conferences 2-3 times per year. Every teacher sends home a weekly classroom letter in addition to a school-wide weekly letter. These letters are posted on the school's website. "Parents and teachers share a warm, informal relationship and communicate often." **Participation requirements:** No requirement for parent participation but it is expected that parents give their time to the extent they can. **Parent education programs offered?** "Yes, such as 'Culture Chats,' sex education, and bullies; we provide many opportunities for parents to discuss child development and parenting."

What Sets the School Apart From Others

"While difficult to describe in words, it's the spirit of the place that really differentiates Presidio Hill. You sense it in the energy of the students, the history of the building, the warmth of the teachers, the dedication of the staff, and the commitment of the parents."

How Parents/Students Characterize School

"The best way to know how the parents and students characterize the school is to visit and ask them directly. We have an admission process that encourages applicant families to get to know our school through visits to the classroom, conversations with our teachers, and ample contact with our current families. We encourage questions and provide many opportunities to do so."

RING MOUNTAIN DAY SCHOOL

70 Lomita Drive
Mill Valley, CA 94941
(415) 381-8181, x31 (Admissions Office) *fax (415) 381-8484*
www.ringmountain.org

Dr. Nancy Diamonti, Head of School, ndiamonti@ringmountain.org
Dana Fitzgerald, Director of Admissions, dfitzgerald@ringmountain.org
Laura Pascal, Assistant Director of Admissions,
   lpascal@ringmountain.org

General

Coed PS-8 day school. Founded in 1976. Independent. Nonprofit. **Member:** Provisional Member of CAIS, NAIS. **Enrollment:** Approx. 95. At full capacity will have 135-140 students. **Average class size:** 15. **Accreditation:** Currently applying for WASC and CAIS. **Endowment:** N/P. **School year:** Sept.-June. **Instructional days:** Approx. 180. **School day:** 8:45 a.m. to 3:15 p.m.

Student Body

Ethnicity: 67% Caucasian (non-Latino), 11% Latino, 8% African-American, 8% other, 4% multi-racial, 2% Asian,

Admission

Applications due: Call for date. **Application fee:** $100. **Application process:** Tour, application, teacher recommendation form, copy of student records, student visit. **No. of applications:** N/P. **No. of K spaces:** 15. **Percentage of K class made up of school's preschool class:** More than 50%. **Admission evaluation requirements for K:** Teacher recommendation, school visit and screening. **Other grades:** Tour, application, teacher recommendation, student records, student visit. **Preferences:** Sibling. **What sort of student do you best serve?** "Most students, as we teach to the individual child."

Costs

Latest tuition: $15,950 for K-4, $16,500 for G5-6, $16,830 for G7-8. **Sibling discount:** None. **Tuition includes:** Lunch: No; Transportation: No; Laptop computer: Yes; Other: N/P. **Tuition increases:** Approx. 8-10% annually. **Other costs:** Approx. $600 for materials; for outdoor education trips, fees are approx. $200 for G3-4 and approx. $1,500+ for G5-8. **Percentage of students receiving financial aid:** 20%. **Financial aid application deadline:** Call for date. Financial aid is based on need. **Average grant:** N/P. **Percentage of grants of half-tuition or more:** 75%. **Donations:** Voluntary cash donations for Annual Fund, Capital Campaign and Auction.

School's Mission Statement

"Ring Mountain Day School's student-centered program creates a dynamic learning environment to stimulate creative thinking, motivate academic excellence and instill a lifelong desire to learn. Small class size enables our faculty to apply an individualized, integrated and rigorous instructional approach that inspires students to realize their talents, strengths, dreams and capabilities. The curriculum emphasizes problem solving in real-life situations, promoting comprehensive understanding of academics and the arts. Students develop overall self-awareness and sense of personal responsibility to their communities: family, school, and the diverse world in which they live."

Academic Program

Philosophy: "A progressive, project-based learning environment where our goals are [to]: - *Develop and nurture a love of learning* with an emphasis on problem solving, creativity and process. - *Achieve mastery of math and language skills* through integrated multi-discipline curriculum instruction. - *Provide individualized instruction* in a multi-age classroom with teaching methods that maximize the benefits of interaction and collaboration among the children and faculty.- *Expose children to art, music, dance and drama. - Promote appreciation of cultural diversity and global awareness* through cultural immersion and outreach - *Encourage children to develop age appropriate physical skills* stressing good sportsmanship and teamwork. - *Help children develop confidence* in themselves, *demonstrate respect for others and assume responsibility* for their own actions." **Foreign languages:** Spanish is a core subject that students study approximately 4 hours per week. **Computer training:** Computer electives offered in Middle School; a technology teacher is on staff as needed for special projects. **No. of computers available for students:** 14 multi-media computers and 25 laptops. **No. of hours weekly of:** Art- 2; Drama- 1; Music- 1; Dance- 1; Computers- "used throughout the curriculum"; Foreign language- 4; PE- 2. **Outdoor education:** "Done throughout the year." **Grading:** A-F, beginning in G5. Students are evaluated twice each year with two parent/teacher conferences and written evaluations through G4. **Average nightly homework:** Approx. 10 min. per grade, including reading (thus 10-15 min. for K; 80-90 min. for G8). Posted on the Internet: Yes. **Percentage of students participating in Johns**

Hopkins Center for Talented Youth Program: N/P. Other indicators of academic success: "ERB Testing." High schools attended by latest graduating class: Bay School, Hawaii Preparatory Academy, Redwood, San Domenico, and University.

Faculty

Ethnicity: 80% Caucasian (non-Latino), 15% other, 5% Latino. Percentage of teachers with graduate degrees: 55%. Percentage with current California credential: 70%. Faculty selection/training: "Experience, degrees, interview with selection committee that also consists of other teachers, observation of sample lesson." Teacher/student ratio: "No more than 1:15 but oftentimes they work in pods of 7 or 1:8. Special subject teachers: Spanish, art, music, drama, dance, PE, computers. Average teacher tenure: 5 years.

Middle School

Description: "Commences in G5." Teacher/student ratio: No more than 1:15 but often break into pods of 7 or 1:8. Elective courses offered: Varies each quarter but has included Student Council, photography, academic chess, knitting, media, student newspaper, and computers. Achievement tracking in: All subjects. Student social events: Back To School Pizza Night, Thanksgiving Circle, Spring Concert, Middle School dances, Spirit Week, annual school play, Earth Day Celebration, all school Angel Island End of the Year Picnic, annual Student Art Show, Step-Up Celebration/Graduation and Picnic in the Park.

Student Support Services

No. of Licensed Counselors on staff: N/P. Counselor/student ratio: N/P. Learning specialists on staff: One. Learning differences/disabilities support: "We accept children with a wide range of learning styles; however, we don't have a learning resource specialist on staff so we determine 'goodness of fit' on a case-by-case basis." High school placement support: "We do SSAT preparation starting in G7. If a student is applying to a private high school they work directly with our Head of School and the High School Counselor. If they are going to a public high school we provide counseling support to make sure the students and families know about the resources that are available to them."

Student Conduct and Health

Code of conduct: "We have high expectations for our students, and the Middle School students are expected to be good role models and leaders. The four guiding principles for behavior are attentive listening, mutual respect, appreciation/no put downs, and right to pass." **Prevention education and awareness addressed in:** "Education on drugs, sex, health and harassment primarily begins in G5."

Athletics

Sports offered: PE is offered twice a week for all students; a variety of sports are offered. Planning is in progress for intramural and/or intermural team play.

Campus/Campus Life

Campus description: "Located in a suburban setting and surrounded by a residential neighborhood, Ring Mountain's new campus has a remodeled interior. Renovations to the existing building include a new science center, an expanded technology laboratory, multimedia, science and Spanish language labs; a multipurpose room; and an art studio with a low-fire kiln and a dark room. The facility is surrounded by grassy playing fields and also features a soccer field, basketball court, outdoor playground and play structure, and in 2006, a space for a community garden and courtyard amphitheater. The campus backs up to public open space, which gives it a country feel." **Library:** Yes. **Sports facilities:** Multi-purpose room, sports field, basketball court, playground, and access to Bay Trail. **Theater/Arts facilities:** "We have a performing arts program on site which includes drama, dance and music. Past productions have included 'Revenge of the Space Pandas,' 'Into the Woods,' and 'Zeus.' **Computer lab:** Yes. **Science lab:** Yes. **Lunch program:** An optional hot lunch program is available, catered by Ann Walker Catering. **Bus service:** No. **Uniforms/dress code:** Dress code. **Opportunities for community service:** "There is a commitment to service learning school wide."

Extended Day

Morning care: Begins at 8 a.m. **After-school care:** Until 6 p.m. **Grade levels:** K-8. **Cost:** No charge for morning care. After-school care is $25/day. **Drop-in care available:** Yes. **Coverage over major holidays:** No. **Homework help:** Yes if needed, before school, at recess and lunch and after school as well. **Snacks:** Not provided. **Staff/student ratio:** 1:4. **After-school classes:** Classes vary each quarter. They have included Science Adventures, academic chess, Aikido, French, lacrosse, Mom & Me Mosaic Classes, cooking, and drama, etc. **Cost:** Varies; contact school.

Summer Programs

The school sometimes offers summer camps, which are typically one-week camps for K-4. Past programs have included Science Adventures, and art and crafts. **Cost:** N/P.

Parent Involvement

"There are many ways to get involved that include working with the Parent Association. There are many events throughout the year that require parent participation including the Annual Walkathon, Book Fair, Teacher Appreciation, Annual Auction/Dinner & Dance and the Annual Art Show." **Parent/teacher communication:** Newsletter, weekly class letters, website, e-mail, conferences, Bagel Breakfasts with Head of School, Back to School Night and Annual State of the School Meetings. **Participation requirements:** 20 hours per family per year. **Parent education programs offered?:** Yes.

What Sets the School Apart From Others

"Small class size with individualized instruction, project-based learning, multi-aged environment, dynamic learning environment with a heart in the arts."

How Parents/Students Characterize School

Parent comment(s): "Ring Mountain Day School is Marin's best kept secret." ✦ "The community has welcomed our family with open arms." "Ring Mountain gave my child the tools she needed to be successful in high school."

Student comment(s): "I never thought learning could be so fun!" "I never thought of myself as a scholar." "Ring Mountain is a place where I feel safe." "RMDS is like my family."

St. Anne School

1320 14th Avenue (between Irving and Judah)(Inner Sunset District)
San Francisco, CA 94122
(415) 664-7977 *fax (415) 661-7904*
www.stanne.com

Mr. Thomas C. White, Principal, white@stanne.com

Coed K-8 parochial day school. Founded in 1920. Catholic. **Member:** WCEA. **Enrollment:** Approx. 500. **Average class size:** 32. **Accreditation:** WASC, March 2000 (6-year term: 2000-06). **Endowment:** $1.8 million. **School year:** Aug.-June. **Instructional days:** 180. **School day:** 8:10 a.m. to 2:50 p.m. for K-3, 8:10 a.m. to 3:05 p.m. for G4-8.

Student Body

Ethnicity: 50% Asian, 35% Caucasian (non-Latino), 8% Latino, 5% multi-racial, 2% African-American.

Admission

Applications due: Ongoing. **Application fee:** $40. **Application process:** N/P. **No. of applications:** 100. **No. of K spaces:** 70. **Percentage of K class made up of school's preschool class:** N/A. **Admission evaluation requirements for K:** Screening. **Other grades:** Test. **Preferences:** Sibling, in-parish Catholics, out-of-parish Catholics, non-Catholics. **What sort of student do you best serve?** N/P.

Costs

Latest tuition: $3,600 for participating parishioners, $4,950 for non-Catholics. **Sibling discount:** Yes (amount N/P). **Tuition includes:** Lunch: No; Transportation: No; Laptop computer: Yes, for school use; Other: N/P. **Tuition increases:** N/P. **Other costs:** N/P. **Percentage of**

students receiving financial aid: 5%. Financial aid application deadline: Feb. (call for date). Financial aid is based on need. Average grant: N/P. Percentage of grants of half-tuition or more: N/P. Donations: N/P.

School's Mission Statement

"St. Anne School Community is committed to carrying out the ministry of Jesus Christ in the education of the youth we serve. We seek to evangelize and strengthen faith formation in partnership with the family and parish. We value the cultural diversity of our school and welcome the unique gift each student contributes to our school community. We seek to develop the whole person, fostering spiritual, intellectual, physical, and psychological growth in a Catholic environment of peace, security, and love."

Academic Program

Philosophy: "St. Anne School strives to challenge the students in a caring and nurturing environment helping them reach their full potential." Foreign languages: None. Computer training: Yes. No. of computers available for students: 96. No. of hours weekly: Art- 1; Drama- N/P; Music- 40 min.; Computers- 40 min.; Foreign language- N/A; PE- 40 min. Outdoor education: Yes, for G6. Grading: A-F, beginning in G3. Average nightly homework: Varies. Posted on the Internet: No. Percentage of students participating in Johns Hopkins Center for Talented Youth Program: None. Other indicators of academic success: N/P. High schools attended by latest graduating class: Lowell, SI, Riordan, SHCP, Mercy, ICA, and other various public schools throughout the Bay Area.

Faculty

Ethnicity: 95% Caucasian (non-Latino), 5% Asian. Percentage of teachers with graduate degrees: N/P. Percentage with current California credential: 98%. Faculty selection/training: N/P. Teacher/ student ratio: 1:30. Special subject teachers: 2 (subjects N/P) Average teacher tenure: 15-25 years.

Student Support Services

No. of Licensed Counselors on staff: One part-time. **Counselor/student ratio:** N/P. **Learning specialists on staff:** Two. **Learning differences/disabilities support:** N/P. **High school placement support:** N/P.

Student Conduct and Health

Code of conduct: "Discipline/behavior policy." **Prevention education and awareness addressed in:** Youth Aware Life Skills Program.

Athletics

Sports offered: N/P. **Team play begins in:** G3 (intermural).

Campus/Campus Life

Campus description: N/P. **Library:** The school's library has 7,000 volumes and 4 computers. **Sports facilities:** N/P. **Theater/Arts facilities:** Moriarty Hall. **Computer lab:** Yes. **Science lab:** Yes. **Lunch program:** Yes. **Bus service:** No. **Uniforms/dress code:** Uniforms. **Opportunities for community service:** Yes.

Extended Day

Morning care: Begins at 7 a.m. **After-school care:** Until 6 p.m. **Grade levels:** All. **Cost:** Varies; contact school. **Drop-in care available:** Yes. **Coverage over major holidays:** No. **Homework help:** Yes. **Snacks:** Provided. **Staff/student ratio:** 1:25. **After-school classes:** Chinese school, karate, ballet, academic chess. **Cost:** Varies; contact school.

Summer Programs: N/P.

Parent Involvement

Parent/teacher communication: Conference, website, e-mail, weekly newsletters. **Participation requirements:** N/P. **Parent education programs offered?:** Yes.

What Sets the School Apart From Others

"The dynamics between the students and faculty the involvement of the parents and the involvement within the parish. The dedication of our parents and staff to our precious children is very evident in the friendly and positive energy that they radiate."

How Parents/Students Characterize School

Parent comment(s): "Our school staff offers a strong educational program for my child." "We looked at all the schools in the area and are extremely happy that our children are at St. Anne School."
Student comment(s): "I love my teachers." "When I need some help I can always count on help from my teachers."

SAINT BRIGID SCHOOL

2250 Franklin Street (Broadway) (Pacific Heights)
San Francisco, CA 94109
(415) 673-4523   fax (415) 674-4187
www.saintbrigidsf.org

Sister Carmen Santiuste, RCM, Head of School,
   principal@saintbrigidsf.org
Director of Admission, office@saintbrigidsf.org

General

Coed K-8 archdiocesan day school. Founded in 1888. Catholic. Nonprofit. **Member:** N/P. **Enrollment:** Approx. 305. **Average class size:** 35. **Accreditation:** WASC (6-year term: 2003-09). **Endowment:** N/P. **School year:** Late Aug. to mid-June. **Instructional days:** 180. **School day:** Begins at 8 a.m. Dismissal is 2:45 p.m. for K-2, 2:55 p.m. for G3-5 and 3 p.m. for G6-8.

Student Body

Ethnicity: 49% Asian, 25% multi-racial, 8% Latino, 8% Caucasian (non-Latino), 6% other, 4% African-American.

Admission

Applications due: Jan. (call for date). **Application fee:** $70. **Application process:** Begins in December. Application forms available at the school or may be downloaded on its website. A kindergarten readiness test is given to all K applicants. **No. of applications:** Approx. 60-70. **No. of K spaces:** 35. **Percentage of K class made up of school's preschool class:** N/A. **Admission evaluation requirements for K:** "We expect the child to be ready for Kindergarten work—follow directions, stay on task, etc. We seek children who pass our entrance test, who are cooperative and behave well, and who have a desire to perform to the best of their abilities." **Other grades:** An entry test given to all transferring students; school visits are held during Open House and Catholic Schools Week in January (call for information). Individual tours may be arranged. Call to schedule. **Preferences:** Siblings, Catholics. **What sort of student do you best serve?** "Families looking for a caring nurturing school family that strives daily to live out the gospel values."

Costs

Latest tuition: $3,950. **Sibling discount:** 15%. **Tuition includes:** Lunch: No; Transportation: No; Laptop computer: No; Other: N/P. **Tuition increases:** Approx. 3-5% annually. **Other costs:** Approx. $120 for uniforms, $325 registration fee. **Percentage of students receiving financial aid:** 16%. **Financial aid application deadline:** March (call for date). Financial aid is based on need. **Average grant:** N/P. **Percentage of grants of half-tuition or more:** 6%. **Donations:** Voluntary for scholarship fund.

School's Mission Statement

"St. Brigid School, in partnership with each family, educates and develops the whole child by teaching the principles of the Catholic faith and by providing a solid academic education. We foster an environment that brings us together as a caring, nurturing school family. We provide the opportunity and motivation for a child to develop spiritually, intellectually, physically, and socially."

Academic Program

Philosophy: "St. Brigid School's curriculum is well known for having strong academic standards. In addition to the traditional classes, students have weekly classes in music, computer, science lab, Spanish, and PE. Additional services available to all students are a fully staffed library, school counselor, and reading specialist." **Foreign languages:** Spanish beginning in G1. **Computer training:** "Students K-8 are taught technology with skills progressing as they move up through the grades." **No. of computers available for students:** 60. **No. of hours weekly of:** Art- 1; Drama- 1; Music- 1; Computers- varies with grade; Foreign language- varies with grade; PE- 1. **Outdoor education:** N/P. **Grading:** A-F, beginning in G3. **Average nightly homework:** "Varies with grade." Posted on the Internet: No. **Percentage of students participating in Johns Hopkins Center for Talented Youth Program:** "40% of G7-8 (60% participate in the UC Irvine Talent Search)." **Other indicators of academic success:** "Students usually get accepted in the high school of their choice." **High schools attended by latest graduating class:** CSH, SI, Lowell, Riordan, Washington, SOTA, ICA, Galileo.

Faculty

Ethnicity: 60% Caucasian (non-Latino), 34% Latino, 6% other. **Percentage of teachers with graduate degrees:** N/P. **Percentage with current California credential:** 100%. **Faculty selection/training:** N/P. **Teacher/student ratio:** N/P. **Special subject teachers:** Music, PE, computer, science, Spanish, math (G6-8), social studies (G6-8). **Average teacher tenure:** N/P.

Middle School

Description: G6-8. **Teacher/student ratio:** 1:35. **Elective courses offered:** N/P. **Achievement tracking in:** N/P. **Student social events:** N/P.

Student Support Services

No. of Licensed Counselors on staff: One. **Counselor/student ratio:** 1:305. **Learning specialists on staff:** One. **Learning differences/disabilities support:** N/P. **High school placement support:** N/P.

Student Conduct and Health

Code of conduct: "The Code of Christian Conduct in the Parent-Student Handbook reiterates that it shall be an expressed condition of enrollment that the parent/guardian of a student shall also conform to the standards of conduct that are consistent with the Christian principles of the school." **Prevention education and awareness addressed in:** Health, taught as a core subject.

Athletics

Sports offered: Basketball and soccer for boys; volleyball for girls. **Team play begins in:** CYO sports in G3-8. The school holds its own mini Olympics open to all students and participates in CYO's Track Meet.

Campus/Campus Life

Campus description: The campus, which spans a block from Franklin Street to St. Brigid's Church (now closed) on Van Ness, includes two buildings with 9 classrooms, library, computer lab, science lab, music room, extended program room, cafeteria, auditorium, and office. **Library:** Library with 20,000 print volumes. **Sports facilities:** School yard. **Theater/Arts facilities:** School Auditorium. **Computer lab:** Yes. **Science lab:** Yes. **Lunch program:** Yes. **Bus service:** No. **Uniforms/dress code:** Yes. **Opportunities for community service:** N/P.

Extended Day

Morning care:: None. **After-school care:** Until 6 p.m. **Grade levels:** K-8. **Cost:** $1,450/year (to 4 p.m.), $2,500/year (to 5 p.m.), and $2,150/year (to 6 p.m.). **Drop-in care available:** Yes. **Coverage over major holidays:** No. **Homework help:** Yes. **Snacks:** Provided. **Staff/student ratio:** N/P. **After-school classes:** Piano and other musical instruments, dance (ballet, hip-hop), and band. **Cost:** N/P.

Summer Programs: None.

Parent Involvement

Parent/teacher communication: Conferences, website, e-mail, monthly newsletter, Wednesday Folder. Parent/teacher conferences are required in the first quarter of the school year. Parents may request evening conferences through the individual teachers. **Participation requirements:** 20 hours per family or 10 hours per parent. **Parent**

education programs: Active Parenting class every other year, Drug Education Parent Night, and Sacraments Program.

What Sets the School Apart From Others

"St. Brigid School is distinguished by the involvement of its parent community and the communications it maintains among parents, teachers, staff, and students. Academic study is complemented with field trips and cultural and environmental enrichment activities. Apart from high academic scores and achievement scores, the school plant itself is kept in excellent condition. St. Brigid School is one of the few schools that has many religious on its staff [including] Sisters of the Immaculate Conception [and a] Sister of the Presentation."

How Parents/Students Characterize School

Parent comment(s): "Very clean and well maintained, very good academic program, prepares the students well for high school."
Student comment(s): "Caring and lots of support."

St. Cecilia School

660 Vicente Street (corner of 18th Ave.) (Parkside/Sunset District) San Francisco, CA 94116
(415) 731-8400 *fax (415) 731-5686*
www.stceciliaschool.org

Sister Marilyn Miller, S.N.J.M., Principal, mmiller@stceciliaschool.org

General

Coed K-8 parochial day school. Founded in 1930. Catholic. Nonprofit. **Member:** N/P. **Enrollment:** Approx. 575. **Average class size:** 30. **Accreditation:** WASC/WCEA (N/P term). **Endowment:** N/P. **School year:** Aug.-June. **Instructional days:** Approx. 183. **School day:** 8 a.m. to 3 p.m. for G1-8, 8 a.m. to 11:45 a.m. for morning K, 11:25 a.m. to 3 p.m. for afternoon K.

Student Body

Ethnicity: 66% Caucasian (non-Latino), 22% Asian, 11% Latino, 1% African-American.

Admission

Applications due: Applications available in the beginning of December (call for due date). **Application fee:** $50. **Application process:** Kindergarten open houses begin in November. **No. of applications:** Approx. 120. **No. of K spaces:** 70. **Percentage of K class made up of school's preschool class:** N/A. **Admission evaluation requirements for K:** 1) Age appropriate language and readiness for reading and math learning; 2) Preschool experience for development of social and group learning skills; 3) Age appropriate screening. Applicants must be five years old by September 1. **Other grades:** N/P. **Preferences:** Siblings, Catholics who are members of the parish, Catholics from other parishes, non-Catholics. **What sort of student do you best serve?** N/P.

Costs

Latest tuition: $4,175 for participating Catholics, $5,000 for non-participating. **Sibling discount:** 30%. **Tuition includes:** Lunch: No; Transportation: No; Laptop computer: No; Other: N/P. **Tuition increases:** Approx. 5% annually. **Other costs:** N/P. **Percentage of students receiving financial aid:** 10%. **Financial aid application deadline:** Call for more information. Financial aid is based on need. **Average grant:** "Varies each year depending on funds available." **Percentage of grants of half-tuition or more:** N/P. **Donations:** No contributions are required.

School's Mission Statement

"St. Cecilia School is a Catholic elementary school of the Archdiocese of San Francisco, whose purpose is to develop students who are active Christians, life-long learners, and responsible citizens."

Academic Program

Philosophy: "St. Cecilia School is a Catholic elementary school dedicated to the religious, academic, social, psychological, cultural, and physical development of each individual. St. Cecilia School is committed to providing instruction and opportunities in a Catholic community of faith which will lead the children to pray, to serve and respect others, and to make Christian choices. Parents, as primary educators, and teachers, as facilitators of learning, work together to provide a quality education that assists students in developing their unique capabilities and prepares them to become responsible citizens. Students develop intellectually by participating in age-appropriate and meaningful activities. As life-long learners, students develop the skills of effective communication and problem-solving to help them face the challenges of the future." **Foreign languages:** N/P. **Computer training:** "Highly developed technology program integrating the curriculum and technology." **No. of computers available for students:** "Numerous wireless laptops in the classrooms." **No. of hours weekly of:** Art- 1; Drama- an elective; Music- .5 hour of classroom singing (instrumental lessons available); Computers- 1; Foreign languages- N/P; PE- 1. **Outdoor education:** N/P. **Grading:** S, N for K; O, S, N for G1-2; A-F for G3-8. **Average nightly homework:** 1 hour. Posted on the Internet: No. **Percentage of students participating in Johns Hopkins Center for Talented Youth Program:** N/P. **Other indicators of academic success:** Junior High Honors Program, high standardized test scores. **High schools attended by latest graduating class:** SI, SHCP, Mercy-SF, Mercy-Burlingame, Serra, Riordan, ICA, CSH, Stuart Hall, Lick, Lowell, Lincoln, Washington, SOTA, CAT, Academy of Arts and Science.

Faculty

Ethnicity: 99% Caucasian (non-Latino), 1% Asian. **Percentage of teachers with graduate degrees:** 30%. **Percentage with current California credential:** 100%. **Faculty selection/training:** Experience, degree, credential. **Teacher/student ratio:** 1:25. **Special subject teachers:** Music, computer, PE, drama. **Average teacher tenure:** 13 years.

Middle School

Description: G6-8, departmentalized. **Teacher/student ratio:** 1:25. **Elective courses offered:** N/P. **Achievement tracking in:** N/P. **Student social events:** N/P.

Student Support Services

No. of Licensed Counselors on staff: Two part-time. **Counselor/student ratio:** N/P. **Learning specialists on staff:** One. **Learning differences/disabilities support:** "Students identified in G1-5 with IEP receive services of the learning specialist." **High school placement support:** N/P. **Other:** Active Student Council.

Student Conduct and Health

Code of conduct: "We expect students to act in a way becoming a Christian student. A primary consideration in all disciplinary decisions is the obligation of the school to maintain a safe place for students and an acceptable learning atmosphere." **Prevention education and awareness addressed in:** Safe Child program (K-3), conflict resolution program (K-8), drug program (G4-8), Take A Stand program (G5-6), Second Step program (G7-8).

Athletics

Sports offered: N/P. **Team play begins in:** G3, through CYO. Sports and Rec program for G6-8 three days a week from 3-4:30 p.m. in the gym.

Campus/Campus Life

Campus description: "Two classrooms of each grade K-8." **Library:** "Fiction and non-fiction, computer." **Sports facilities:** Gymnasium. **Theater/Arts facilities:** Auditorium with stage. **Computer lab:** Yes. **Science lab:** No. **Lunch program:** One day per week. **Bus service:** No. **Uniforms/dress code:** Uniforms. **Opportunities for community service:** N/P.

Extended Day

Morning care: Begins at 7:10 a.m. **After-school care:** Until 6 p.m. **Grade levels:** K-8. **Cost:** N/P. **Drop-in care available:** No. **Coverage over major holidays:** No. **Homework help:** Yes. **Snacks:** Provided. **Staff/student ratio:** 1:10. **After-school classes:** N/P.

Summer Programs: N/P.

Parent Involvement
Parent/teacher communication: Conferences, website, e-mail, newsletter. **Participation requirements:** None. **Parent education programs offered?** Yes.

What Sets the School Apart From Others
"A strong academic program within a Christian environment. We engender a family spirit within our school community."

How Parents/Students Characterize School: N/P.

ST. GABRIEL SCHOOL
2550 – 41st Ave. (between Ulloa and Vicente) (Parkside/Sunset)
San Francisco, CA 94116
(415) 566-0314 *fax (415) 566-3223*
www.stgabrielsf.com

Sister Mary Pauline Borghello R.S.M., Principal, office@stgabrielsf.com

General
Coed K-8 parochial day school. Founded in 1948. Catholic. Nonprofit. **Member:** N/P. **Enrollment:** Approx. 465. **Average class size:** 27. **Accreditation:** WASC/WCEA (term N/P). **Endowment:** N/A. **School year:** Aug.-June. **Instructional days:** Approx. 183. **School day:** Begins at 8 a.m. for morning K and G1-8. Dismissal is 2:45 p.m. for G1-3, and 3 p.m. for G4-8.

Student Body
Ethnicity: 41% Caucasian (non-Latino), 33% Asian, 20% other, 5% Latino, 1% African-American.

Admission
Applications due: "Applications available end of November." (Call for due date). **Application fee:** $50. **Application process:** Kindergarten open house is held during business hours at the end of November. Parents may visit in the morning on designated tour days twice monthly,

or by appointment. **No. of applications:** Approx. 120 applicants to K. **No. of K spaces:** 60. **Percentage of K class made up of school's pre-school class:** N/A. **Admission evaluation requirements for K:** (Note: Applicants but be four years, 9 months by September 1.) 1) Preschool experience for development of social and group learning skills; 2) age appropriate language and readiness for reading and math learning; 3) "independence." A short standardized screening is administered to entering K students. **Other grades:** Applicants to G1-7 take an entrance test in the spring. **Preferences:** First, Catholics who are members of the parish, next Catholics from other parishes and then siblings. **What sort of student do you best serve?** N/P.

Costs
Latest tuition: $4,980. **Sibling discount:** Available for families who complete parent participation and participate in the parish (amount N/P). **Tuition includes:** Lunch: No; Transportation: No; Laptop computer: No; Other: N/A. **Tuition increases:** Approx. 5% annually. **Other costs:** N/P. **Percentage of students receiving financial aid:** 11%. Financial aid is based on need. **Average grant:** Varies each year with funds available. **Percentage of grants of half-tuition or more:** N/P. **Donations:** No contributions are required.

School's Mission Statement
"Our mission is to provide excellent Catholic elementary education that is true to our philosophy and responsive to the needs of the families we serve."

Academic Program
Philosophy: "Our philosophy is grounded in the belief that each student should cultivate a lifestyle based on the teachings of the Catholic faith, the experience of a Christian community, and the striving for truth." **Foreign languages:** Cantonese after-school program. **Computer training:** A full computer lab with computer specialist teachers. Networked classrooms, and library with Internet access. **No. of hours weekly of:** Art and Drama- integrated into regular classroom activities; Music- 1; Computers- 1- Foreign language- after school; PE- 1.

Outdoor education: Integrated into science program. **Grading:** Letter grades in G3-5; percentages in G6-8. **Average nightly homework:** Varies by grade. **Posted on the Internet:** For G7-8. **Percentage of students participating in Johns Hopkins Center for Talented Youth Program:** N/P. **Other indicators of academic success:** "St. Gabriel School has placed first in the San Francisco Archdiocesan Academic Decathlon six out of eight years." **High schools attended by latest graduating class:** SI, SHCP, Riordan, Mercy-SF, Mercy-Burlingame, ICA, CSH, Lowell, Lincoln, and Lick.

Faculty

Ethnicity: N/P. **Percentage of teachers with graduate degrees:** 40%. **Percentage with current California credential:** 100%. **Faculty selection/training:** N/P. **Teacher/student ratio:** 1:10 in K, 1:14 in G1, 1:27 in G2-7 with teacher aides available part of the day. **Special subject teachers:** Art, music, PE, library, computers, science. **Average teacher tenure:** 17 years.

Middle School

Description: G7-8, departmentalized. **Teacher/student ratio:** Approx. 1:27. **Elective courses offered:** N/P. **Achievement tracking in:** "Based on the Iowa Test of Basic Skills." **Student social events:** N/P.

Student Support Services

No. of Licensed Counselors on staff: One part-time 3 days/week. **Counselor/student ratio:** 1:465. **Learning specialists on staff:** Two. **Learning differences/disabilities support:** Accommodations and/or modifications are offered for qualified students. **High school placement support:** N/P.

Student Conduct and Health

Code of conduct: "Based on Christian values." **Prevention education and awareness addressed in:** Drug and family life education.

Athletics

Sports offered: Basketball. **Team play begins:** G3-8, through CYO Athletic League.

Campus/Campus Life

Campus description: N/P. **Library:** 7,000 volumes, 4 computers. **Sports facilities:** Gymnasium and paved playground. **Theater/Arts facilities:** The school uses the gym. **Computer lab:** Yes. **Science lab:** Yes. **Lunch program:** Twice weekly. **Bus service:** No. **Uniforms/dress code:** Uniforms. **Opportunities for community service:** "Encouraged and rewarded."

Extended Day

Morning care: Begins at 7 a.m. **After-school care:** Until 6 p.m. **Grade levels:** K-8. **Cost:** $2.50/hour. **Drop-in care available:** No. **Coverage over major holidays:** No. **Homework help:** Supervision. **Snacks:** Provided. **Staff/student ratio:** N/P. "Adult supervision in all areas." **After-school classes:** Cantonese. Cost: N/P.

Summer Programs

St. Gabriel School offers a 5-week academic summer school program from late June through July. Classes in language arts, reading, and math are held from 9 a.m. to noon. No extended care is offered. **Cost:** G1-6, $225 for G1-6; $115, science and math program for G7-8.

Parent Involvement

Parent/teacher communication: Conferences, website, e-mail, newsletter. **Participation requirements:** 40 hours per year per family, 20 hours for single parent families. **Parent education programs:** A parent support group offered for parents of students with learning differences.

What Sets the School Apart From Others:

"St. Gabriel School is accredited by the Western Catholic Educational Association and the Western Association of Schools and Colleges and is served by a fully credentialed staff. We offer a comprehensive

Kindergarten through eighth grade curriculum and a wide variety of enrichment and support services which include a computer specialist teacher, a Science Discovery Center and a science specialist teacher, individual and family counseling, and learning specialist instruction. Our curriculum reflects the St. Gabriel philosophy of developing the total child through a variety of educational activities. By acknowledging the uniqueness of each child, the staff helps students to develop a positive self image and a sense of self-discipline. A challenging yet supportive environment fosters moral, intellectual, physical, emotional, and aesthetic growth. Favorable teacher to student ratios ensure academic progress. Children learn to recognize and appreciate the many unique ethnic and cultural contributions of their classmates. Community service opportunities contribute to the growth of positive social values and willingness to accept responsibility."

How Parents/Students Characterize School
Parent comment(s): N/P.
Student comment(s): N/P.

St. James School
321 Fair Oaks St. (btwn. 24th & 25th Street) (Noe Valley/Mission)
San Francisco, CA 94110
(415) 647-8972 fax (415) 647-0166
www.saintjamessf.org

Sister Mary Susanna Vasquez, O.P., Head of School, sms@saintjamessf.org
Mrs. Lucia Vazquez Harp, Director of Admission,
    office@saintjamessf.org

General
Coed K-8 parochial day school. Founded in 1924. Catholic. Nonprofit. **Member:** NCEA. **Enrollment:** Approx. 210. **Average class size:** 24. **Accreditation:** WASC (term N/P). **Endowment:** N/P. **School year:** Aug.-June. **Instructional days:** 180. **School day:** 7:45 a.m. to 2:30 p.m. for K-3, 2:45 p.m. dismissal for G4-8.

Student Body

Ethnicity: 70% Latino, 10% Caucasian (non-Latino), 10% Asian, 6% African-American, 4% multi-racial.

Admission

Applications due: Feb.-Aug. (call for date). **Application fee:** $40. **Application process:** Parents should call to schedule a visit to the school. If interested, parents fill out an application and their child is tested. The child can also shadow the class for a half or whole day. **No. of applications:** 25. **No. of K spaces:** 20. **Percentage of K class made up of school's preschool class:** N/A. **Admission evaluation requirements for K:** Readiness (Brigance Screening method) and school visit. **Other grades:** Screening, past report card, recommendations, visitation and interview. **Preferences:** First preference goes to siblings, followed by parishioners, then Catholics from other parishes. **What sort of student do you best serve?** "For all students, we look at the all around student and the parents interested in participation."

Costs

Latest tuition: $4,050 Catholic, $4,502 non-Catholic, payable in 10, 11 or 12 installments. **Sibling discount:** Yes (amount N/P). **Tuition includes:** Lunch: No; Transportation: No; Laptop computer: No; Other: N/A. **Tuition increases:** Approx. 1% annually. **Other costs:** Registration fee of $332 for K-5 and $362 for G6-8; uniforms for $100-150; and $110 for the Parent Guild. **Percentage of students receiving financial aid:** 23%. **Financial aid application deadline:** May (call for date). Financial aid is based on need. **Average grant:** $500-$1,000. **Percentage of grants of half-tuition or more:** 25%. **Donations:** Voluntary.

School's Mission Statement

"St. James School has developed a mission and philosophy consistent with the belief that each student is a unique child of God, that the parents are the primary educators, that the faculty instills Catholic Christian values and the curriculum educates the whole child. Our learning philosophy emphasizes that our students will be faith-filled persons preaching the word of God. St. James strives to help students deepen their relationship with God and to manifest this relationship with words, deeds and actions. We encourage our students to be responsible through Christian behavior and respectful attitudes. This philosophy holds true whether the students are in the classroom, at liturgy, playing in the yard or being cared for in extended care. Our philosophy notes that our students will be committed to personal growth and intellectual competence. The teaching faculty provides a basic curriculum that enables each student to develop intellectually, according to the individual's potential. We also encourage a personal sense of value so that our students learn to love and respect self and others. The learning expectation of being a person dedicated to working for others is accomplished through our social goals. Students are provided with a variety of experiences to promote the social goals of effective communication, cooperation, leadership and community involvement. In the area of personal growth, we aid students to meet the physical goals."

Academic Program

Philosophy: N/P. **Foreign languages:** None. **Computer training:** Yes. **No. of computers available for students:** 30. **No. of hours weekly of:** Art- N/P; Drama- 1; Music- 1; Computers- 1; Foreign language- None; PE- 1. **Outdoor education:** N/P. **Grading:** A-F, beginning in G3. **Average nightly homework:** 1 hour. Posted on the Internet: No. **Percentage of students participating in Johns Hopkins Center for Talented Youth Program:** N/P. **Other indicators of academic success:** "First & Second Honors." **High schools attended by latest graduating class:** ICA, Mercy-SF, SI, SHCP, Riordan, Lowell, Leadership, Wallenberg, and CAT.

Faculty

Ethnicity: 70% Caucasian (non-Latino), 20% Latino, 10% Asian. **Percentage of teachers with graduate degrees:** 93%. **Percentage with current California credential:** 93%. **Faculty selection/training:** Experience and degree. **Teacher/student ratio:** 1:15. **Special subject teachers:** Music, drama, dance, computers, health and PE. **Average teacher tenure:** 8 years.

Middle School

Description: G6-8. Teacher/student ratio: 1:20. Elective courses offered: None. Achievement tracking in: N/P. Student social events: Quarterly Jr. High dances, Spirit Days, sporting events, choir events.

Student Support Services

No. of Licensed Counselors on staff: One part-time. Counselor/student ratio: N/P. Learning specialists on staff: One. Learning differences/disabilities support: N/P. High school placement support: N/P.

Student Conduct and Health

Code of conduct: "Discipline/behavior policy." Prevention education and awareness programs: The school provides education on drugs, sex, health, and harassment.

Athletics

Sports offered: Basketball, volleyball, soccer, baseball. Team play begins in: G3 (inter/intramural).

Campus/Campus Life

Campus description: N/P. Library: Yes. Sports facilities: No. Theater/Arts facilities: Stage and auditorium. Computer lab: Yes. Science lab: Yes (G6-8). Lunch program: Yes. Bus service: No. Uniforms/dress code: Khaki shorts and pants for boys and girls, plaid skirt for girls, navy blue sweater or sweatshirt with school emblem, white polo or button down shirt. Opportunities for community service: Toys for Tots, Coins for Kids, food drives for parish and SF Food Bank.

Extended Day

Morning care: Begins at 7 a.m. After-school care: Until 5:30 p.m. Grade levels: All. Cost: N/P. Drop-in care available: Yes. Coverage over major holidays: No. Homework help: Yes. Snacks: Provided. Staff/student ratio: 1:6. After-school classes: Homework Club (after school help for G5-8).

Summer Programs: None.

Parent Involvement

Parent/teacher communication: Conferences, website, e-mail, newsletter. **Participation requirements:** Service hours. **Parent education programs offered?:** Yes.

What Sets the School Apart From Others: N/P.

How Parents/Students Characterize School: N/P.

St. John's School

925 Chenery Street (at Diamond) (Glen Park)
San Francisco, CA 94131
(415) 584-8383   *fax (415) 584-8359*
www.stjohnseagles.com

Kenneth Willers, Head of School and Director of Admission,
   principal@stjohnseagles.com

General

Coed K-8 parochial day school. "Current school building founded in 1967. Elementary school offered since 1917." Catholic. Nonprofit. **Member:** N/P. **Enrollment:** Approx. 260. **Average class size:** 30. **Accreditation:** WASC (6-year term: 2005-11). **Endowment:** N/P. **School year:** Aug.-mid-June. **Instructional days:** 180. **School day:** 8 a.m. to 3 p.m.

Student Body

Ethnicity: 30% Latino, 30% Caucasian (non-Latino), 19% Asian, 13% African-American, 8% other.

Admission

Applications due: Open. **Application fee:** $25. **Application process:** "Form/assessment." **No. of applications:** 40. **No. of K spaces:** 25. **Per-**

centage of K class made up of school's preschool class: N/A. Admission evaluation requirements for K: Screening. **Other grades:** N/P. **Preferences:** N/P. **What sort of student do you best serve?** N/P.

Costs

Latest tuition: $4,750 payable over 10 months. **Sibling discount:** Yes (amount N/P). **Tuition includes:** Lunch: No; Transportation: No; Laptop computer: Laptops are available; Other: N/A. **Tuition increases:** Approx. 5% annually. **Other costs:** Registration fee of $350; approx. $75 for uniforms and $30 in other fees. **Percentage of students receiving financial aid:** 10%. **Financial aid application deadline:** Feb.-Sept. (call for date). Financial aid is based on need. **Average grant:** $1,000. **Percentage of grants of half-tuition or more:** None. **Donations:** $200 is requested from each family.

School's Mission Statement

"St. John's mission is to provide an academic environment in which students can develop the knowledge, skills, attitudes and values necessary for a productive Catholic Christian life and to foster Catholic values for the families it serves by teaching and modeling Christian moral development, service, community, respect and self-esteem."

Academic Program

Philosophy: N/P. **Foreign languages:** After-school Spanish. **Computer training:** Yes. **No. of computers available for students:** 36. **No. of hours weekly of:** Art- 1; Drama- integrated into curriculum; Music- 1; Computers- integrated into the curriculum; Foreign languages- not offered; PE- 1. **Outdoor education:** N/A. **Grading:** A-F, beginning in G3. **Average nightly homework:** 30 min. to 1.5 hrs. Posted on the Internet: N/P. **Percentage of students participating in Johns Hopkins Center for Talented Youth Program:** N/A. **Other indicators of academic success:** N/P. **High schools attended by latest graduating class:** SHCP, SI, Riordan, ICA, Mercy-SF, Mercy-Burlingame, Lincoln, SOTA, Leadership, Alameda High, Christian High School, Deer Valley, School of the Arts Academy, and Gateway.

Faculty

Ethnicity: 95% Caucasian (non-Latino), 5% other. **Percentage of teachers with graduate degrees:** 50%. **Percentage with current California credential:** 100%. **Faculty selection/training:** "Experience, degree, philosophy, references." **Teacher/student ratio:** 1:30. **Special subject teachers:** Music, PE, fine arts. **Average teacher tenure:** N/P.

Middle School

Description: G6-8. **Teacher/student ratio:** 1:35. **Elective courses offered:** N/P. **Achievement tracking in:** N/P. **Student social events:** "[For] families of G6-8 students, kite day, Grad Dinner Dance, 8th Grade Retreat, Knighting Ceremony, Fine Art Production, Student Council service days, Traffic outing, Spring Fling and Fall Dinner, Talent show, Halloween Carnival, prayer services."

Student Support Services

No. of Licensed Counselors on staff: One. **Counselor/student ratio:** 1:260. **Learning specialists on staff:** One. **Learning differences/disabilities support:** "Assist with assessment, intervention, testing, and evaluation." **High school placement support:** Provided by 8th grade teacher and principal.

Student Conduct and Health

Code of conduct: "Respect, responsibility and reverence for each other are imperative to create an atmosphere where optimal learning/growing can take place." **Prevention education/awareness program:** N/P.

Athletics

Sports offered: League play in girls volleyball, basketball, and baseball and boys soccer, basketball, and baseball. **Team play begins in:** G3 (inter-city league).

Campus/Campus Life

Campus description: "Glen Park Neighborhood, warm, bright, and large classrooms." **Library:** "Web-based browsing." **Sports facilities:** Gym. **Theater/Arts facilities:** Portable stage. **Computer lab:** Yes and mobile laptops. **Science lab:** No. **Lunch program:** Yes. **Bus service:** No. **Uniforms/dress code:** Uniform. **Opportunities for community service:** Yes.

Extended Day
Morning care: Begins at 6:45 a.m. **After-school care:** Until 6 p.m. **Grade levels:** K-8. **Cost:** $4/hour. **Drop-in care available:** Yes. **Coverage over major holidays:** No. **Homework help:** Yes. **Snacks:** "Not provided but can purchase." **Staff/student ratio:** N/P. **After-school classes:** Drama, science, math, dance, gymnastics, hip/hop, guitar, piano. **Cost:** Varies; contact school.

Summer Programs
"Day Camp." Cost: $100/week.

Parent Involvement
Parent/teacher communication: Conferences, website, on-line grading, e-mail, newsletter, phone. **Participation requirements:** 20 hours with participation in a school event, function or school need. **Parent education programs:** Varies.

What Sets the School Apart From Others
"Innovation with wireless technology and integrated technology program managed by our students. Fine Arts integrated into the curriculum. Our diversity ratio mirrors the city of SF. The principal and administration listens to the voice of the parents when planning and visioning for the future."

How Parents/Students Characterize School
Parent comment(s): "Warm, inviting, strong academics and child centered."
Student comment(s): "Teachers really care about you and students really get a chance to lead and serve."

Saint Mark's School

39 Trellis Drive
San Rafael, CA 94903
(415) 472-8007 fax (415) 472-0722
www.saintmarksschool.org

Damon Kerby, Head of School, dkerby@saintmarksschool.org
Barbara Finley, Director of Admission, bfinley@saintmarksschool.org

General

Coed K-8 day school. Founded in 1980. Independent. Nonprofit. **Member:** NAIS, CAIS, BADA. **Enrollment:** Approx. 380. **Average class size:** 20 in K-3, 22 in G4-8 (two sections of each grade). **Accreditation:** CAIS (6-year term: 2002-08). **Endowment:** $8.3 million. **School year:** Aug.-June. **Instructional days:** 183. **School day:** 8:30 a.m. to 3:15 p.m.

Student Body

Ethnicity: 76% Caucasian (non-Latino), 10% Latino, 9% Asian, 3% other, 2% African-American.

Admission

Applications due: Early Jan. (call for date). **Application fee:** $100 (waived for financial aid candidates). **Application process:** Parent Information Nights and Observation Mornings (assembly and classroom visitations) are held November-January for interested parents.

Individual tours are given of the whole campus on the interview date. Upon submission of the application and fee, a parent interview will be scheduled. Students applying to K-1 will be screened; those entering G2-8 will have a student visit and testing. Transfer students submit prior years' transcripts. All applicants submit teacher recommendations. **No. of applications:** 100-120. **No of K spaces:** 40. **Percentage of K class made up of school's preschool class:** N/A. **Admission evaluation requirements for K:** Developmental readiness (average to above average), no behavioral problems, good teacher recommendation, parents to work in partnership with the school. **Other grades:** "We seek to admit students of average to above average ability who demonstrate developmental readiness, who have a successful class visit and strong school recommendations, and who score commensurately with current Saint Mark's students." **Preferences:** Sibling. **What sort of student do you best serve?** "We enroll students who will benefit from rigorous academic and creative challenges designed to help them meet their potential."

Costs

Latest tuition: $16,850. **Sibling discount:** None. **Tuition includes:** Lunch: No; Transportation: No; Laptop computer: No. **Tuition increases:** Approx. 7-8% annually. **Other costs:** Approx. $300-400 for books, $250-675 for outdoor education (G3-8). **Percentage of students receiving financial aid:** 17%. **Financial aid application deadline:** Early Jan. (call for date). Financial aid is based on need. **Average grant:** $12,400. **Percentage of grants of half-tuition or more:** 89%. **Donations:** "Parents are encouraged to participate in the annual fund which raises money to fill the gap between tuition and the actual cost of educating each child."

School's Mission Statement

"Saint Mark's School provides a challenging academic program in a nurturing community that values respect, responsibility and trust. An independent, nonsectarian school, Saint Mark's enrolls students in kindergarten through grade eight who will benefit from rigorous academic and creative challenges. The curriculum emphasizes mastery of basic academic disciplines while providing broad exposure to the arts, athletics and world cultures. The school works in partnership with families to foster academic success and personal growth. Saint Mark's recognizes that a diverse community enriches the learning of all students and promotes global understanding and citizenship."

Academic Program

Philosophy: "The school's curriculum includes reading, vocabulary, literature, composition, handwriting, grammar, spelling, mathematics, history, geography, and science. Art, music, French (K-8), Spanish (K-8), PE, drama, and computers (G3-8) are taught by specialists. Most of the curriculum and the pedagogy are traditional, although innovative teaching strategies and methods are encouraged and supported." **Foreign languages:** Spanish or French beginning in K. **Computer training:** "The use of technology is integrated into the daily life of the classroom in G4-8. The formal computer curriculum begins in G3 with keyboarding and basic skills instruction. Basic skills continue to be emphasized in a project-based curriculum through G4. In G5-8 the computer curriculum is integrated with the core curricula through projects and special units of study. Technology resources include a computer lab, a mobile laptop lab, classroom computer clusters/mounted LCD projectors, and a media center." **No. of computers available for students: 80. No. of hours weekly of:** Art- 1–2; Drama- 40 min.; Music- 1-1.5; Computers (beginning G3)- 40-80 min.; Foreign language- 1.5-3; PE- 2.5-3.5. **Outdoor education:** "The Outdoor Education program (G3-8) exposes students to a variety of environmental venues, with a view to educating each student to outdoor educational skills and self-reliance. Venues include Yosemite, Big Basin, and Pinnacles." Other: The school also has a nationally ranked chess team, open to K-8. **Grading:** "Comprehensive comments for all students." Letter grades begin in G5. **Average nightly homework:** Approx. 15 min. per grade (i.e. 30 min. for G2; 1.5 hours for G6). Posted on the Internet: Yes for G7-8. **Percentage of students participating in Johns Hopkins Center for Talented Youth Program:** "71% of 5th-8th graders invited to participate." **Other indicators of academic success:** "Our students are accepted by the finest private high schools and continue at wonderful colleges. High schools report back on how well our students do and how prepared they are. Students demonstrate respect, responsibility, caring, trust, community, involvement, honesty, fairness, courage, and citizenship." **High schools attended by latest graduating class: Branson,** MA, MC, University, SI, Redwood, San Rafael, and Andover.

Faculty

Ethnicity: 85% Caucasian (non-Latino), 5% Asian, 5% Latino, 3% other, 2% African-American. **Percentage of teachers with graduate degrees:** 42%. **Percentage with current California credential:** 71%. **Faculty selection/training:** "Interested teaching candidates undergo a rigorous selection process, which includes teaching and interviewing with faculty, administration, and students." **Teacher/student ratio:** 1:10 in K-3, 1:11 in G4-8. **Special subject teachers:** Art, music, drama, technology, media studies, PE. **Average teacher tenure:** 11 years at Saint Mark's, 17 years in teaching.

Middle School

Description: The school's middle division consists of G4-6; upper division is G7-8. "In middle and upper divisions, the methodology becomes more sophisticated, moving students from the concrete to the conceptual. There is also a focus on organizational and study skills, problem solving, and critical thinking. The skills are hierarchically arranged." **Teacher/student ratio:** 1:10. **Elective courses offered:** "Electives are offered in G7-8 with an emphasis on the arts. Further programs are offered through PALS (philosophy, arts/media studies, and life issues). Media Literacy is taught in G5-8 with intensive studies on the subject in G7-8." Outdoor education is offered in G3-8. **Achievement tracking in:** Students are not tracked; however, in the 7th and 8th grade the school offers two math groupings/classes. The school has learning specialists on site to reinforce students' learning strengths. K-6 specialists independently contract with parents and the G7-8 specialists provide a course called 'classroom support' which is graded and taught in lieu of a foreign language. **Student social events:** Dances for G7-8. Sixth graders may attend the last dance. Students may bring guests.

Student Support Services

No. of Licensed Counselors on staff: One part-time. **Counselor/student ratio:** 1:380. **Learning specialists on staff:** One; also, for G1-5, Bay Area Speech & Learning independently contracts with families to provide a support program during the school day. For G6-8, a classroom support class (about 6 students) is offered. This is a graded course which students take in lieu of a foreign language. **Learning differences/disabilities support:** See above re: tracking. **High school placement support:** "The Head of the Upper School works closely with students and families throughout the 8th grade year to assist them with high school placement. Graduates attending local private and public schools return to speak to 8th graders about their experience."

Student Conduct and Health

Code of conduct: Zero tolerance for drug and alcohol use. Vulgar language is handled on an individual basis. Sexual harassment is governed by a written policy forbidding sexual harassment by any student, parent or teacher. **Prevention education and awareness programs:** Drug/alcohol education is taught through a mentor (advisor) program. Outside experts are involved. Sex education starts with a short unit in G3-6 and a fall half-year course in G7. Annual diversity workshops are offered for G3, G5, and G7-8. Diversity is also addressed in the curriculum. A parent education program is included, as well.

Athletics

Sports offered: Basketball, volleyball, flag football, cross-country, track and field. **Team play begins in:** G6.

Campus/Campus Life

Campus description: The school is located on 10 acres in the residential neighborhood of Terra Linda. Buildings include a new gymnasium, media center, and arts and science center. **Library:** "Together with the Media Center, over 10,000 volumes." **Sports facilities:** "A new state-of-the-art gymnasium and recently enhanced athletic field." **Theater/Arts facilities:** "Drama class takes place in our drama room, complete with stage and professional lighting. Two major annual productions are shown at the Marin Civic Center." **Computer lab:** Yes. **Science lab:** Yes, used primarily by G7-8. **Lunch program:** Optional organic hot lunch program. **Bus service:** None. Extensive carpool network. **Uniforms/dress code:** None, except students wear a Saint Mark's collared shirt for special events. **Opportunities for community service:** Community service is a part of the Saint Mark's curriculum. In addition to several all-school programs throughout the year, each grade organizes its own outreach. Recent service opportunities include visits to senior centers, environmental clean-up, and serving meals to the homeless.

Extended Day

Morning care: Begins at 7:30 a.m. **After-school care:** Until 6:30 p.m. **Grade levels:** K-8. **Cost:** $6/hour (discount for students receiving financial aid). **Drop-in care available:** Yes. **Coverage over major holidays:** No. **Homework help:** Yes. **Snacks:** Provided. **Staff/student ratio:** 1:8. **After-school classes:** The offerings of the school's After School Adventures program change each trimester. Recent classes include: Band, ceramics, hip hop dance, and computer game creation. Cost: Varies; contact school.

Summer Programs

"The Early Learners Program is offered for incoming kindergartners and first graders to assist them in getting to know the school and each other better. Children become familiar with the campus as they play indoors and out, do art projects, sing, dance, and do variety of other activities with current Saint Mark's teachers. The program is offered in 2- or 4-week sessions. Contact the school for current costs. Arts in Action is a camp especially designed for incoming students to G1-4 graders to explore art to the fullest. Performing and visual arts programs focus on encouraging each child's creativity and imagination. Super Tech camp invites incoming students to G5-7 to experience technology first hand. Students work with clay animation, flash animation, robotics and rocketry in our state-of-the-art computer lab, science/art building and media center." **Cost:** Varies; contact school.

Parent Involvement

Parent/teacher communication: Weekly newsletter, updated website, frequent letters from faculty and administration, parent conferences in fall and spring. **Participation requirements:** "No parent participation required, but strongly encouraged." **Parent education programs offered?** Yes.

What Sets the School Apart From Others

"Saint Mark's challenges students in a nurturing environment, where their love of learning is celebrated. The community lives out our '7 Pillars of Character'—honesty, caring, fairness, responsibility, courage, respect, and citizenship—on a daily basis."

How Parents/Students Characterize School

Parent comment(s): "The level of commitment, the caring, and the sense of community at Saint Mark's are all amazing. The staff is dedicated, the kids are happy, and the parents are involved."
Student comment(s): "I think the teachers are great. All of the faculty cares for each student in a different way. Classes are small enough that teachers can spend one-on-one time." –6th grade student ◆ "You can be the best of whatever you want to be at Saint Mark's." –5th grade student ◆ "At Saint Mark's, it's cool to be smart." – 8th grade student

ST. MARY'S CHINESE DAY SCHOOL

910 Broadway (at Mason) (Chinatown)
San Francisco, CA 94133
(415) 929-4690   *fax (415) 929-4699*
www.stmaryschinese.org

Mary Ng, Principal, stmaryssf@yahoo.com
Father Daniel McCotter, Director of Admission, stmaryssf@yahoo.com

General

Coed K-8 parochial day school. Founded in 1921. Catholic. Nonprofit. **Member:** NCEA, WASC, WCEA. **Enrollment:** Approx. 240.

Average class size: 25-30. **Accreditation:** WASC/WCEA (6-year term: 2005-11). **Endowment:** N/P. **School year:** Sept.-June. **Instructional days:** 182. **School day:** 8 a.m. to 3 p.m. for K-6, 8 a.m. to 3:15 p.m. for G7-8.

Student Body
Ethnicity: 97% Asian, 2% multi-racial, 1% Caucasian (non-Latino).

Admission
Applications due: Open. **Application fee:** $55. **Application process:** Upon receipt of completed application with a copy of birth certificate, testing will be arranged. **No. of applications:** N/P. **No. of K spaces:** 25. **Admission evaluation requirements for K:** Must be 5 years old by Dec. 1st. **Other grades:** Entrance exams are given to all applicants to determine readiness for grade. **Preferences:** Siblings, children of alumni. **What sort of student do you best serve?** "Serious, motivated, and academic minded."

Costs
Latest tuition: $4,500. **Sibling discount:** 25%. **Tuition includes:** Lunch: No; Transportation: No.; Laptop: No. **Tuition increases:** Approx. 5% annually. **Other costs:** Approx. $650 for books/registration fees, materials, insurance, ITBS, and about $100 for uniforms. **Percentage of students receiving financial aid:** 10%. **Financial aid application deadline:** Call for date. Financial aid is based on need. **Average grant:** N/P. **Percentage of grants of half-tuition or more:** 25%. **Donations:** The school solicits parents for voluntary cash donations for the annual fund, capital campaign, and auctions.

School's Mission Statement
"St. Mary's Chinese Day School is a Catholic School whose existence is an integral part of the mission of the Church. Our core values of Catholic Identity, Dignity, Excellence and Justice are included in all our curriculum and in all our programs."

Academic Program

Philosophy: "We recognize the uniqueness of each person and maintain an academic program which enables all students to fully cultivate their abilities." **Foreign languages:** Cantonese. **Computer training:** Yes. **No. of computers available for students:** N/P. **No. of hours weekly of:** Art, music, and drama are combined for a total of 90 min. in K-3 and 60 min. in G4-8; Computers-"formal class 45 min."; Foreign language-1; PE- 1. **Outdoor education:** Incorporated in science. **Grading:** A-F, beginning in G3. **Average nightly homework:** 30 min. for G1-2; 60 min. for G3-4; 90 min. for G5-6; 120 min. for G7-8. Posted on the Internet: "Not at this time." **Percentage of students participating in Johns Hopkins Center for Talented Youth Program:** N/A. **Other indicators of academic success:** "Our students do well on standardized and high school acceptance tests." **High schools attended by latest graduating class:** "45% to Lowell; other acceptances to SI, SHCP, Riordan, Mercy-SF, Wallenberg, Lincoln, and Washington."

Faculty

Ethnicity: 45% Asian, 45% Caucasian (non-Latino), 10% other. **Percentage of teachers with graduate degrees:** 25%. **Percentage with current California credential:** 80%. **Faculty selection/training:** "Experience, degree, buy into philosophy of the school." **Teacher/student ratio:** 1:25. **Special subject teachers:** Cantonese, music, PE, computer, reading/learning specialist. **Average teacher tenure:** 10 years.

Middle School

Description: G6-8 are considered the school's middle-jr. high division; G7-8 are departmentalized. **Teacher/student ratio:** 1:25. **Elective courses offered:** N/A. **Achievement tracking in:** All core academic subjects. **Student social events:** Dances, fairs, class trips.

Student Support Services

No. of Licensed Counselors on staff: One part-time. **Counselor/student ratio:** N/P. **Learning specialists on staff:** One. **Learning differences/disabilities support:** One After-school Tutoring-Learning Specialist. **High school placement support:** The principal and 8th grade teacher assists parents and students in the placement process.

Student Conduct and Health

Code of conduct: "All are expected to maintain a pattern of respect, cooperation, courtesy and refinement in our words and actions." **Prevention education and awareness addressed in:** Taught as part of the Family Life Program, in which issues of drugs, sex, health, and harassment are addressed.

Athletics

Sports offered: Basketball and track. **Team play begins in:** G3 (intramural).

Campus/Campus Life

Campus description: "We are currently in a temporary site and a new school and campus is being built with completion targeted in a couple of years." **Library:** "Our library consists of books and computers (in the adjacent computer room). Students are also taken to the branch libraries in the neighborhood in a cooperative program with these facilities." **Sports facilities:** The school rents gym space off campus. **Theater/Arts facilities:** No. **Computer lab:** Yes. **Science lab:** No. **Lunch program:** Yes. **Bus service:** No. **Uniforms/dress code:** Uniforms for class and for PE. **Opportunities for community service:** Students visit senior facilities, hospitals; the school's choir performs at such facilities, serve at soup kitchens, collect food and clothing for the poor, and participate in various drives as situations arise.

Extended Day

Morning care: None. **After-school care:** Extended academic study halls from 3-5 p.m. **Grade levels:** K-8. **Cost:** $45 per month. **Drop-in care available:** No. **Coverage over major holidays:** No. **Homework help:** Yes. **Snacks:** Provided. **Staff/student ratio:** 1:20. **After-school classes:** A Tutoring-Learning Specialist assists student for 45 minutes per day with learning needs and works in collaboration with classroom teachers on individual child's needs. Cost: $90/month.

Summer Programs

The school has a 5-week summer program. The morning session (8-11:30 a.m.) consists of an academic program including math, reading, English, computer education and fine arts. The afternoon session (12-4 p.m.) consists of a sports, recreation and crafts program. **Cost:** The program costs $375 for the morning session and $600 for the entire day. Lunch and snacks are provided.

Parent Involvement

Parent/teacher communication: Conferences, website, e-mail, newsletter. **Participation requirements:** At least 15 hours per year, per family. **Parent education programs:** Citizenship classes. The school is currently working on a student special needs program and computer literacy program.

What Sets the School Apart From Others

"In addition to normal school offerings and activities, St. Mary's takes into account the cultural heritage of our student population. Efforts are made to accentuate the values of the Chinese tradition."

How Parents/Students Characterize School

Parent comment(s): "St. Mary's offers our children opportunities to be proud of their heritage and teaches values that prepare them for life, as well as preparing them to be successful in high school."
Student comment(s): "St. Mary's is a family."

Saint Monica School

5950 Geary (at 24th Avenue) (Richmond District)
San Francisco, CA 94121-2007
(415) 751-9564 *fax (415) 751-0781*
www.stmonicasf.org

Mr. Bret E. Allen, Head of School and Director of Admission,
allen@stmonicasf.org

General

Co-ed K-8 parochial day school. Founded in 1919. Catholic. Nonprofit. **Member:** NCEA. **Enrollment:** Approx. 190. **Average class**

size: 21. **Accreditation:** WASC/WCEA (6-year term: 2002-08). **Endowment:** $1.3 million. **School year:** Aug.-June. **Instructional days:** 180. **School day:** 8 a.m. to 3 p.m.

Student Body

Ethnicity: 50% Asian, 20% Pacific Islander, 20% Caucasian (non-Latino), 5% multi-racial, 4% Latino, 1% African-American.

Admission

Applications due: Jan.-April. **Application fee:** $50. **Application process:** N/P. **No. of applications:** 55-65. **No. of K spaces:** 25. **Percentage of K class made up of school's preschool class:** N/A. **Admission evaluation requirements for K:** School tour by parents, admission evaluation, recommendations by pre-school. **Other grades:** School tour by parents, classroom visitation day for student, admission test, grades from previous school. **Preferences:** Siblings from current families, new Catholic families, non-Catholic families. **What sort of student do you best serve?** "Highly motivated, well-rounded students with strong parental support."

Costs

Latest tuition: $4,390-$4,990. **Sibling discount:** 70% of one child tuition. **Tuition includes:** Lunch: No; Transportation: No; Laptop computer: Yes, for junior high; Other: None. **Tuition increases:** Approx. 8-10% annually. **Other costs:** "Approx. $250 for books, supplies, insurance, testing (parent responsibility), and uniforms; $50 Parent Club fee." **Percentage of students receiving financial aid:** 15-20%. **Financial aid application deadline:** Feb. (call for date). Financial aid is based on need. **Average grant:** $1,300. **Percentage of grants of half-tuition or more:** 10%. **Donations:** Parents are required to complete 20 service hours annually, participate in the SCRIP program, and two mandatory fundraisers.

School's Mission Statement

"The Mission of St. Monica School is to provide a vigorous, comprehensive academic curriculum which stimulates the full range of a child's spiritual, intellectual, physical, social and cultural development; create a fulfilling, supportive, Christ-centered environment in which children can discover and develop their individual attributes and abilities; engage children in the learning process, and foster a life-long love of and respect for education; build a community in which teachers, parents, and students come together to support the common goal of learning and to recognize their responsibility to contribute to the welfare of the larger community."

Academic Program

Philosophy: "As an integral part of the mission of education of the Catholic Church, St. Monica School exists to cooperate with parents in developing the religious, intellectual, moral, social, cultural and physical aspect of each child. Under the inspiration of the Holy Spirit the school community strives to develop and live Jesus' message of respect, love and concern for one another in our contemporary, multi-cultural world." **Foreign languages:** Mandarin and Cantonese (after school). **Computer training:** Yes, as part of the overall curriculum. **No. of computers available for students:** 50. **No. of hours weekly of:** Art- 1.5; Drama- 2 after school; Music- .5; Computers- 1; Foreign language- 4 after school; PE- 1.5. **Outdoor education:** N/A. **Grading:** A-F, beginning in G3. **Average nightly homework:** 30 to 120 min. based on grade level. Posted on the Internet: No. **Percentage of students participating in Johns Hopkins Center for Talented Youth Program:** N/A. **Other indicators of academic success:** "All G2-8 score from the 70th to the 90th percentile on the ITBS test and 85+% of students are at grade level or above in Math, Reading and Language Arts. St. Monica School ranks as one of the highest scoring academic schools in the Archdiocese of San Francisco." **High schools attended by latest graduating class:** SI, SHCP, Mercy-SF, Riordan, and Lowell.

Faculty

Ethnicity: 81% Caucasian, 13% Asian, 6% Hispanic/Latina. **Percentage of teachers with graduate degrees:** 50%. **Percentage with current California credential:** 100%. **Faculty selection/training:** "Experience, degree, and credential." **Teacher/student ratio:** 1:12.5. **Special subject teachers:** Art, music, computers, PE, and reading K-4. **Average teacher tenure:** 14 years.

Middle School

Description: "G6-8 are departmentalized with teachers instructing their home room in language arts. Science, social science and math/algebra are taught by specialized teachers to the entire junior high level. Students also have art, music, PE and computer integration skills." **Teacher/student ratio:** 1:17. **Elective courses:** Co-curricular programs in Chinese language, drama, student choir, summer school. **Achievement tracking in:** N/A. **Student social events:** School picnic, monthly family potluck, bi-monthly Student Choir performance, Christmas show.

Student Support Services

No. of Licensed Counselors on staff: One part-time. **Counselor/student ratio:** 1:10. **Learning specialists on staff:** Reading specialist for K-4. **Learning differences/disabilities support:** "Yes." **High school placement support:** The junior high school team assists students with high school the application/entrance process, including entrance test preparation and parent meetings.

Student Conduct and Health

Code of conduct: "Discipline in the school is to be considered as an aspect of moral guidance and not a form of punishment. It is a means of training the child to assume more and more the control of her/his own conduct, whether this conduct has physical, mental, or moral aspects, so that she/he can progressively grow in self-competency and maturity." **Prevention education and awareness addressed in:** Taught in conjunction with Science and Religious Education classes.

Athletics

Sports offered: Through the Catholic Youth Organization, basketball, soccer and volleyball for girls; basketball, soccer and baseball for boys. **Team play begins in:** G3. Students in K-2 participate in a Micro-soccer league.

Campus/Campus Life

Campus description: The campus contains one large building which houses all classrooms. There are two paved play areas comprising approximately one-quarter acre and a full gymnasium. **Library:** The library has hundreds of volumes. Students may check out books for two week periods. The library collection is computerized and students may access materials by author, subject, or title. **Sports facilities:** Gymnasium and outdoor sports courts. **Theater/Arts facilities:** Drama Club uses the parish hall stage facilities and produces a spring play yearly. **Computer lab:** Yes. **Science lab:** No. **Lunch program:** Yes. **Bus service:** No. **Uniforms/dress code:** Uniforms. **Opportunities for community service:** Children in each grade participate in age-appropriate service in community outreach programs to the elderly, veterans, and the homeless.

Extended Day
Morning care: Begins at 7:15 a.m. **After-school care:** Until 6 p.m. **Grade levels:** K-8. **Cost:** $2,015/year for 1 child, $3,225/year for 2, full-time. **Drop-in care available:** Yes. **Coverage over major holidays:** No. **Homework help:** Yes. **Snacks:** Provided occasionally. **Staff/student ratio:** 1:14. **After-school classes:** Chinese language classes 4 days a week in Cantonese and Mandarin writing, reading, speaking, history and culture; Drama Club and peer tutoring are offered twice weekly. Costs: N/P.

Summer Programs
"The Summer School Program is an enrichment program where students will explore subjects that they would not necessarily learn during the regular school year. Students will be grouped by age for academic studies in the morning, but will have the opportunity of cross-grade instruction during creative/artistic classes in the afternoons. There will also be sports and athletics for all grades. Academic subjects include, integrated science, geography, math, history, and language arts. Computer skills will be taught in conjunction with academic subjects throughout the program to all grades. There will be an assessment of student progress at the end of the session. Courses will also use film and video as supplements, and field trips will be held each Friday, except for the last day of instruction. The costs associated with fieldtrips are additional to the cost of the program." The five-week program runs

mid-June to late July from 9 a.m. until 3 p.m. Monday through Friday." **Cost:** $700. Extended care from 3 p.m. until 6 p.m. is $200.

Parent Involvement

Parent/teacher communication: Conferences, website, e-mail, and telephone calls; a weekly communication envelope goes home to each family. **Participation requirements:** Parents are required to complete 20 hours of service to the school per year and to participate in one mandatory fundraiser per year and in the Scrip/e-Scrip program. **Parent education programs offered?:** None.

What Sets the School Apart From Others

"St. Monica School provides a Christ-centered, academically-rich, nurturing environment where students thrive."

How Parents/Students Characterize School

Parent comment(s): "St. Monica School has an excellent academic program, and strong, dedicated teachers who care about children. The environment emphasizes Christian moral values and prepares students for success in life."
Student comment(s): "St. Monica is a school that makes learning fun, challenging and exciting."

St. Paul's Elementary School

1690 Church Street (at 29th Street) (Mission/Noe Valley)
San Francisco, CA 94131
(415) 648-2055 *fax (415) 648-1920*
www.stpaulsf.net

Arleen Guaraglia, Head of School, aguaraglia@stpaulsf.net

General

Coed PS-8 parochial day school. Founded in 1916 by BVM Sisters. Roman Catholic. Nonprofit. **Member:** NCEA. **Enrollment:** Approx. 260. **Average class size:** 32. **Accreditation:** WASC/WCEA (6-year term: 2005-11). **Endowment:** N/P. **School year:** Aug.-June. **Instructional days:** 181. **School day:** 8 a.m. to 3:15 p.m.

Student Body

Ethnicity: 47.1% Latino, 28.3% Caucasian (non-Latino), 18% Asian, 4.4% multi-racial, 1.4% African-American, 1.4% other.

Admission

Applications due: Jan. 31st for K; open for G1-8. **Application fee:** $75. **Application process:** Grade level assessment, previous school questionnaire, transcripts, interview with principal. **No. of applications:** N/P. **No. of K spaces:** 33. **Percentage of K class made up of school's preschool class:** 40%. **Admission evaluation requirements for K:** Screening, school visit and tour, preschool recommendations. **Other grades:** Entrance test, transcript, previous school teacher questionnaire and interview with principal. **Preferences:** Siblings, pre-school applicants from St. Paul Parish program, St. Paul Parish members, Roman Catholics. **What sort of student do you best serve?** "We serve urban and suburban families interested in a faith-based curriculum in the Roman Catholic tradition within a family atmosphere that is gifted in cultural diversity. We strive to educate the whole child preparing him/her for the competitive secondary schools to which they apply and to which they are accepted—in most cases, to their first choice school."

Costs

Latest tuition: $4,107 for Catholics, $4,557 for non-Catholic. **Sibling discount:** Yes (amount N/P). **Tuition includes:** Lunch: No; Transportation: No; Laptop computer: No; Other: N/P. **Tuition increases:** Approx. 3% annually. **Other costs:** $325 registration fee; approx. $25 for books and supplies and $150 for uniforms. **Percentage of students receiving financial aid:** 15%. **Financial aid application deadline:** Call for date. Financial aid is based on need. **Average grant:** $500. **Percentage of grants of half-tuition or more:** 5%. **Donations:** A financial agreement stipulates that families will raise $400 in school sponsored fundraisers such as the walkathon, candy sale, e-script, holiday gift sale, among other opportunities.

School's Mission Statement

"We are called as a Catholic School to teach as Jesus taught. In partnership with parents, St. Paul's School attempts to educate students for what they can be spiritually, intellectually, psychologically, socially and aesthetically. We encourage and support the role of parents as primary educators by helping students to live as responsible Christians in the St. Paul parish and school community and the larger community of San Francisco. We hope as adults they will continue to grow in Christian development."

Academic Program

Philosophy: "It is the goal of St. Paul's School to provide for the development of each child to his or her fullest potential as an integrated individual: spiritually, socially, emotionally, aesthetically and physically. We offer a solid curriculum in religion, reading/literature, English, mathematics, science and social studies. We supplement that core curriculum with art, music, PE and computer classes." **Foreign languages:** After-school Spanish, at an additional cost. **Computer training:** Yes. **No. of computers available for students:** 15 in lab, 3-5 in classrooms. **No. of hours weekly of:** Art- 40 min.; Drama- N/P; Music- 30 min.; Computers- 40 min.; Foreign language- N/A (after-school Spanish); PE- 1. **Outdoor education:** One full day with Yosemite Institute at the Marin Headlands. **Grading:** A-F, beginning in G3. **Average nightly homework:** 20-30 min. for G1; 20-40 min. for G2-3; 35-55 min. for G4; 45-60 min. for G5; 60-90 min. for G6; and 60-110 min. for G7-8. Posted on the Internet: "Optional for teachers." **Percentage of students participating in Johns Hopkins Center for Talented Youth Program:** 1%. **Other indicators of academic success:** "St. Paul graduates are accepted at the private and public academic high schools of their first choice." **High schools attended by latest graduating class:** Riordan, SHCP, Lick, SI, ICA, Mercy-SF, CAT, Lowell, Washington, Capuchino, and the Academy of Arts and Sciences.

Faculty

Ethnicity: 90% Caucasian (non-Latino), 8% Latino, 2% Asian. **Percentage of teachers with graduate degrees:** 30%. **Percentage with current California credential:** 100%. **Faculty selection/training:**

"Successful elementary school experience, degree, compatibility with mission of school, preferably a practicing Roman Catholic." **Teacher/ student ratio:** 1:30. **Special subject teachers:** Science, music, PE, computers. **Average teacher tenure:** 12 years.

Middle School
Description: G6-8, departmentalized in math and English in G7-8. **Teacher/student ratio:** 1:30. **Elective courses offered:** None. **Achievement tracking in:** Math, science, English/literature, social studies, religion. **Student social events:** "Grade appropriate field trips, CYO sports, S.F. Giants baseball games, annual family picnic, field-day and carnival, monthly Family Mass and pancake breakfast, retreats, 8th grade family dinner/dance, music program with Davies Symphony Hall, Lawrence Hall of Science Hands-on Assemblies and Labs, Family bingo night, Christmas and Spring Concert (Outstanding Parish and School Choir)."

Student Support Services
No. of Licensed Counselors on staff: One part-time. **Counselor/student ratio:** 1:260. **Learning specialists on staff:** One day per week (reading specialist). **Learning differences/disabilities support:** "Supervised Doctoral student program through St. Mary's Hospital called Project School Care which does initial screening and assessments." **High school placement support:** N/P. Other: Middle Grade Resource Person (G3-5).

Student Conduct and Health
Code of conduct: "Discipline within St. Paul's is considered an aspect of moral guidance and not a form of punishment. It is a means of training the students to take control of their own choices and to assume responsibility for their own actions. Our main purpose at St. Paul's School is to learn and to grow both individually and also as a Catholic Christian Community. At St. Paul's School the expectation is that relationships are based on mutual respect, patience, and kindness." **Prevention education and awareness addressed in:** Family Life Education, Health Education (PE). (Students also receive vision screening.)

Athletics

Sports offered/team play begins in: Through the CYO, students beginning in G3 play basketball, baseball, volleyball, and soccer (boys). K-2 students participate in t-ball and micro-soccer programs through the local recreation department.

Campus/Campus Life

Campus description: "St. Paul's Elementary School serves approximately 260 students in kindergarten through grade 8. Our new school building opened in 1999. We have a preschool program located on campus in a separate school, called Littlest Angles Preparatory Preschool (415-824-5437). **Library:** Yes. The library has a computer lab (16 computers) adjacent to it. **Sports facilities:** Gym. **Theater/Arts facilities:** None. **Computer lab:** Yes. **Science lab:** Yes. **Lunch program:** Twice a week. **Bus service:** None. The school is located on the J-MUNI line which provides access to various points around the city and to BART. **Uniforms/dress code:** "All students are required to wear the school uniform each day unless otherwise informed. Unavoidable circumstances for a lack of uniform will require a note from the parent to the classroom teacher. Students are expected to be clean and neatly groomed during the school day and properly attired at school." **Opportunities for community service:** Students in G8 are required to complete 20 hours of community service before graduation. The school community sponsors toy drives, food drives, special fundraising for international emergencies and an annual coat drive for the homeless.

Extended Day

Morning care: Begins at 7 a.m. **After-school care:** Until 6 p.m. **Grade levels:** K-8. **Cost:** $220/mo. (a.m. and p.m.). **Drop-in care available:** Yes. **Coverage over major holidays:** No. **Homework help:** Yes. **Snacks:** Provided. **Staff/student ratio:** 6:5. **After-school classes:** Art and Spanish. Cost: "Minimal."

Summer Programs: None.

Parent Involvement

Parent/teacher communication: Parent-teacher conferences, school website, e-mail, weekly newsletter, voicemail. **Participation requirements:** 40 hours per year for two-parent families and 20 hours for single families. **Parent education programs offered?:** Yes.

What Sets the School Apart From Others

"The administration, faculty and staff of St. Paul's give attentiveness to each student to help them succeed academically and assist them in developing a personal moral value system and service-orientated attitude that will become the basis for civic responsibility. Secondly, we value the partnership developed within our parent community to help both our students and families develop a strong sense of faith and family centered well-being."

How Parents/Students Characterize School

Parent comment(s): "In a 2004 WASC survey, when asked to comment on the strengths of St. Paul's School, parents indicated the top five areas in order of priority as: a dedicated and caring staff, the Catholic values of the school, a sense of community, excellent instruction and a safe environment. Other areas listed as the strengths of the school included: the parents, the pastor, the principal, the clean environment, the athletic program, and the extended care program."

Student comment(s): "St. Paul's school is a clean, safe, friendly, and nurturing environment for learning … the curriculum is challenging and well-rounded." ✦ "I relate well to my teachers and the school staff. I think my teachers are fair, helpful, caring and the staff listen and respond to our needs." ✦ "At St. Paul's, we have a real sense of community—all of us feel respected by teachers and staff. We think it is a fun, safe place to learn and we are happy *Sister Act* [the movie] was filmed here."

St. Peter's School

1266 Florida Street (at 25th Street) (Mission District)
San Francisco, CA 94110
(415) 647-8662 fax (415) 647-4618
www.sanpedro.org

Victoria Butler, Principal and Director of Admission, vbutler@sanpedro.org

General
Coed K-8 parochial day school. Founded in 1878. Catholic. Non-profit. **Member:** N/P. **Enrollment:** Approx. 500. **Average class size:** 30. **Accreditation:** WASC (6-year term: 2003-09). **Endowment:** N/A. **School year:** Aug.-June. **Instructional days:** 180. **School day:** 8 a.m. to 3 p.m.

Student Body
Ethnicity: 97% Latino, 1% Asian, 1% African-American, 1% multi-racial.

Admission
Applications due: May (call for date). **Application fee:** $15. **Application process:** "Parents call the school to set up a time for entrance testing. Entrance testing is $15 and is used to determine the skills the child has so he/she will be able to succeed in the expected curriculum of the grade applied for. The family and child also need to have an interview with the principal." **No. of applications:** N/P. **No. of K spaces:** 30. **Percentage of K class made up of school's preschool class:** N/A. **Admission evaluation requirements for K:** Brigance test. **Other grades:** Entrance test. **Preferences:** N/P. **What sort of student do you best serve?** "Students eager to succeed."

Costs
Latest tuition: $2,700 for 1 child, $4,400 for 2, $5,300 for 3. **Sibling discount:** See above. **Tuition includes:** Lunch: No; Transportation: No; Laptop computer: No; Other: No. **Tuition increases:** N/P. **Other costs:** Approx. $100 uniforms, $250 for other fees. **Percentage**

of students receiving financial aid: 60%. Financial aid application deadline: May-June (call for date). Financial aid is based on need. Average grant: N/P. Percentage of grants of half-tuition or more: N/P. Donations: N/P.

School's Mission Statement

"St. Peter's Elementary School was founded by the Sisters of Mercy in 1878. Since its founding, St. Peter's continues to serve all economic levels of the community. Through our partnership with parents, we recognize as the primary educators of their children, we provide a strong Catholic education. We strive to deepen each child's understanding of the life of Christ through worship, example and by providing opportunities for them to practice their Catholic faith. It is expected that upon graduation all students will exhibit not only an understanding of their Catholic identity, but also an ability to put this understanding into practice."

Academic Program

Philosophy: N/P. Foreign languages: None. Computer training: "Yes." No. of computers available for students: 60. No. of hours weekly of: Art- 1; Drama- none; Music- 2; Computers- 1; Foreign language- none; PE- 2. Outdoor education: N/A. Grading: Letter grades begin in G3. Average nightly homework: "Yes." Posted on the Internet: Yes. Percentage of students participating in Johns Hopkins Center for Talented Youth Program: None. Other indicators of academic success: N/P. High schools attended by latest graduating class: SI, Mercy-SF, ICA, Riordan, SHCP, Lowell and other public schools."

Faculty

Ethnicity: 70% Caucasian (non-Latino), 29% Latino, 1% Asian. Percentage of teachers with graduate degrees: N/P. Percentage with current California credential: 100%. Faculty selection/training: N/P. Teacher/student ratio: N/P. Special subject teachers: Music, computers. Average teacher tenure: 20 years.

Middle School

Description: "G6-8. We provide quality Catholic education. We challenge our students in all areas of the curriculum so as to prepare each for successful entrance into high school." **Teacher/student ratio:** N/P. **Elective courses offered:** N/P. **Achievement tracking in:** N/P. **Student social events:** N/P.

Student Support Services

No. of Licensed Counselors on staff: Two part-time. **Counselor/student ratio:** N/P. **Learning specialists on staff:** None. **Learning differences/disabilities support:** N/P. **High school placement support:** None.

Student Conduct and Health

Code of conduct: "The students' interest in receiving a quality, morally based education can be served if students, parents and school officials work together. It shall be an express condition of enrollment that the students behave in a manner, both in and off campus that is consistent with the Christian principles of the school as determined by the school." **Prevention education and awareness addressed in:** Provided through the Archdiocese of San Francisco.

Athletics

Sports offered: Basketball for boys and girls, girls volleyball, boys soccer and baseball. **Team play begins in:** G3.

Campus/Campus Life

Campus description: "We have a computer lab, a music room, gym, an excellent PE program and an attractive daycare facility. Although the school was built in 1878, it was rebuilt in 1978 and supports a comfortable environment for learning. We have two school yards for student recess." **Library:** "Yes, well-stocked and with a school librarian." **Sports facilities:** Gym. **Theater/Arts facilities:** N/P. **Computer lab:** Yes. **Science lab:** No. **Lunch program:** Yes. **Bus service:** No. **Uniforms/dress code:** Uniforms. **Opportunities for community service:** "St. Peter's School is known for our exceptional outreach program.

Our active Student Council leads our students in ongoing projects of outreach and mercy. We bring care to shut-ins, we visit the sick, and we support our mission projects in Peru, El Salvador, and within our own neighborhood. In every national disaster, our children are present to help and support in numerous ways."

Extended Day
Morning care: Begins at 8 a.m. **After-school care:** Until 6 p.m. **Grade levels:** K-6. **Cost:** $3.50/hour. **Drop-in care available:** Yes. **Coverage over major holidays:** No. **Homework help:** Yes. **Snacks:** Provided. **Staff/student ratio:** N/P. **After-school classes:** None.

Summer Programs
"Please call for a brochure."

Parent Involvement
Parent/teacher communication: Parent meetings, newsletter, conferences. **Participation requirements:** "Yes." **Parent education programs offered?:** None.

What Sets the School Apart From Others
"St. Peter's School is a remarkable school and has been for the last 126 years. We educate, we love, we offer faith and commitment, and amongst everything, we continue to be a family. Our school exceeds in educational excellence and in the richness of being a family centered school."

How Parents/Students Characterize School
Parent comment(s): N/P.
Student comment(s): N/P.

St. Philip School

665 Elizabeth Street (at Diamond Street) (Noe Valley)
San Francisco, CA 94114
(415) 824-8467   fax (415) 282-5746
www.saintphilipschool.com

Sister Ann Cronin, BVM, Head of School and Director of
  Admission, anncronin@saintphilipschool.com

General

Co-ed K-8 parochial day school. Founded in 1938. Roman Catholic. Nonprofit. **Member:** NCEA. **Enrollment:** Approx. 205. **Average class size:** 24. **Accreditation:** WASC (6-year term: 2004-10). **Endowment:** N/P. **School year:** Aug-June. **Instructional days:** 180. **School day:** 8 a.m. to 3 p.m.

Student Body

Ethnicity: 42% multi-racial, 20% African-American, 20% Caucasian (non-Latino), 10% Latino, 6% other, 2% Asian.

Admission

Applications due: No deadline. **Application fee:** $30. **Application process:** Call for appointment. **No. of applications:** N/P. **No. of K spaces:** 28. **Percentage of K class made up of school's preschool class:** N/A. **Admission evaluation requirements for K:** School visit, screening, recommendations. **Other grades:** Test scores and report card from previous school. **Preferences:** Sibling and religious affiliation. **What sort of student do you best serve?** "English speaking."

Costs

Latest tuition: $4,609. **Sibling discount:** None. **Tuition includes:** Lunch: No; Transportation: No; Laptop computer: No. **Tuition increases:** Approx. 8% annually. **Other costs:** Approx. $150 for uniforms. **Percentage of students receiving financial aid:** 2%. **Financial aid application deadline:** Feb. (call for date). Financial aid is based on need. **Average grant:** $1,500. **Percentage of grants of half-tuition or more:** 3%. **Donations:** N/P.

School's Mission Statement

"St. Philip School is committed to being a child-centered, family sensitive school that consistently endeavors to address the unique spiritual, intellectual, physical, social and emotional needs of our students." **Philosophy:** "We strive to develop Christian students through formal religious instruction and a prevailing spirit of respect and service. We feel that each child has the right to approach life with a sense of self-worth and respect for others. We offer positive learning experiences which encourage each child to communicate and think critically and creatively and solve problems effectively. This enables each child to succeed, while respecting the various learning styles of our other students. Our rigorous academic program provides opportunities for students to take pride in and responsibility for their work and to discover the benefits of learning through a variety of spiritual, intellectual, cultural and physical activities. We strive to develop a respect for diversity and a pride in the children's cultural heritage. We affirm that parents are the first and primary educators of their children. We invite them to join us in partnership with the parish and entire Christian community in the continuing educative process. As a Catholic school, we hope to influence students and families to be dynamic agents of change in society in the areas of social justice, human dignity, freedom and peace. We provide an environment that fosters a belief in the sacredness of the human person and awareness that we are born into one worldwide human family. As Catholic educators, we the faculty of St. Philip School, realize that we are the role model as well as the teacher. We, therefore, strive to be a community dedicated to Gospel values and to promote by our own example of caring and committed leadership, a Christian atmosphere which is joyful, accepting, just and sensitive to the needs of others."

Academic Program

Philosophy: See above. **Foreign languages:** After-school Spanish. **Computer training:** Part of curriculum. **No. of computers available for students:** 50. **No. of hours weekly of:** Art- 1; Drama- N/P; Music- 1; Computers- varies per grade; Foreign language- N/P; PE- 1. **Outdoor education:** N/P. **Grading:** A-F, beginning in G3. **Average**

nightly homework: 1 hour. Posted on the Internet: No. **Percentage of students participating in Johns Hopkins Center for Talented Youth Program:** N/A. **Other indicators of academic success:** "High test scores." **High schools attended by latest graduating class:** SI, Riordan, Mercy-SF SHCP, ICA. Lowell, SOTA, Lick and University.

Faculty

Ethnicity: 75% Caucasian (non-Latino), 22% other, 3% Latino. **Percentage of teachers with graduate degrees:** 80%. **Percentage with current California credential:** 100%. **Faculty selection/training:** Education and experience. **Teacher/student ratio:** 2:20. **Special subject teachers:** Music and PE. **Average teacher tenure:** 6 years.

Middle School

Description: G6-8; departmentalization for language arts, math, social studies, and science. **Teacher/student ratio:** 1:24. **Elective courses offered:** N/A. **Achievement tracking in:** Language arts, math, social studies and science. **Student social events:** Church related.

Student Support Services

No. of Licensed Counselors on staff: One part-time. **Counselor/student ratio:** 1:10. **Learning specialists on staff:** None. **Learning differences/disabilities support:** "We have a group of teachers that make up a special needs team." **High school placement support:** By the G8 teacher, principal and pastor.

Student Conduct and Health

Code of conduct: "Discipline in a Catholic School is to be considered an aspect of moral guidance. The purpose of discipline is to promote student development, increase respect for authority and provide a classroom situation conducive to learning. All concerns should first be addressed to the classroom teacher and then to the principal." **Prevention education and awareness addressed in:** The school brings speakers on campus to discuss drug abuse, harassment, etc.

Athletics

Sports offered: T-ball, soccer, football, basketball, volleyball and baseball are offered through CYO. **Team play begins in:** G1.

Campus/Campus Life

Campus description: "We are a small school located in a quiet neighborhood." **Library:** "Newly renovated and small, but it serves the needs of our students." **Sports facilities:** "Limited." **Theater/Arts facilities:** "Very limited." **Computer lab:** Mobile laptops. **Science lab:** Yes. **Lunch program:** Yes. **Bus service:** No. **Uniforms/dress code:** Uniforms. **Opportunities for community service:** In the middle school grades.

Extended Day

Morning care: Begins at 6:30 a.m. **After-school care:** Until 6 p.m. **Grade levels:** K-8. **Cost:** $4/hour. **Drop-in care available:** Yes. **Coverage over major holidays:** No. **Homework help:** Yes. **Snacks:** Provided. **Staff/student ratio:** 1:24. **After-school classes:** Spanish. **Cost:** N/P.

Summer Programs: None.

Parent Involvement

Parent/teacher communication: E-mail, telephone, in person communications, newsletters, meetings. **Participation requirements:** Auction and festival plus 20 hours of service. **Parent education programs:** Offered through PTA meetings.

What Sets the School Apart From Others

"St. Philip the Apostle School has a long tradition of academic excellence. Students come to our school from all neighborhoods of San Francisco. Today, we are one of the most ethnically and financially diverse Catholic elementary schools in San Francisco, serving a student body population of 205 children in grades K-8. We strive to develop respect for diversity and pride in the cultural heritage of our children. Our goal is to instruct our students in a program that emphasizes basic skills, which will provide them with a strong foundation in the areas of language arts, mathematics, social studies and science. Teachers employ a wide variety of techniques and activities to meet the differing needs of children's learning abilities."

How Parents/Students Characterize School

Parent comment(s): "St. Philip's is a good school where our children receive an excellent education."
Student comment(s): "Our teachers are nice and take good care of us. They work hard to make learning a good experience."

Saint Vincent de Paul School

2350 Green Street (at Pierce) (Pacific Heights/Cow Hollow)
San Francisco, CA 94123
(415) 346-5505   fax (415) 346-0970
www.svdpsf.com

Mrs. Barbara Harvey, Head of School, Bharv1@aol.com
Mrs. Maria Balestrieri, Director of Admission,
  Mbalestrieri62@yahoo.com

General

Coed K-8 parochial day school. Founded in 1924. Catholic. Non-profit. **Member:** N/P. **Enrollment:** Approx. 250. **Average class size:** 30 ("with a primary teacher, and a full- or part-time aide. Many classes such as computers, music, drama, art are carried out in half-class groups. Some classes have reading and math groupings that provide for smaller groups and allow for smaller student: teacher ratio"). **Accreditation:** WASC/WCEA (term N/P). **Endowment:** N/P. **School year:** Aug.-June. **Instructional days:** 180. **School day:** 8:10 a.m. to 3:20 p.m.

Student Body
Ethnicity: "74% Caucasian (non-Latino)."

Admission
Applications due: Approx. Dec. 1 (call for date). **Application fee:** $75. **Application process:** Application and fee, parent interview, kindergarten screening or standardized test, recommendation(s); class visit and report cards for children entering G1-8. **No. of applications:** N/P. **No. of K spaces:** 30. **Percentage of K class made up of school's preschool class:** N/A. **Admission evaluation requirements for K:** A preschool recommendation and a Kindergarten readiness screening will be administered in January on an individual basis which will last approximately 15 minutes. A Kindergarten applicant must be 5 years old by Dec. 1 of the admission year. **Other grades:** Class visit, recommendation, previous report cards and standardized tests. **Preferences:** Parish Catholics, siblings, non-parish Catholics and non-Catholics (in that order). **What sort of student do you best serve?** "Each student is unique and valuable because his or her life comes from God. We believe the purpose of Catholic education is to assist each student to become a life-long learner, to identify and communicate his or her personal worth and message, to be aware of the same dignity in others, and to acquire a sense of responsibility to society."

Costs
Latest tuition: Ranges from $5,000 per year for Catholics in the Parish who perform service hours for the school to $7,750 for non-Catholics who are not able to perform service hours. **Sibling discount:** $500 for 3rd and subsequent child. **Tuition includes:** Lunch: No; Transportation: No; Laptop computer: No; Other: Books. **Tuition increases:** Approx. 8% annually. **Other costs:** $100 uniforms, $500 other fees.

Percentage of students receiving financial aid: 5%. **Financial aid application deadline:** April (call for date). Financial aid is based on need. **Average grant:** Varies. **Percentage of grants of half-tuition or more:** 1%. **Donations:** $200 or more requested per family.

School's Mission Statement

"The mission of Saint Vincent de Paul School is to educate our students in the Catholic tradition. We aspire to teach as Jesus did, with a focus on Gospel values. As facilitators of learning, we recognize parents as the primary educators of their children. We strive to acknowledge and celebrate the cultural differences in each individual student. We encourage our students to be responsible and sensitive to Church, school, and neighboring communities. We challenge our students to be self-motivated, life-long learners who will share their God-given gifts and talents with the global community."

Academic Program

Philosophy: "It is the goal of St. Vincent de Paul School to provide for the development of each child to his or her fullest potential as a whole person: spiritually, morally, socially, physically, intellectually, and emotionally. We strive to do this by offering an excellent curriculum in religion, mathematics, reading, science, English, social studies and Spanish. To assist each child in further development, we also include art, library skills, drama, music and PE. Computer skills are integrated throughout the curriculum. Sacramental programs for Catholic students are also offered in G2 (Reconciliation and First Eucharist) and G7-8 (Confirmation)." **Foreign languages:** Spanish. **Computer training:** N/P. **No. of computers available for students:** 20. **No. of hours weekly of:** Art- 1; Drama- 1; Music- 1; Computers- 1; PE- 1. **Outdoor education:** N/P. **Grading:** Letter grades begin in G3. **Average nightly homework:** "Depends on grade level." Posted on the Internet: N/P. **Percentage of students participating in Johns Hopkins Center for Talented Youth Program:** N/A. **Other indicators of academic success:** N/P. **High schools attended by latest graduating class:** Riordan, CSH, SI, SHCP, Stuart Hall, and SOTA.

Faculty

Ethnicity: N/P. **Percentage of teachers with graduate degrees:** N/P. **Percentage with current California credential:** N/P. **Faculty selection/training:** N/P. **Teacher/student ratio:** N/P. **Special subject teachers:** N/P. **Average teacher tenure:** N/P.

Middle School

Description: G7-8. **Teacher/student ratio:** 1:30. **Elective courses offered:** N/P. **Achievement tracking in:** N/P. **Student social events:** N/P.

Student Support Services

No. of Licensed Counselors on staff: N/P. **Counselor/student ratio:** N/P. **Learning specialists on staff:** N/P. **Learning differences/disabilities support:** N/P. **High school placement support:** N/P.

Student Conduct and Health

Code of conduct: N/P. **Prevention education and awareness addressed in:** N/P.

Athletics

Sports offered: Volleyball, soccer and basketball for girls; soccer, basketball and baseball for boys. **Team play begins in:** G3 (intramural) and students in G3-8 may participate in the De Paul Youth Club, which offers sports and participation in city-wide sports competition. Membership also allows students to participate in a supervised free play period each afternoon until 4 p.m.

Campus/Campus Life

Campus description: "We have the distinct advantage of being located next door to our parish church. We have a main building, built in 1924, which houses our administrative offices, K-5, our library, faculty lounge, cafeteria and full operating kitchen. We also have an annex which contains our gym, junior high, computer lab, special needs classroom, music room, art room, Spanish, and learning specialist room. **Library:** Yes. **Sports facilities:** Gymnasium and auditorium. **Theater/Arts facilities: Theatrical stage. **Computer lab:** Yes. **Science lab:** Yes. **Lunch program:** Yes. **Bus service:** No. **Uniforms/dress code:** Uniforms. **Opportunities for community service:** Yes.

Extended Day

Morning care: N/P. **After-school care:** Until 6 p.m. **Grade levels:** K-8. **Cost:** $210/month, full-time. **Drop-in care available:** Yes. **Coverage over major holidays:** No. **Homework help:** For one hour. **Snacks:** Provided. **Staff/student ratio:** N/P. **After-school classes:** Band and Science Club. **Cost:** Varies; contact school.

Summer Programs: None.

Parent Involvement

Parent/teacher communication: N/P. **Participation requirements:** Yes (requirements: N/P). **Parent education programs offered?** Yes.

What Sets the School Apart From Others

"Serving generations of families, the mission of Saint Vincent de Paul School is to educate students in the Catholic tradition and to provide for the development of the whole person. With a science center, music department, Spanish department, drama program, school band and journalism club, it is the school's philosophy to provide a variety of activities to stimulate intellectual curiosity and to build an individual's sense of personal worth. Saint Vincent de Paul is proud of its many achievements as a school family, and as a community we are dedicated to realizing every student's potential."

How Parents/Students Characterize School

Parent comment(s): N/P.
Student comment(s): N/P.

San Domenico School

1500 Butterfield Road
San Anselmo, CA 94960
(415) 258-1905 *fax (415) 258-1906*
www.sandomenico.org

Dr. Mathew Heersche, Head of School, mheersche@sandomenico.org
Wendy Feltham, Director of Admission, wfeltham@sandomenico.org

General

Coed PreK-8 day school, girls day and boarding G9-12. Founded in 1850. Independent. Catholic, "Welcoming students of all faiths." (50% Catholic). **Member:** CAIS, NAIS, NCGS, TABS, CBSA, BADA, BAAD. **Enrollment:** Approx. 570, with 400 in PreK to G8. **Average class size:** N/P. **Accreditation:** WASC/CAIS (6-year term: 2001-07). **Endowment:** $5.5 million. **School year:** Aug.-June. **Instructional days:** 178. **School day:** 8:15 a.m. to 3 p.m.

Student Body

Ethnicity: 82% Caucasian (non-Latino), 12% Asian, 3% multi-racial, 2% African-American, 1% Latino.

Admission

Applications due: Jan. (call for date). **Application fee:** $100. **Application process:** Call to request a tour and application packet. **No. of applications:** N/P. **No. of K spaces:** 44. **Percentage of K class made up of school's preschool class:** 80-85%. **Admission evaluation requirements for K:** Parent tour and meeting, student screening and school visit, PreK teacher's recommendation. **Other grades:** Parent tour and meeting, student interview and campus visit, transcripts, teacher recommendations, standardized test scores (ISEE for G6-8). **Preferences:** N/P. **What sort of student do you best serve?** "Engaged students and creative thinkers."

Costs

Latest tuition: $8,700 for PreK, $14,712 for K, $16,636 for G1-8. **Sibling discount:** None. **Tuition includes:** Lunch: Yes; Transportation: Yes; Laptop computer: No; Other: N/P. **Tuition increases:** N/P. **Other costs:** Approx. $390-$440 for Science Camp in G5-8. **Percentage of students receiving financial aid:** N/P. **Financial aid application deadline:** Feb. (call for date). Financial aid is based on need. **Average grant:** N/P. **Percentage of grants of half-tuition or more:** N/P. **Donations:** Voluntary cash donations for the annual fund, auctions, and endowment.

School's Mission Statement

"We celebrate diversity recognizing God's presence in ourselves and in all of creation. We explore and develop the unique gifts of each individual in mind, heart, body and spirit. We inspire inquiry and provide a strong academic foundation for life long intellectual growth. We recognize what it means to be human in a global community and respond with integrity to the needs and challenges of our time."

Academic Program

Philosophy: "The overall philosophy of San Domenico's curriculum, PreK through 12, is to ensure a dynamic, relevant educational program by using a model of connected learning that is based upon integrated, inter-disciplinary and thematic learning." **Foreign languages:** Spanish in G1-5, Spanish and French in G6-8. **Computer training:** In Primary and Middle School computer labs. **No. of computers available for students:** 150. **No. of hours weekly of:** Art- 2-3; Drama- N/P; Music- 2; Computers- 2; Foreign language- 2-6; PE- 2-3. **Outdoor education:** "0-4." **Grading:** A-F, beginning in G3. **Average nightly homework:** 20 min. to 2 hours. Posted on the Internet: Yes. **Percentage of students participating in Johns Hopkins Center for Talented Youth Program:** "N/P but 10% of students participate in the Stanford EPGY program." **Other indicators of academic success:** "Standardized tests, academic performance, and school median profile on ERB/CTP scores is above independent school median profile." **High schools attended by latest graduating class:** San Domenico, Bay School, Branson, Drew, MA, MC, SI, Urban, Drake, Marin School of Arts & Technology, Redwood, and Tamalpais.

Faculty

Ethnicity: 97% Caucasian (non-Latino), 3% African-American. **Percentage of teachers with graduate degrees:** 82%. **Percentage with current California credential:** N/P. **Faculty selection/training:** N/P. **Teacher/student ratio:** 1:12. **Special subject teachers:** (G1-8) Art, vocal music, music conservatory, computers, science, PE, Religion/Campus Ministry, sustainability, Spanish, and in middle school only, French. **Average teacher tenure:** 13 years.

Middle School

Description: G6-8, "departmentalized with experienced teachers." **Teacher/student ratio:** 1:12. **Elective courses offered:** "Many." **Achievement tracking in:** Math. **Student social events:** Daily morning meeting, quarterly Pizza & Movie Nights, 1-2 day retreats, Spirit Week and week-long science camps, excursions and parties.

Student Support Services

No. of Licensed Counselors on staff: Two full-time. **Counselor/student ratio:** 1:200. **Learning specialists on staff:** One. **Learning differences/disabilities support:** "We can work successfully with students with mild to moderate learning differences, and assist parents in locating support services; after-school support available in Middle School." **High school placement support:** Counseling by Division Head and Head of School; 7th grade Parent Night and a High School Packet.

Student Conduct and Health

Code of conduct: "San Domenico is a community dedicated to learning. The primary focus of discipline is directed towards helping students become responsible and mature, to accept the consequences of their actions, and to become persons of integrity and self-discipline." **Prevention education/awareness addressed in:** Integrated into the curriculum, including Life Skills workshops and counselor support.

Athletics

Sports offered/team play begins: In the Primary School, students in G3-5 engage in cross-country in the fall (G3-5), CYO volleyball in the fall (G5 girls only); CYO basketball in the winter; and CYO track and field intramurals, soccer & basketball in the spring. Students in the Middle School play flag football (boys only), CYO volleyball (girls only), and cross-country in the fall; CYO basketball in the winter; and CYO & Marin Junior High Track & Field, and girls soccer in the spring. The school has intramurals in flag football and basketball. Cost: All except CYO basketball cost $50 (family rate is $65); the CYO basketball fee is $120 (or $160 for families with more than one child participating). San Domenico's Equestrian Center offers private ($65/hour), semi-private ($50/45 minutes) and group lessons ($50/hour) in hunt seat equitation."

Campus/Campus Life

Campus description: "515 spectacular acres of hills and fields, creek and organic garden." **Library:** Three separate areas for Primary, Middle and Upper School students with 23,000 volumes and 8 computers. **Sports facilities:** "State-of-the-art Athletic Center, dance and yoga studio, sports fields, pool, and tennis courts." **Theater/Arts facilities:** Primary School and Middle School Art Studios, brand new Performing Arts center, two auditoriums for smaller performances. **Computer labs:** For Primary and Middle Schools. **Science lab:** "We have 2-3 well-equipped science labs per division." **Lunch program:** "Yes-delicious, healthy foods with choice of hot entrees including vegetarian." **Bus service:** Marin, to San Francisco and the East Bay. **Uniforms/dress code:** Uniforms. **Opportunities for community service:** "San Domenico is dedicated to service learning in our community and globally."

Extended Day

Morning care: None. **After-school care:** Until 2:50 p.m. for PreK and 4:20 p.m. for K-5th. **Grade levels:** PreK to G5. **Cost:** $7-10/hour. **Drop-in care available:** No. **Coverage over major holidays:** Yes. **Homework help:** Yes. **Snacks:** Provided. **Staff/student ratio:** 1:15. **After-school classes:** In addition to sports, the school offers drama for school musicals; private music lessons for piano, violin, cello, flute, saxophone, clarinet, voice, recorder, guitar, viola, oboe and harp. Cost: For PreK-1 (30 min./week) $1,560/year.; for G2-8 (40 min./week) $2,000/year. Ensemble coaching is available to all students taking private lessons for $330-$410/semester.

Summer Programs

The school offers a variety of summer programs, most recently, SportsKids for G2-7 ($215/week or $400/two weeks); Volleyball for G4-8 ($200/week); Bay Area Naturalists for G3-5 ($400/week); Summer Arts Intensive for G6-8 ($400/week); Chamber Music for G4-8 ($400/week); Piano Ensemble for G3-8 ($400/week); Northern CA Elite Basketball Camp for G7-8 ($350/week for day campers or $600/week if boarding in dorms); and Go Coastal Overnight for G6-8 ($900/week).

Parent Involvement

Parent/teacher communication: Conferences, meetings with Division Head and Head of School, website, e-mail, newsletter. **Participation requirements:** Parent participation is welcomed and encouraged, and is coordinated by the Parent Service Association. **Parent education programs:** Meetings, lectures and workshops.

What Sets the School Apart From Others

"San Domenico is an innovative and challenging school in a spectacular setting with a state-of-the-art Music Conservatory, arts and athletic facilities. Our talented faculty helps students develop qualities of leadership, independent thinking and spiritual development. We are known for our commitment to sustainability, service learning and joyful celebrations."

How Parents/Students Characterize School

Parent comments: "A San Domenico education encompasses the whole child: academically, athletically and spiritually." "I amazed at how much the teachers know about my kids, how they learn and think." "San Domenico has given our entire family a sense of community and friendship."

Student comments from 4th graders: "Mother Nature came through and spread her magic on San Domenico!" "At San Domenico, there is something for everyone." "We are so lucky to go to San Domenico with all the opportunities we have here." And from a Kindergartner: "I love having really fun teachers!"

San Francisco Day School

350 Masonic Ave. (at Golden Gate) (Western Edition/Inner Richmond)
San Francisco, CA 94118
(415) 931-2422 fax (415) 931-1753
www.sfds.net

John C. Lin, Head of School, jlin@sfds.net
Margarita Rhodes, Director of Admission, mrhodes@sfds.net

General

Coed K-8 day school. Founded in 1981. Independent. Nonprofit.
Member: CAIS, NAIS, ISBOA, ALA, BAISL, BADH, Bay Area
POCIS, and BADA. **Enrollment:** Approx. 400. **Average class size:**
22-23. **Accreditation:** CAIS (6-year term: 2000-06). **Endowment:**
Approx. $6.9 million. **School year:** Sept.-June. **Instructional days:**
Approx. 170. **School day:** 8:30 a.m. to 2:15 p.m. for K-1, 8:30 a.m. to
3:30 p.m. for G2-4, 8 a.m. to 3:30 p.m. for G5-8. (G2-8 have 3 p.m.
dismissal on Mondays and Fridays.)

Student Body

Ethnicity: 67% Caucasian (non-Latino), 13% Asian, 8% Latino, 7%
African-American, 5% other.

Admission

Applications due: Typically the 1st week of January (call for date). **Application fee:** $75. **Application process:** Starts with an evening open
house where prospective families get a chance to hear from administrators, tour the school, and talk to teachers. If interested, families submit
an application and then schedule a 30-minute parent interview (October-early January) and a student visit (K visits take place in January, G1-8 visits typically take place in February). Optional daytime
tours are also available to families that have submitted an application.
No. of applications: N/P. **No. of K spaces:** Varies. **Percentage of K
class made up of school's preschool class:** N/A. **Admission evaluation requirements for K:** Age 5 by August 1st of K year; screening,
school visit, parent interview, and recommendations. **Other grades:**

Screening, school visit, grades, test scores, parent interview, recommendations, and parts of the ERB. **Preferences:** Sibling. **What sort of student do you best serve?** "Children with intellectual curiosity and social skillfulness who come from families committed to supporting the school and their child's school experience."

Costs

Latest tuition: $18,760 for K-8, payable in 1 payment, 2 payments, or through a 10-month payment plan for a fee. **Sibling discount:** None. **Tuition includes:** Lunch: No; Transportation: No; Laptop computer: No; Other: No. **Tuition increases:** Approx. 7% annually. **Other costs:** None. **Percentage of students receiving financial aid:** Approx. 21%. **Financial aid application deadline:** Jan. (call for date). Financial aid is based on need. **Average grant:** $12,821. **Percentage of grants of half-tuition or more:** 80%. **Donations:** "All families are asked to support the growth of the school's programs and facilities by making the school a top priority for their annual giving. In the past two years, the school has celebrated 100% participation from the parents, faculty, and staff. San Francisco Day School also hosts an annual auction to fundraise for tuition assistance, as well as other smaller fundraisers throughout the year. There is a gap of approximately $1,800 between the tuition fee and the cost of education per child."

School's Mission Statement

"San Francisco Day School educates, nurtures, and inspires girls and boys of diverse backgrounds to achieve their highest academic and creative potential, to embrace ethical values, and to become active contributors to their communities. The cornerstones of San Francisco Day School are: *Academic excellence; Diversity & inclusiveness* in our community, *Strong partnership* between family and school; *Shared values* of compassion, integrity, and responsibility; *Active involvement* in the city."

Academic Program

Philosophy: "Students acquire the skills of lifelong learners, well equipped for the world beyond the Day School. They have command of the essential skills of reading, writing, speaking, computing, and problem solving. They are expected to master technology to access and exchange information, to solve problems, and to assist in individual research. They learn to value and appreciate their creative potential in the arts and master a wide range of physical skills. They are aware of their gifts and challenges as learners and come to understand their own and other learning styles. The curriculum developed at San Francisco Day School relies significantly on students thinking critically and working collaboratively." **Foreign languages:** All students in G4-6 take Spanish; G7-8 students may take either Spanish or Latin. **Computer training:** "Integrated into the classroom curriculum for all students. Up-to-date iMac lab as well as roving carts of wireless laptops for class and individual use." **No. of computers available for students:** Approx. 100. **No. of hours weekly of:** Art- 1.5; Drama- varies; Music- 1-1.5; Computer- varies; Foreign language- 1.5 in G4, 2.5 in G5, 3.75 in G6-8; PE- 1.5; Library- 1. **Outdoor education:** Varies. **Grading:** Twice yearly progress reports consisting of narrative and progress grid. Letter grades begin in G5. **Average nightly homework:** 20 min. for G2; 30 min. for G3; 1 hr. for G4; 1.5 hrs. for G5-6; 2 hrs. for G7; 2.5 hrs. for G8. Posted on the Internet: Yes. **Percentage of students participating in Johns Hopkins Center for Talented Youth Program:** N/P. **Other indicators of academic success:** N/P. **High schools attended by latest graduating class:** "The majority go on to attend top-rated, independent high schools."

Faculty
Ethnicity: 79% Caucasian (non-Latino), 10% Asian, 6% Latino, 3% African-American, 2% other. **Percentage of teachers with graduate degrees:** Approx. 50%. **Percentage with current California credential:** Approx. 50%. **Faculty selection/training:** "BA/BS and relevant teaching experience." **Teacher/student ratio:** 1:10-11 in K-5, 1:22-23 in G6-8. **Special subject teachers:** Art (3), music (3), PE (4), technology (2). **Average teacher tenure:** Approx. 8 years.

Middle School
Description: "The Upper School (middle school) at SFDS is G5-8. In G5 the students are in homeroom based settings for core subjects and morning meeting. In G6-G8 the students transition to an advisory

program and different teachers for all core and extracurricular subjects. In the second semester of G5, the students begin to receive letter grades as well as narrative comments and a rubric based assessment. Students in G6-8 participate in small advisory groups each school day. Faculty advisors facilitate a program to develop character values, build peer relationships, improve student performance, and work on service learning projects together. Service learning is a teaching and learning strategy that combines principles of experiential learning with service to the community. Each grade level has a theme to guide students' study and work in service learning. The SFDS Student Council is made up of 22 girls and boys. There are four elected representatives for each grade, one boy and one girl per class. In addition to the reps, there are two treasurers, two secretaries, and two presidents. Student Council is in charge of planning fundraisers, food days, spirit weeks, dances, and parties. Students Striving for Diversity is a self-selected group that meets once a week during lunch to discuss issues of diversity and multiculturalism. They make presentations during school assemblies. Some of the topics they have covered are self-identity, homophobia, and human rights activists." **Teacher/student ratio:** 1:10-11 in G5, 1:22-23 in G6-8. **Elective courses offered:** N/P. **Achievement tracking in:** Algebra. **Student social events:** School picnics, performances, Concert for Community, Copa Soccer Tournament, Sally's Day Out, 8th Grade Graduation, dances.

Student Support Services

No. of Licensed Counselors on staff: Two part-time. **Counselor/student ratio:** N/P. **Learning specialists on staff:** Two full-time, 1 part-time. **Learning differences/disabilities support:** "The learning resource center is a 3 person department providing assessment, direct instruction, and consultation with faculty, administrators, and parents to help students reach their full academic potential. The services include the following: early screening in K and G1; educational screening for learning strengths and weaknesses in G2-8 as needed; referrals for outside in-depth testing and/or remediation; remedial instruction in language arts skills for students in G1-3 needing additional support; weekly support in G4 with language arts curriculum; assistance to teachers regarding strategies and accommodations for students with learning differences; learning specialists attend weekly grade level meetings; office hours for upper school students requesting additional support; assistance with interpretation and analysis of ERB testing in G3-7. The school holds the same expectations and course requirements for all students, but will make reasonable efforts to provide accommodations for students with learning differences. If the accommodations/modifications cannot fully address the identified needs of a student, the school will confer with the student's family to discuss alternatives, including other school placements." **High school placement support:** "The high school counseling program is for 8th graders and their families. The secondary school placement counselor works closely with students/parents to gather information about high schools, assess students' strengths, and make sound choices for continuing their education." Other: Advisory Program.

Student Conduct and Health

Code of conduct: "When the school's behavioral expectations are not met, classroom teachers will intervene and communicate with the parents. A teacher may issue a discipline slip to document the event. If the inappropriate behavior is particularly harmful or is a repeated infraction, the Division Head will contact the parents to discuss ways to resolve the situation and help the student meet community standards. Students who demonstrate a pattern of repeated occurrences may be placed on probation while the administration considers whether continued enrollment at SFDS is appropriate. In instances of extremely inappropriate, persistent, or disruptive behavior, the administration may take more severe measures, including suspension or expulsion from school." **Prevention education and awareness addressed in:** "The school recognizes the primary role of the family in educating children about sexuality and drugs. Classes are prepared with the age level of students in mind and with the expectation that students and parents will discuss these topics at home. The presentation of these subjects at school is matter-of-fact, with a focus on the natural development of the human body and the effects harmful agents can produce. Teachers and the school counselor create a safe and comfortable forum in which students discuss situations they are likely to encounter while growing up in today's society. The G5 curriculum covers biology of reproduction and puberty, and sexual choice. The G6 curriculum covers drugs and alcohol. The G7 curriculum covers sexuality/intimacy. The G8 curriculum covers HIV/AIDS, review of substance use, sexuality and social pressures."

Athletics

Sports offered: The SFDS sports program offers, for boys, soccer, cross-country, volleyball, baseball, and basketball; for girls, soccer, basketball, and volleyball; and for boys and girls, cross-country. **Team play begins in:** G5. The school emphasizes fitness, sports skills, and sportsmanship in K-4. Students in G5-8 may participate in the sports program.

Campus/Campus Life

Campus description: The school has a California mission-style campus with several courtyards on the corner of Masonic and Golden Gate Ave. The campus includes a large library, classrooms, computer lab, science labs, cafeteria, gym, two music rooms, and two art studios. **Library:** Large two-floor library with 20,000 volumes; 23 computers for student use, all with internet access; 20 subscription databases; and remote access for all catalogs and databases. **Sports facilities:** Gym, rooftop and ground level play areas. The school uses the USF field across the street for sports and physical education. **Theater/Arts facilities:** Gym/performing arts center. **Computer lab:** One lab, two traveling carts with enough laptops for class use, and a computer area in the library. **Science lab:** 3 labs. **Lunch program:** Lunches may be purchased daily for approximately $3.25. **Bus service:** No. The school is centrally located in the city and it is on or near several major MUNI lines. **Uniforms/dress code:** "All students are expected to wear clean and neat clothing." **Opportunities for community service:** Available for all grades and families.

Extended Day

Morning care: The school opens at 7:30 a.m. with teacher supervision until school begins. **After-school care:** Until 6 p.m. for K-8. The school tries to make the extended day program as much like home as possible for K-3, whose afternoon consists of outdoor play, games, sports, cooking, art, music, and drama. Extended care students G4-8 are usually involved in after-school enrichment classes, sports, or study hall. K-4 spend their afternoon in a large classroom on the ground floor with a kitchen and an adjacent yard with a play structure. The program also makes use of the roof play space and the gym. **Cost:** $7/hour with pre-paid blocks of 25 hours or more. **Drop-in care available:** Yes. All children not picked up at 3:30 p.m. are automatically sent to the extended care program as "drop-ins" at the cost of $8/hour. Any parent may arrange for drop-in care on the same day of use. **Coverage over major holidays:** No. **Homework help:** Yes. **Snacks:** Provided. **Staff/student ratio:** Approx. 1:10. **After-school classes:** Art, computer, film making, theater, karate, supervised study, gymnastics, jewelry making, Spanish, and Mandarin language have been offered. Classes change each quarter and are available to all students. Cost: $11.25 per class. No charge for extended care when children are in classes. Also, musical instrument lessons are available through the music department for $33 a lesson (45-60 min.) or approx. $495 for a semester.

Summer Programs

"San Francisco Day School has offered in past years: Ray of Light Theater Camp and Dolphin Sports Camps taught by SFDS faculty. As part of our commitment of service to the community and our active involvement in the city, the school hosts Summerbridge, a five-week mentoring program for public and parochial school students in G5-6 who wish to improve their academic skills." **Cost:** None (since program is only open to economically qualified students).

Parent Involvement

Parent/teacher communication: Weekly all-school newsletter from head of school, e-mail/voicemail available for all faculty and staff, and weekly classroom newsletters. Twice yearly parent/teacher conferences. **Participation requirements:** "Parents are not required, but are encouraged to give time to the school. Opportunities include fundraising, mailings, art studio volunteers, tour guides, room parents, library assistants, gardening, and bringing any special talents or knowledge they have to the classroom and the community." **Parent education programs:** The parent-led and run Education Committee meets several times a year to discuss current topics in education and child/adolescent development. The committee also sponsors events like movie nights and lectures.

What Sets the School Apart From Others

"Exceptional faculty, well-equipped facility, strong commitment to best educational practices in each discipline, supportive families, thoughtful approach to benefits of coeducation, student leadership opportunities, active use of cultural and artistic resources of the city, and a diverse and multicultural community."

How Parents/Students Characterize School

Parent comment(s): "The community is truly warm and welcoming and the education program is outstanding."
Student comment(s): "Teachers really know and care about us."

SAN FRANCISCO FRIENDS SCHOOL
117 Diamond Street (at 18th St.) (Upper Market/Castro)
San Francisco, CA 94114
(415) 552-8500 *fax (415) 552-8501*
www.sffriendsschool.org

Cathy Hunter, Head of School, chunter@sffriendsschool.org
Yvette Bonaparte, Director of Admission,
    ybonaparte@sffriendsschool.org

General

Coed K-3 day school. Founded in 2002. Independent. Nonprofit. **Member:** CAIS New School Services Program, CASE, BADA, BAISHA, POCIS. **Enrollment:** 160; growing a grade each year. K-3 in the 2005-06 school year. **Average class size:** 20. **Accreditation:** Friends Council of Education (FCE) (term N/P). **Endowment:** N/P. **School year:** Sept.-June. **Instructional days:** 175. **School day:** 8:30 a.m. to 3 p.m.; 2:30 p.m. dismissal for K.

Student Body

Ethnicity: "26% of our families are Latino, African-American, Asian-American, or bi-racial."

Admission

Applications due: Jan. (call for date). **Application fee:** $70. **Application process:** School tours including evening coffees and open houses, application, teacher recommendation, parent interview, student visit; school tours begin mid-October. **Number of applications:** Approx. 200. **No. of K spaces:** 40. **Percentage of K class made up of school's preschool class:** N/A. **Admission evaluation requirements for K:** Screening/playdate, school visit, recommendations, parent interview. **Other grades:** All of the above and school records from previous school. **Preferences:** Siblings, Quaker affiliation. **What students do you best serve?** "We seek students and families who value the school's Quaker mission and philosophy."

Costs

Latest tuition: $18,245. **Sibling discount:** None. **Tuition includes:** Lunch: No; Transportation: No; Laptop computer: No. **Tuition increases:** N/P. **Other costs:** N/P. **Percentage of students receiving financial aid:** 28%. **Financial aid application deadline:** Jan. (call for date). Based on need. **Average grant:** N/P. **Percentage of grants of half-tuition or more:** N/P. **Donations:** Voluntary and appreciated.

School's Mission Statement

"San Francisco Friends School is dedicated to educating, inspiring, and nurturing girls and boys in the tradition of Quaker learning. The daily life of our school is rooted in the Quaker values of simplicity, integrity, mutual respect, peaceful problem-solving, and service to others. We strive to develop in each child intellectual curiosity and passion for learning. We challenge students with academic rigor, while honoring individual strengths and abilities. We seek to create a community that embraces children and families of all backgrounds, recognizing that diversity is essential to the vitality of our school. We engage with the larger world around us, working toward the Quaker ideal of a caring and just society."

Academic Program

Philosophy: "SFFS provides a nurturing and stimulating environment in which we encourage each child's natural love of learning; a focus on simplicity and clarity; a respectful, kind, and inclusive community; cooperative and collaborative learning; the development of independence, resourcefulness, and responsibility; an appropriate balance of challenges and successes." **Foreign languages:** Spanish. **Computer training:** Computer curriculum begins in G1. **No. of computers available for students:** 10. **No. of hours weekly of:** Art- 1.5; Drama- 1.5; Music- 1.5; Computers- 1 in G1 and above; Foreign language- 2, PE- 2.25. **Outdoor education:** Built into science curriculum starting in K. **Grading:** Written comments each semester. **Average nightly homework:** Beginning in G2, 1 hour. Posted on the Internet: No. **Percentage of students participating in Johns Hopkins Center for Talented Youth Program:** "N/A, currently do not have a middle school." **Other indicators of academic success:** N/P. **High schools attended by latest graduating class:** N/A. The school's first 8th grade class will be graduating in the year 2011.

Faculty

Ethnicity: "29% diversity." **Percentage of teachers with graduate degrees:** 28%. **Percentage with current California credential:** 33%. **Faculty selection/training:** "Several years of experience, degree, Quaker affiliation." **Teacher/student ratio:** 1:10. **Special subject teachers:** 5, in art, music, drama, Spanish and PE. **Average teacher tenure:** "The majority of teachers have remained since the school was founded 2002."

Middle School

"N/A. SFFS is growing a grade each year and will have an 8th grade in 2010."

Student Support Services

No. of Licensed Counselors on staff: None. **Counselor/student ratio:** N/A. **Learning specialists on staff:** One part-time. **Learning differences/disabilities support:** One part-time Educational Therapist.

High school placement support: N/A. First graduating class will be 2011.

Student Conduct and Health

Code of conduct: "School-based behavioral program-responsive classroom. Honor each community member." **Prevention education and awareness addressed in:** Included in health curriculum, which starts in K.

Athletics

Sports offered: Intramural and/or intermural team play will begin when G5 is added.

Campus/Campus Life

Campus description: The school is located in a 1929 former parish school in the Castro. The building consists of three floors with ten classrooms, two large meeting rooms and nine offices. **Library:** "Welcoming and growing collection, warm and heart of the community; computerized card catalog; 2 computers." **Sports facilities:** The Eureka Valley Recreation Center is adjacent to the school, with a full-size gymnasium and field. **Theater/Arts facilities:** Large multi-purpose room. **Computer lab:** Computers are in classroom pods. **Science lab:** N/P. **Lunch program:** Bag lunches are delivered daily through "Kid Chow" at an additional charge. **Bus service:** No. **Uniforms/dress code:** "Clothing must be neat, comfortable and appropriate." **Opportunities for community service:** "At SFFS, community service is built into the curriculum and introduced in gentle, age-appropriate ways. Students begin by serving their own immediate community. Each child completes a daily chore, such as cleaning work areas, tending our school garden, or collecting the recycling. Writing letters of appreciation or condolence to school community members is an emphasis in the early writing program. Children learn that service to others and thoughtful stewardship of the environment or institutions such as libraries, parks and museums creates ties and builds community. At SFFS service to others includes the sharing of love, respect, created or collected material goods and most especially-purposeful work."

Extended Day

Morning care: Begins at 7:45 a.m. **After-school care:** Until 6 p.m. **Grade levels:** All grades. **Cost:** Approx. $7/hour. Support is available for students with tuition assistance. **Drop-in care available:** Yes. **Coverage over major holidays:** Yes. **Homework help:** Yes. **Snacks:** Provided. **Staff/student ratio:** 1:8. **After-school classes:** Enrichment classes such as yoga, Mandarin, chess, woodworking, crafts, and Spanish." Cost: Approx. $10/hour. Tuition assistance is available.

Summer Programs

Five week-long summer sessions are offered to all students at the school. Children may enroll for single or multiple weeks. Each week includes a field trip and special guests. Extended care is available from 2:30 - 5:30 p.m. **Cost:** $300/week; $7/hour for extended care.

Parent Involvement

Parent/teacher communication: Two conferences annually. Special link for parents to website, e-mail communication with parents, weekly newsletter. **Participation requirements:** "Voluntary and most welcomed." **Parent education programs offered?** Yes. Topics include Quaker values, child development, parenting workshops.

What Sets the School Apart From Others

"Only Quaker-based program in the Bay Area. SFFS is dedicated to educating, inspiring and nurturing girls and boys in the tradition of Quaker learning. Friends Schools have a 300-year tradition of academic excellence and thoughtful concern for the emotional and spiritual growth of children. Friends schools are much admired for their outstanding academic programs, grounded by strongly-held values. Friends educators attend to the growth and development of each child's capacity for independent thought, creativity, and reflection."

How Parents/Students Characterize School

Parent comment(s): "The San Francisco Friends School curriculum is 'narrow and deep'—the Quaker values of service, silent reflection, peaceful problem-solving and simplicity infuse the curriculum, and all of the programs and activities at the school." —1st grade parent.

Student comment(s): "All my friends are at Friends. My favorite subjects are science and chess—we do experiments in science, and then we write about what we learned. Sometimes when we go for a hike in Muir Woods, we sit and have quiet time so we can write about what we see in our journals."

The San Francisco School

300 Gaven Street (at Boylston) (Excelsior/Portola District)
San Francisco, CA 94134
(415) 239-5065 *fax (415) 239-4833*
www.sfschool.org

Terry Edeli, Head of School, tedeli@sfschool.org
Nina Wang, Director of Admission, nwang@sfschool.org

General

Coed PS-8 day school. Founded in 1966. Independent. Nonprofit. **Member:** CAIS, BADA POCIS. **Enrollment:** Approx. 275. **Average class size:** 20. **Accreditation:** WASC/CAIS (term: N/P). **Endowment:** Approx. $1 million. **School year:** Aug.-June. **Instructional days:** 175. **School day:** 8:30 a.m. to 3 p.m.

Student Body

Ethnicity: 59% Caucasian (non-Latino), 15% Asian, 15% Latino, 11% African-American.

Admission

Applications due: Jan. (call for date). **Application fee:** $70. **Application process:** Applicants must attend an open house prior to signing up for a tour. They then submit records and recommendations. Interviews are scheduled after the January application due date. **No. of applications:** 250. **No. of K spaces:** Only 1-5 because key point of entry is 3-year old class. **Percentage of K class made up of school's preschool class:** Generally 100%. **Admission evaluation requirements for K:** Interview, recommendation, screening. **Other grades:** Screening, school visit, grades, test scores, recommendations. **Preferences:**

Siblings. **What sort of student do you best serve?** "Academically prepared, inquisitive, compassionate and eager for the challenges ahead."

Costs

Latest tuition: $15,600 for preschool and elementary, $16,820 for middle school. **Sibling discount:** None. **Tuition includes:** Lunch: Yes; Transportation: No; Laptop computer: No; Other: Camping, trips to Yosemite and Mexico. **Tuition increases:** Approx. 9% annually. **Other costs:** Approx. $25 for other fees. **Percentage of students receiving financial aid:** 25%. **Financial aid application deadline:** Feb. (call for date). Financial aid is based on need. **Average grant:** N/P. **Percentage of grants of half-tuition or more:** N/P. **Donations:** Voluntary.

School's Mission Statement

"The San Francisco School cultivates and celebrates the intellectual, imaginative and humanitarian promise of each student in a community that practices mutual respect, embraces diversity and inspires a passion for learning."

Academic Program

Philosophy: See Mission Statement above. **Foreign languages:** Spanish G2-8. **Computer training:** "Some." **No. of computers available for students:** 24 in computer lab plus laptops. **No. of hours weekly of:** Art- 3; Drama- varies; Music- 5; Computers- varies; Foreign language- N/P.; PE- varies. **Outdoor education:** Yosemite trips, camping. **Grading:** A-F, beginning in middle school. **Percentage of students participating in Johns Hopkins Center for Talented Youth Program:** N/P. **Other indicators of academic success:** N/P. **High schools attended by latest graduating class:** Bay School, Crystal, Drew, Gateway, IHS, Leadership, Lick, Lincoln, Lowell, Midland, Riordan, SHCP, SOTA, Stevenson, Stuart Hall, SI, Thacher, University, Urban, Waldorf, and Washington.

Faculty

Ethnicity: 70% Caucasian (non-Latino), 13% African-American, 10% Asian, 7% Latino. **Percentage of teachers with graduate degrees:**

17%. **Percentage with current California credential:** N/P. **Faculty selection/training:** Experience, degree. **Teacher/student ratio:** Approx. 1:10. **Special subject teachers:** Approx. 15, in art, music, computers. **Average teacher tenure:** 12 years.

Middle School

Description: "Commences in G6. SFS middle school students learn accountability in an atmosphere that continually asks them to make decisions and to reflect on the wisdom of their choices." **Teacher/student ratio:** 1:15. **Elective courses offered:** N/A. **Achievement tracking in:** N/A. **Student social events:** Dances.

Student Support Services

No. of Licensed Counselors on staff: One part-time. **Counselor/student ratio:** 1:275. **Learning specialists on staff:** Three part-time. **Learning differences/disabilities support:** The school works with student, teachers and family to identify strengths, learning styles and sources of learning difficulties, and to recommend in-class, at-home, and outside services and interventions as necessary. The school also has an on-campus tutorial program as part of its extended care program. **High school placement support:** "The school counselor acts as 20% High School Placement Counselor. At SFS, our faculty and administration advisers are well-versed in guiding families through the application process and helping them select the schools that best fit the strengths of each student."

Student Conduct and Health

Code of conduct: "The middle school program is specifically designed to nurture and guide students on their journey to becoming responsible, thoughtful and actively engaged adults." **Prevention education and awareness programs:** Programs cover drugs, sex, health and harassment.

Athletics

Sports offered: Volleyball, basketball, tennis, soccer, and track. **Team play begins in:** K (intramural).

Campus/Campus Life

Campus description: "The school resembles a quiet village tucked in a corner of a bustling metropolis." **Library:** Yes. **Sports facilities:** Outdoor basketball courts, use of nearby fields and gymnasium. **Theater/Arts facilities:** Multi-purpose room and large art studio with kilns. The school rents nearby theaters for performances. **Computer lab:** Yes. **Science lab:** Yes, for middle school. **Lunch program:** Yes. **Bus service:** No. **Uniforms/dress code:** "Respectful." **Opportunities for community service:** Yes.

Extended Day

Morning care: Begins at 7:30 a.m. **After-school care:** Until 6 p.m. **Grade levels:** All. **Cost:** Approx. $6/hour. **Drop-in care available:** Yes. **Coverage over major holidays:** No. **Homework help:** Yes. **Snacks:** Provided. **Staff/student ratio:** 1:10. **After-school classes:** Elementary students sign up for specialty classes, including cooking, art, music, academic enrichment and team sports. Middle school students can also choose student government, supervised homework or other specialty clubs and classes. **Cost:** N/P.

Summer Programs

"SFS offers a variety of day camps at the school, including one for pre-school students, ages 4 to 6. Elementary and middle school students can choose from a variety of academic and athletic programs and a Shakespeare camp. Current offerings can be referenced online." **Costs:** N/P.

Parent Involvement

Parent/teacher communication: Conferences, website, e-mail, newsletter. **Participation requirements:** "Expected but not required." **Parent education programs offered?** Yes.

What Sets the School Apart From Others

"Three aspects make us stand out among excellent schools. Our educational approach teaches students to think and work like the professionals they will become. Secondly, we focus student attention on big questions that are central to a subject. And finally, the SFS program is structured to help students find and nurture their passions in an environment where each child feels safe bringing his/her whole self to school."

How Parents Characterize School

Parent comment(s): "Like a small town in the big city."
Student comments: N/P.

SAN FRANCISCO WALDORF SCHOOL

2938 Washington Street (at Divisadero) (Pacific Heights)
San Francisco, CA 94115
(415) 931-2750   fax (415) 931-0590
www.sfwaldorf.org

Joan Caldarera, Head of School, jcaldarera@sfwaldorf.org
Lori Grey, Enrollment Coordinator, lgrey@sfwaldorf.org

General

Coed PS-8 day school. High school is on a separate campus. Founded in 1979. Independent. Nonprofit. **Member:** AWSNA. **Enrollment:** 275. **Average class size:** 25. **Accreditation:** WASC, AWSNA (7-year term: 2002-09). **Endowment:** N/P. **School year:** Sept.-June. **Instructional days:** 172. **School day:** 8:30 a.m. to 3:20 p.m.

Student Body

Ethnicity: 70% Caucasian (non-Latino), 13% other, 8% Asian, 6% Latino, 3% African-American.

Admission

Applications due: Jan. (call for date). **Application fee:** $75. **Application process:** Tour, interview. **No. of applications:** 80. **No. of K spaces:** 30. **Percentage of K class made up of school's preschool class:** 65%. **Admission evaluation requirements for K:** Interview. **Other grades:** Interview, transcripts, class visit. **Preferences:** Siblings. **What sort of**

student do you best serve? "Waldorf education meets the needs of the developing human being, and therefore serves a very wide range of students."

Costs

Latest tuition: $12,530-$13,830. **Sibling discount:** 10%. **Tuition includes:** Lunch: No; Transportation: No; Laptop computer: No; Other: None. **Tuition increases:** Approx. 3-5% annually. **Other costs:** Approx. $200-$650 which include tuition insurance, sports program fees, and field trip fees. **Percentage of students receiving financial aid:** 16%. **Financial aid application deadline:** Jan. (call for date). Financial aid is based on need. **Average grant:** $5,500. **Percentage of grants of half-tuition or more:** 40%. **Donations:** Voluntary—Annual Fund Campaign, Scrip Program and Benefit Auction.

School's Mission Statement

"Our purpose is to provide a Waldorf education in San Francisco for children from early childhood through high school. Academic excellence, social responsibility, and the recognition of each individual's gifts are the guiding educational ideals. The curriculum integrates the student's developmental needs with intellectual and artistic skills. Our deeply committed faculty works together to foster each student's sense of self-reliance, concern for community, and moral purpose. The student's educated, disciplined imagination will be the foundation for leadership into the future."

Academic Program

Philosophy: "Each child is viewed as a growing human being of body, soul and spirit, all of which must be nurtured by education. The school places human development and art at the center of its work and curriculum. It prepares young people to meet the world with inner confidence, to trust in the value of each human being, and to think and work with initiative in their lives." **Foreign languages:** Spanish and German G1-8. **Computer training:** None. **No. of computers available for students:** N/A. **No. of hours weekly of:** N/P. **Outdoor education:** N/P. **Grading:** Narrative evaluations. **Average nightly homework:** .5-2 hours for G4 and up. Posted on the Internet: N/A.

Percentage of students participating in Johns Hopkins Center for Talented Youth Program: N/P. Other indicators of academic success: "Happy, healthy, self-confident children." High schools attended by latest graduating class: SF Waldorf, Urban, Drew, Gateway, Lick, SI, SOTA, and University.

Faculty

Ethnicity: 84% Caucasian (non-Latino), 10% Latino, 3% Asian, 3% African-American. Percentage of teachers with graduate degrees: 25%. Percentage with current California credential: N/P. Faculty selection/training: Experience, bachelor's degree or more, Waldorf teacher training. Teacher/student ratio: 1:25. Special subject teachers: Music, languages, handwork, woodwork, Eurythmy, PE. Average teacher tenure: 12 years.

Middle School

Description: Students in G1-8 have a class teacher with them through the entire 8 years providing continuity. Special subject teachers work throughout these years with additional resource teachers in academic areas working in G6-8. Teacher/student ratio: 1:20. Elective courses offered: None. Achievement tracking in: N/P. Student social events: N/P.

Student Support Services

No. of Licensed Counselors on staff: N/P. Counselor/student ratio: N/P. Learning specialists on staff: One tutor. Learning differences/ disabilities support: "Faculty care group, tutor." High school placement support: A high school placement counselor works with all 8th graders.

Student Conduct and Health

Code of conduct: Policy is stated in Parent Handbook. The upper grades have a Student Handbook as well which students in G6-8 are required to read and sign, with discipline slips being issued for violations. Multiple violations result in detention and possible suspension. Prevention education and awareness addressed in: Class teachers develop individualized programs to meet the needs of their class.

Athletics

Sports offered/team play begins in: CYO basketball for both boys and girls begins in G6. Girls volleyball is offered for G7-8 teams.

Campus/Campus Life

Campus description: "A small oasis in an urban setting." **Library:** On campus library. **Sports facilities:** Multi-purpose hall, nearby park and additional basketball practice space. **Theater/Arts facilities:** Multi-purpose hall. **Computer lab:** N/P. **Science lab:** No. **Lunch program:** No. **Bus service:** No. **Uniforms/dress code:** Warm and dry, neat and clean, modest and functional. These concepts are grounded in each class teacher's judgment of the age-appropriate needs of each grade and of unique class requirements. **Opportunities for community service:** Weekly community service in 8th grade.

Extended Day

Morning care: None. **After-school care:** Until 5:30 p.m. **Grade levels:** K-5. **Cost:** $6.50/hour. **Drop-in care available:** Yes. **Coverage over major holidays:** Spring break camp only. **Homework help:** None. **Snacks:** Provided. **Staff/student ratio:** 1:10 for K, 1:16 for G1-5. **After-school classes:** Weekly craft day, baking day and local park trips included. Cost: N/P.

Summer Programs

Separate one-month programs for nursery, K and 6-9-year-olds. Two-week drama program for 9-14-year-olds. **Cost:** Approx. $400 per two weeks.

Parent Involvement

Parent/teacher communication: Parent evenings by class approximately every two months, individual conferences twice a year. **Participation requirements:** Voluntary participation in field trips, special projects, library and festival celebrations. **Parent education programs offered?** Yes.

What Sets the School Apart From Others

"The sense of aesthetics and the full integration of the arts into the academics are quite unique and palpable. This wholeness allows students to absorb material through all their senses and develop a full range of capacities for expressing themselves and their knowledge of material presented."

How Parents/Students Characterize School

Parent comment(s): "SFWS not only opens doors for my child, but more to the point, doesn't close them. Each year, as she grows and develops, I am thrilled that she has not been pigeon-holed and can discover new and unexpected abilities." "In an urban setting, it is wonderful to have a school that is so beautiful to walk into and that sees and welcomes nature everywhere."

Student comment(s): "Our class teacher sees us grow both as opinionated individuals and as a whole. The teacher becomes somewhat of a co-parent and a major authority figure in the student's life."

STUART HALL FOR BOYS

2222 Broadway (between Fillmore and Webster) (Pacific Heights)
San Francisco, CA 94115
(415) 563-2900 *fax (415) 929-6928 (Admissions)*
www.sacredsf.org

Jaime Dominguez, Head of School, dominguez@sacredsf.org
Pamela Thorp, Director of Admission, thorp@sacredsf.org

General

Boys K-8 day school. Founded in 1887. Catholic (55%). Stuart Hall for Boys along with Convent Elementary School, Convent of the Sacred Heart High School and Stuart Hall High School, is one of the four Schools of the Sacred Heart in San Francisco. Independent. Nonprofit. **Member:** CAIS, Network of Sacred Heart Schools, NAIS, IBSC, NCEA, ERB, CASE, BADA. **Enrollment: 324. Average class**

size: 15-20. **Accreditation:** CAIS/WASC (6-year term: 2005-11), Network of Sacred Heart Schools. **Endowment:** $9 million. **School year:** Sept.-June. **Instructional days:** N/P. **School day:** From 8:15 a.m. to 2:45 p.m. Monday-Thursday for K. Dismissal for G1-8 is between 3 p.m. and 3:30 p.m. Friday dismissal for K is 1:45 p.m. and for G1-8, between 2 p.m. and 2:30 p.m.

Student Body
Ethnicity: "26% students of color."

Admission
Applications due: Mid-Dec. for K, for G1-8, early Jan. (call for date). **Application fee:** $75. **Application process:** Parent tours are held two hours on weekday morning beginning in late September. The Head of School meets with parents for a question and answer period during tour. Parents are also invited to meet with the Head of School when child attends play group activity. **No. of applications:** N/P. **No. of K spaces:** 40. **Percentage of K class made up of school's preschool class:** N/A. **Admission evaluation requirements for K:** Applicants to K must be five years old by the first of August. Assessment for readiness to begin the full-day program offered by the school includes both individual screening and a play group date. Preschool evaluations are also part of each child's application. **Other grades:** Includes a parent tour, teacher recommendation, previous grades and testing. **Preferences:** Siblings. **What sort of student do you best serve?** "Students and families who will support the school's Mission Statement."

Costs
Latest tuition: $17,450 for K-4, $17,850 for G5-8. Tuition payable in 1, 2 or 10 installments (10-month plan carries a fee). **Sibling discount:** None. **Tuition includes:** Lunch: No; Transportation: No; Laptop computer: N/P; Other: N/P. **Tuition increases:** Approx. 7% annually. **Other costs:** Approximately $200 for K uniform including shoes. Uniforms are also available through school's thrift shop, Seconds To Go. **Other costs:** N/P. **Percentage of students receiving financial aid:** 15%. **Financial aid application deadline:** Jan. (call for date). Financial aid is based on need. **Average grant:** N/P. **Percentage of grants of**

half-tuition or more: N/P. **Donations:** Parents are solicited to participate in annual giving; participation is voluntary.

School's Mission Statement

"Founded in 1887 as an independent Catholic school, Schools of the Sacred Heart, San Francisco, carry on the educational mission of the Religious of the Sacred Heart. We share with the other members of the nationwide Network of Sacred Heart Schools five common goals and the commitment to educate to: A personal and active faith in God; A deep respect for intellectual values; A social awareness which impels to action; The building of community as a Christian value; Personal growth in an atmosphere of wise freedom. A K-12, four-school complex, Schools of the Sacred Heart, San Francisco offer the unique experience of single-sex education within a coed community. Students are expected to achieve their highest level of scholarship while learning to assume leadership roles as responsible, compassionate and contributing members of society."

Academic Program

Philosophy: "Sacred Heart schools were founded upon a firm commitment to academic excellence. While the Program of Studies at Stuart Hall has evolved over the years, the rigor that underpins Sacred Heart schools remains a constant. Stuart Hall's academic program provides a balance between the best of traditional (concepts, skills, facts, disciplines) and progressive (experiential learning, projects, cross-curriculum) methodologies and pedagogy. The spirit of the Program of Studies provides an environment that is a center of sound learning, new discovery, and the pursuit of wisdom. The challenges are many and met with exuberance. The emphasis is always on the student as a whole child." **Foreign languages:** Spanish or French offered beginning in G3. Latin is mandatory in G6. **Computer training:** Beginning in K and continuing through G8. **No. of computers available for students:** "Approximately 100 state-of-the art computers. Computers are located in the Unkefer Computer Lab, the elementary school library and stations outside the classroom." **No. of hours weekly of:** "Art, drama, music, computers, foreign language, PE and outdoor education: Times vary weekly with grade of child." **Outdoor education:** N/P. **Grading:**

Narrative report in K-4 and letter grades in G5-8. **Average nightly homework:** The school's guidelines are 30-60 min. for G1-3; 60-90 min. for G4-5; and 120 min. for G6-8. Posted on the Internet: No. **Percentage of students participating in Johns Hopkins Center for Talented Youth Program:** N/P. **Other indicators of academic success:** "Stuart Hall for Boys students are well prepared for their high school experience. They maintain high academic standards and participate in the full life of high school including sports, clubs and leadership roles in student government. Graduates also continue to maintain a high level of commitment to community service." **High schools attended by latest graduating class:** "Schools include Stuart Hall, Lick, University, SI, Lowell, SHCP, Bay School, Groton and Stevenson."

Faculty

Ethnicity: "22% are faculty of color." **Percentage of teachers with graduate degrees:** N/P. **Percentage with current California credential:** N/P. **Faculty selection/training:** Experience, college degree and/or credential. "Professional teacher development is an integral part of the school's program." **Teacher/student ratio:** 1:10 in the Lower Form; 1:15-20 in the Middle Form. **Special subject teachers:** Art, music, computers and the after-school program (which also includes private instrumental music lessons in piano, flute, violin and guitar). **Average teacher tenure:** 8 years.

Middle School

Description: "The Middle Form Program at Stuart Hall for Boys introduces the Advisory System where students and teachers are grouped together in small teams that meet weekly to discuss both academic and social life at the school. Students further develop their critical thinking skills within a community that promotes cooperative learning. Writing, both creative and expository, is emphasized in all subject areas. Stuart Hall students build upon their experience in a science lab and the scientific method of discovery. The values of citizenship continue to be stressed through the Goals and Criteria of Sacred Heart Education. There is a strong esprit de corps among the students and faculty within the classroom and across the school. Departmentalization begins in G5." **Teacher/student ratio:** 1:15-20. **Elective courses offered:** N/P.

Achievement tracking: None. **Student social events:** With Convent Elementary School students: dances, drama club, and the after-school program including orchestra.

Student Support Services

No. of Licensed Counselors on staff: One full-time. **Counselor/student ratio:** N/P. **Learning specialists on staff:** Two. **Learning differences/disabilities support:** "Educational resources as needed." **High school placement support:** A High School Counselor counsels students and families. Students may re-enroll to Stuart Hall High School.

Student Conduct and Health

Code of conduct: "As articulated in the Goals and Criteria of Sacred Heart Schools." **Prevention education and awareness addressed in:** Health classes, mandatory in K-8. (Fitness is also included).

Athletics

Sports offered: Soccer, cross-country, basketball, baseball, lacrosse, and golf. **Team play begins in:** G5 (intermural) through ISAL and CYO.

Campus/Campus Life

Campus description: Stuart Hall for Boys occupies the former Hammond House and is located on the same campus as Convent Elementary School and Convent of the Sacred Heart High School. Stuart Hall High School is located several blocks away at Pine and Octavia. **Library:** Houses 20,000 volumes including fiction, non-fiction and reference books, periodicals, books on tape, CD ROMs, videos, and computers. **Sports facilities:** A gymnasium with a basketball court and a running track. **Theater/Art facilities:** Two theaters. The newest is the Syufy Theater used for school presentations including plays, musicals and guest lectures. The Siboni Art and Science Center houses all art, music and science classrooms for Stuart Hall, Convent Elementary School and Convent of the Sacred Heart High School. **Computer lab:** Yes. **Science lab:** Yes. **Lunch program:** Yes (hot lunch). **Bus service:** A private bus service from St. Francis Wood/Forest Hills is available through an independent company. **Uniforms/dress code:** Uniforms. **Opportunities for community service:** "From its inception Sacred Heart education has had a deep and abiding commitment to social service. Community service and justice education are guided by the school's ministry team which oversees and supports both classroom and school-wide service endeavors. Community service helps students understand the needs of others, cultivates a spirit of cooperation and collaboration and fosters a comprehension of leadership today and tomorrow."

Extended Day

Morning care: Begins at 7:30 a.m. **After-school care:** Until 6 p.m. (coed) **Grade levels:** K-4. **Cost:** No charge for a.m. care. For a 5 p.m. pick up, $2,550; for a 6 p.m. pick up, $3,300. **Drop-in care available:** Yes. **Coverage over major holidays:** No. **Homework help:** Yes. **Snacks:** Provided. **Staff/student ratio:** 1:15. **After-school classes:** Classes (for K-8, all coed) have included Taekwando, Spanish, robotics, fencing, art, pee wee sports, drama, chess, gymnastics, cooking, yoga, SSAT preparation and debate club. Music lessons are also available. Cost: Varies; contact school.

Summer Programs

Classes are coeducational and designed for children entering grades K-8. Two 3-week sessions offered. The program includes academic enrichment, basic skills, technology, cooking, drama, art, sports, test preparation, counselor-in-training and a community service program. Extended care is available from 8-9 a.m. and from 4-6 p.m. **Cost:** Varies; contact school.

Parent Involvement

Parent/teacher communication: Conferences are scheduled twice yearly and as needed. Special scheduling needs are accommodated. Parents also utilize e-mail, the schools' web site, Thursday Notes and a monthly newsletter for K-4. **Participation requirements:** Parents are encouraged to volunteer for activities assisting with the Schools' annual fund raising activity auction/dinner and Saturday block party, creating gift items for the boutique and as well as assisting with phoning and mailings. Parents also volunteer to help on class field trips and in the school library. **Parent education programs offered?** Yes.

What Sets the School Apart From Others

"Among the oldest independent schools in California, Schools of the Sacred Heart are a part of a worldwide network of Sacred Heart Schools having their beginnings in the Society of the Sacred Heart founded in Paris in 1800. Our independent Catholic school draws on the rich tradition of Sacred Heart education worldwide, including strong intellectual challenge, faith development, social awareness and growth of the individual as a community member. Stuart Hall for Boys offers the benefits of single sex education in a coed environment and prepares boys to assume leadership responsibilities as intelligent, compassionate, self-confident and contributing members of society."

How Parents/Students Characterize School

Parent comment: "A top notch academic school that offers a nurturing and safe environment where the faculty really cares about the students."

Student comment: "My classes are fun and interesting and my teachers are really nice."

SYNERGY SCHOOL

1387 Valencia Street (at 25th St.) (Mission District)
San Francisco, CA 94110
(415) 567-6177   fax (415) 567-0607
www.synergy.pvt.k12.ca.us

Tammy Damon, Head of School, tammy@synergyschool.org
Elena Dillon, Director of Admission, elena@synergyschool.org

General

Coed K-8 day school. Founded in 1973. Independent. Nonprofit. **Member:** "Haven't applied." **Enrollment:** Approx. 185. **Average class size:** In K-3, 24 to 27 with 2 full teachers in each class; 20 in G4-5 with

1 teacher and 1 aide; 22 in middle school. **Accreditation:** "Haven't applied." **Endowment:** $1,235,000. **School year:** Sept.-June. **Instructional days:** 172. **School day:** 8:30 a.m. to 3 p.m.

Student Body

Ethnicity: 53% Caucasian (non-Latino), 15% African-American, 14% Asian, 11% Latino, 7% multi-racial.

Admission

Applications due: Jan. (call for date). **Application fee:** $50. **Application process:** Call to schedule a tour; applications are given out on the tour. **No. of applications:** Approx. 100. **No. of K spaces:** Six for young K (2-year kindergarten), 18 for K. **Percentage of K class made up of school's preschool class:** N/A. **Admission evaluation requirements for K:** Playdate, plus Synergy calls the child's preschool for a recommendation. **Other grades:** School visit, grades, recommendations. **Preferences:** Siblings. **What sort of student do you best serve?** "We have an inclusive community with many types of students."

Costs

Latest tuition: $10,900. **Sibling discount:** None. **Tuition includes:** Lunch: No; Transportation: No; Laptop computer: No; Other: Farm school trip and most field trips. **Tuition increases:** Approx. 6.9% annually. **Other costs:** Approx. $35 for middle school books, $130 for snow trip (financial aid available), and $20 for a yearbook. **Percentage of students receiving financial aid:** 33%. **Financial aid application deadline:** Jan. (call for date). Financial aid is based on need. **Average grant:** $4,400. **Percentage of grants of half-tuition or more:** 48%. **Donations:** Voluntary for annual fund; each family is required to solicit or give 2 auction item donations.

School's Mission Statement

"The mission of Synergy School is to provide a quality education by empowering children to flourish academically, to blossom as individuals, and to become self-confident, creative learners. The Synergy educational journey takes place in an environment based on encouragement, cooperation, mutual respect, and responsibility. Our approach inspires confidence and allows each child to work and develop at her/his own pace. An excellent teacher-student ratio helps each child feel known and valued and able to take personal risks. Education at Synergy is both challenging and joyful. Active, hands-on learning fosters each child's curiosity, critical thinking skills, and love of discovery. Strong conceptual foundations are built through challenging explorations in all academic subjects. A rich and varied curriculum is taught with the expectation that each child will strive for personal and academic excellence. At Synergy there is a commitment to developing global awareness and to learning to appreciate and honor differences both inside and outside the school community. We affirm the necessity of creating and sustaining a socially just, equitable environment which actively works against racism and all forms of bias. We accomplish these goals through ongoing curriculum development, teacher selection and training, and by actively recruiting a diverse student population. Synergy's approach to children's behavior is based on cooperation, logical and natural consequences, and the belief that we all have the ability to look at ourselves honestly, to change and to grow. The Agreement System is a vehicle through which our philosophy is expressed. It is a unifying force in the school and involves parents, staff, and children in a common goal: the creation of a supportive educational environment where children's enthusiasm for learning is fostered."

Academic Program

Philosophy: "Synergy is a progressive school, providing numerous opportunities for hands-on, project-based learning. We provide the skills and encouragement for students to become competent, independent, and enthusiastic learners throughout their lives. Academic skills are achieved with a non-competitive and cooperative atmosphere. Children work at their individual ability levels and pace, participating in whole class activities, small groups, and individual learning centers."
Foreign languages: Spanish. **Computer training:** Keyboarding, word processing, file sharing, photoshop elements, internet research, in G4-5. Middle school adds web design, yearbook design and production, more advanced research, multi–media, publisher, and spreadsheets. **No. of computers available for students:** In G4-8, 4 to 6 per classroom plus computers available in the library. **No. of hours weekly**

of: Art- "integrated into the curriculum on regular basis (students work with a fine arts specialist weekly); Drama- each class works intensively on 1 play per year; Music- 1.5; Computers- depends upon grade level, specific projects, etc.; Foreign language- ranges from 45 min. in K to 3 hours in middle school; PE- 1.5. **Outdoor education:** In G4-8, 1-2 weeks per year; students in K-5 have one overnight trip per year ranging from 1-3 nights. **Grading:** Non-graded skills checklist in K-5. Letter grades begin in G6. **Average nightly homework:** 30 min. in G1, increasing every year up to 2 hours in middle school. Posted on the Internet: For middle school. **Percentage of students participating in Johns Hopkins Center for Talented Youth Program:** N/A. (The school does not participate.) **Other indicators of academic success:** "The enthusiasm for learning demonstrated in so many ways by our students. Our students are welcomed enthusiastically by diverse high schools." **High schools attended by latest graduating class:** Lick, Urban, Drew, JCHS, SHCP, SI, Bay School, Lowell, Gateway, and CAT.

Faculty

Ethnicity: 53% Caucasian (non-Latino), 31% African-American, 11% Latino, 5% Asian. **Percentage of teachers with graduate degrees:** 16%. **Percentage with current California credential:** 75%. **Faculty selection/training:** Extensive interview process, experience in grade level and subject matter, philosophical match with the school, degree. **Teacher/student ratio:** 1:12 in K, 1:13 in G1-3, 1:15 in G4-5, 1:22 in middle school (not counting specialists). **Special subject teachers:** Art, music, PE, drama, Spanish, computers in middle school. **Average teacher tenure:** "8.5 years. This is little misleading because we doubled our teaching staff 6 years ago when we expanded. Seven of our teachers have been at the school for 9 to 27 years."

Middle School

Description: "Our middle school program (G6-8) remains committed to the goals set forth in our Mission Statement with particular emphasis on providing an optimum environment to meet the specific needs of younger adolescents within a supportive K-8 community of learners. Young people undergo more rapid and profound personal changes during the years between 10 and 15 than any other period of our lives. Synergy's program development and implementation recognizes that young adolescents require the following: a rigorous, challenging and engaging academic program; continued opportunities for concrete, experiential learning along with bridging to their growing capacity for more abstract thinking: a safe community in which to explore their growing sense of self; emphasis on problem solving and critical thinking skills; on-going education in and understanding of diversity and equity issues; service learning connected to real life issues and problems; leadership opportunities within the school community and beyond; regular physical fitness and health activities; an environment that encourages a lifelong love of learning and strong sense of community. Departmentalization commences in G6." **Teacher/student ratio:** 1:22 not including specialists. **Elective courses offered:** "Students have 6 elective courses per year. Four or 5 electives are offered each session. This year they have included: web design, swimming, community service, softball, astronomy, art of many types." **Achievement tracking in:** All subject areas. **Student social events:** Dances, parties.

Student Support Services

No. of Licensed Counselors on staff: None. **Counselor/student ratio:** N/A. **Learning specialists on staff:** One half-time. **Learning differences/disabilities support:** "We have an active parent/teacher Unique Learners Committee which provides support to parents and educational events. Synergy has been a pilot school for 4 years with California Pacific Medical Center's Learning Institute in implementing Mel Levine's 'Schools Attuned' philosophy. A minimum of one member of each teaching team is trained in this approach and receives regular mentoring." **High school placement support:** Regular meetings for parents and students with the High School Placement Counselor, weekly newsletter sent home during fall G8 with key dates and critical information to help parents stay organized through the process, application essay writing feedback, and practice interviews. SSAT preparation is offered on site.

Student Conduct and Health

Code of conduct: "The Agreement System is based on agreements that the students and teachers make with the school and must keep to be a part of the school. The six basic agreements of Synergy are: I agree to make Synergy a respectful learning community, free of bias, by: 1. keeping a safe place, without prejudices, for everyone's body and feelings; 2. respecting all property; 3. participating academically; 4. participating in all other school activities; 5. being in a designated space; 6. agreeing to leave quickly and quietly when waved out. (A wave out is a non-punitive, nonverbal reminder from a teacher to a student that his/her classroom behavior is not appropriate. Wave outs are used only after students are very clear about classroom expectations for behavior. After one wave out, a student has the opportunity to regroup and stay with the class; after a second wave out, the student must go to a different area to complete work.) This system helps eliminate time-consuming verbal interruptions during class. **Prevention education and awareness programs:** Programs on drug awareness and "sex ed" are offered through the regular classrooms at age appropriate levels. In middle school the advisory program brings in outside facilitators in addition to middle school teacher-advisors. In addition, Synergy uses several programs that address issues of bullying in an anti-bias curriculum.

Athletics

Sports offered: Cross-country, basketball. **Team play begins in:** G6 (intramural). There are many informal teams organized by parents for K-5 students in soccer, basketball and softball.

Campus/Campus Life

Campus description: "Bright airy building in the heart of the Mission." **Library:** On-site library with 5,000 volumes plus periodicals. The collection provides curriculum support and reading enhancement. K-5 classes visit the library weekly. **Sports facilities:** Outdoor basketball and volleyball courts on campus. The school also utilizes sports facilities in the neighborhood including Garfield Pool, City College's outdoor courts, and Precita and Dolores Park. **Theater/Arts facili-**

ties: A multipurpose room provides space for the whole school for class performances. Larger theatrical productions are performed at other sites in the neighborhood. The school has a dedicated art room with kiln. **Computer lab:** Computers are in the classrooms and library. **Science lab:** Yes. **Lunch program:** No. **Bus service:** No. **Uniforms/ dress code:** Dress code. **Opportunities for community service:** Middle school students work with the San Francisco Garden Project and have worked with neighborhood preschools. The choir performs for the senior center at a local church during the winter holidays and meets with the seniors.

Extended Day

Morning care: Begins at 7 a.m. **After-school care:** Until 6 p.m. **Grade levels:** K-8. **Cost:** $210/month for 5 days a week until 6 p.m.; $5/hour for drop in. **Drop-in care available:** Yes. **Coverage over major holidays:** Yes. **Homework help:** Yes. **Snacks:** Provided. **Staff/student ratio:** 1:13. **After-school classes:** Chess, yoga, art, dance, rocketry. **Cost:** Varies; contact school.

Summer Programs

The school offers two 4-week summer programs from 9 a.m.-3 p.m. Students entering K-5 have a wide range of classes in poetry, art, dance, science and sports coupled with weekly "Out and About" field trips. Students in G6-8 have classes in math, writing and study skills coupled with leadership training, field trips and community service activities. **Cost:** $600/session for 5 days/week; $480 for 3 days/week.

Parent Involvement

Parent/teacher communication: Scheduled conferences twice per year; teachers are available by phone, e-mail or additional conferences as needed. Regular weekly newsletter and website with current middle school homework posted. **Participation requirements:** Each family is asked to participate on a committee that organizes and runs one of two fundraising events or on a committee that provides a service to the school—library, yard, technology, etc. Each family is also asked to support the two fundraising events and one all-school clean up day. **Parent education programs offered?** Yes, based on parent interest.

What Sets the School Apart From Others

"Our teacher cooperative structure gives teachers a strong voice in what happens in their classroom and in the school as a whole. They are therefore very committed to and empowered within the school. This contributes to our low teacher turnover. The second factor is our approach to working with students around behavior. The Agreement System is based on logical and natural consequences for behavior and is used consistently throughout all classes in the school. A third factor is our combination classrooms which permit students and teachers to work together for two years and which create strong teaching teams. Finally, Synergy has an ongoing commitment to maintaining a diverse community which reflects the racial, economic and family structure diversity in San Francisco. This affects all aspects of our growth and development, from curriculum to admissions to hiring. We work hard to keep our tuition in the lowest 5% of Bay Area Independent Schools."

How Parents/Students Characterize School

Parent comment(s): "Synergy is more like a community than just a school—that whole families are often present and involved, in various ways, from the infant siblings being passed around in the hallways to the grandparents showing up at the school plays. For a private school, the families at Synergy are pretty diverse—in family structure and class as well as ethnic background." ◆ "I truly appreciate the teachers' commitment to the student as a whole person—not just an academic learner but a member of our society that they are mentoring, influencing and sharing ideas with there as well." ◆ "Synergy's academic program encourages creativity and critical thinking." ◆ "Synergy teachers excel at what they do because they are encouraged to be innovative in the classroom."

Student comment(s): "Synergy has built my confidence academically and socially." ◆ "At my old school the students weren't as enthusiastic about their work as they are here at Synergy. At my old school we had more homework, but I learn so much more here. We have more intellectual work instead of stressful and time-consuming work that we didn't get anything out of." ◆ "I'm in 8th grade and I've been here since kindergarten. Instead of being sick of the school, I'm sad to leave."

Town School for Boys

2750 Jackson Street (at Scott) (Pacific Heights)
San Francisco, CA 94115
(415) 921-3747   fax (415) 921-2968
www.townschool.com

W. Brewster Ely IV, Head of School, ely@townschool.com
Lynn McKannay, Director of Admission, mckannay@townschool.com

General

K-8 boys day school. Founded in 1939. Independent. Nonprofit. **Member:** NAIS, IBSC, CASE, CAIS, WASC, ERB, ISAL, POCIS, BADA. **Enrollment:** Approx. 400. **Average class size:** 22. **Accreditation:** WASC (term N/P). **Endowment:** $13 million. **School year:** Sept.-June. **Instructional days:** Approx. 176. **School day:** Begins at 8:30 a.m. for K-4 and 8:10 a.m. for G5-8. Dismissal times are staggered from 2 p.m. to 3:20 p.m.

Student Body

Ethnicity: N/P.

Admission

Applications due: Jan. (call for date). **Application fee:** $75. **Application process:** Families tour the school, meet the Headmaster and have an interview with the Director of Admission. **No. of applications:**

N/P. **No. of K spaces:** 44. **Percentage of K class made up of school's preschool class:** N/A. **Admission evaluation requirements for K:** Play date at the school and recommendations from preschool. **Other grades:** Full-day visit, recommendation and records from current school and testing, if appropriate. **Preferences:** N/P. **What sort of student do you best serve?** N/P.

Costs
Latest tuition: $17,950. **Sibling discount:** None. **Tuition includes:** Lunch: No; Transportation: No; Laptop computer: Families purchase laptop computers in G5; Other: N/P. **Tuition increases:** N/P. **Other costs:** Approx. $300 for activity fees. **Percentage of students receiving financial aid:** N/P. **Financial aid application deadline:** Feb. (call for date). Financial aid is based on need. **Average grant:** N/P. **Percentage of grants of half-tuition or more:** N/P. **Donations:** Voluntary.

School's Mission Statement
"Town School for Boys is committed to educational excellence. We encourage each student to strive for high academic achievement and to fulfill his individual potential. The school fosters personal development and the values of integrity, citizenship and respect for others. Our school values a diverse and inclusive school community. The school's programs balance academic effort, social interaction, physical activity and artistic expression in a stimulating and caring environment. As an all boys school, we design our programs to address the distinctive developmental styles and energy levels of boys."

Academic Program
Philosophy: N/P. **Foreign languages:** Spanish, French, Latin. **Computer training:** Training in Lower School and families purchase laptop computers in G5. **No. of computers available for students:** N/P. **No. of hours weekly of:** N/P. **Outdoor education:** N/P. **Grading:** A–F, beginning in G5. **Average nightly homework:** N/P. Posted on the Internet: Yes. **Percentage of students participating in Johns Hopkins Center for Talented Youth Program:** N/P. **Other indicators of academic success:** N/P. **High schools attended by latest graduating

class: Bay School, Branson, Cate, Lick, Lowell, MA, Middlesex, Proctor Academy, SI, University, and Urban.

Faculty
Ethnicity: N/P. **Percentage of teachers with graduate degrees:** N/P. **Percentage with current California credential:** N/P. **Faculty selection/training:** N/P. **Teacher/student ratio:** 1:11. **Special subject teachers:** Art, music, drama, science, digital photography, and woodworking. **Average teacher tenure:** N/P.

Middle School
Description: "The goals of the Upper School are designed to provide a challenging, enriching, and effective education for the fifth through eighth grader. Building on the skills taught in the K-4 division of the School, the curriculum is designed to develop competency while emphasizing the academic and character developmental needs of the students. In order to develop independence and responsibility, students are no longer taught in self-contained classrooms." **Teacher/student ratio:** 1:11 and some classes smaller. **Elective courses offered:** Drama, woodshop, bells, introduction to digital design, Lego Logo, and digital photography. **Achievement tracking in:** N/P. **Student social events:** N/P.

Student Support Services
No. of Licensed Counselors on staff: One full-time. **Counselor/student ratio:** N/P. **Learning specialists on staff:** Two. **Learning differences/disabilities support:** N/P. **High school placement support:** Yes.

Student Conduct and Health
Code of conduct: "Students in the Town School for Boys community are expected to show respect, courtesy, kindness, and consideration for others. Each individual is expected to act with regard for the safety and welfare of others." **Prevention education and awareness addressed in:** Part of the curriculum.

Athletics

Sports offered: Cross-country, soccer, basketball, baseball, and lacrosse. **Team play begins in:** Intermural play begins in K and intramural play begins in G5.

Campus/Campus Life

Campus description: The school has a 60,000 sq. ft. building with classrooms and offices, gym, library and media center, computer lab, science lab, art studio, music rooms, dining room, performing arts theater, and a woodworking shop. **Library:** "18,000 print volumes." **Sports facilities:** The school currently leases Morton Field in the Presidio. **Theater/Arts facilities:** Yes. **Computer lab:** Yes. **Science lab:** Yes. **Lunch program:** Yes. **Bus service:** No. **Uniforms/dress code:** "No uniform but dress code." **Opportunities for community service:** "The goal of community service at Town School for Boys is to provide opportunities for boys to actively contribute to and enrich the broader community in which they live. Opportunities are available at each grade level."

Extended Day

Morning care: N/P. **After-school care:** Until 6 p.m. **Grade levels:** All. **Cost:** Varies; contact school. **Drop-in care available:** Available with sufficient notice. **Coverage over major holidays:** Yes. **Homework help:** Yes. **Snacks:** Provided. **Staff/student ratio:** N/P. **After-school classes:** Lego engineering, language, video, cartooning, cooking, chess, roller hockey, lacrosse, Tree Frog Treks Science, and fencing. **Cost:** Varies; contact school.

Summer Programs

The school offers three 2-week sessions of Town Tiger Camp, a coed camp offering a variety of courses and activities. **Cost:** $325/session.

Parent Involvement

Parent/teacher communication: Conferences, website, Wednesday packet, e-mail, newsletter and any other communication upon request. **Participation requirements:** "No required hours." **Parent education programs offered?** Yes.

What Sets the School Apart From Others

"Where boys come first, learning is prized, and love of school is essential."

How Parents/Students Characterize School

Parent comment(s): "I love shaking the Headmaster's hand each day, walking through the halls, seeing the smiles, the engagement and hearing the laughter."

Student comment(s): "Town's awesome!"

WEST PORTAL LUTHERAN SCHOOL

Grades Kindergarten - 3
3101 Moraga Street (at 37th Avenue) (Sunset)
San Francisco, CA 94122

Grades 4 - 8
200 Sloat Blvd (at 19th Avenue) (Lakeshore/Lakeside)
San Francisco, CA 94132
(415) 665-6330 *fax* (415) 242-8876
www.westportallutheran.org

Margaret Finley, Head of School and Director of Admission

General

Coed K-8 day school. Founded in 1951. Lutheran. Nonprofit. **Member:** N/P. **Enrollment:** Approx. 515. **Average class size:** 30. **Accreditation:** WASC/NLSA (6 year term: 2004-10). **Endowment:** N/P. **School year:** Sept.-June. **Instructional days:** 180. **School day:** 8:30 a.m. to 2:45 p.m. for K, 8:30 a.m. to 3 p.m. for G1-3, 8:30 a.m. to 3:15 p.m. for G4-8.

Student Body

Ethnicity: N/P.

Admission

Applications due: Open except for K, which are due in January (call for date). **Application fee:** $50. **Application process:** Parents attend an open house; application packets are provided at the open house. **No. of applications:** N/P. **No. of K spaces:** 60. **Percentage of K class made up of school's preschool class:** N/A. **Admission evaluation requirements for K:** Preschool recommendation. **Other grades:** School visit, grades, test scores. **Preferences:** West Portal Lutheran Church members; siblings. **What sort of student do you best serve?** "Those who desire a Christian environment of nurturing and are motivated to learn and value an education highly."

Costs

Latest tuition: $5,373 for K, $5,148 for G1-8. **Sibling discount:** N/P. **Tuition includes:** Lunch: No; Transportation: No; Laptop computer: No; Other: N/P. **Tuition increases:** Approx. 3.5-4% annually. **Other costs:** N/P. **Percentage of students receiving financial aid:** N/P. **Financial aid application deadline:** N/P. Financial aid is based on N/P. **Average grant:** N/P. **Percentage of grants of half tuition or more:** N/P. **Donations:** N/P.

School's Mission Statement

"By the grace of God, West Portal Lutheran Church operates a Christian Day School in our Evangelical Lutheran tradition. Our goals: to offer a high-quality academic experience; to nurture and help each child grow as a whole, happy, and healthy person; to minister to the spiritual, moral, educational, interpersonal, cultural, and physical needs of each child; to strive to touch the hearts and lives of the families of the children in a caring, Gospel context."

Academic Program

Philosophy: N/P. **Foreign languages:** Spanish or German in G7-8. **Computer training:** G1-8. **No. of computers available for students:** 15 in the computer lab. **No. of hours weekly of:** Art- N/P; Drama- N/P; Music- 45 min.; Computers- 45 min.; Foreign language- daily (G7-8); PE- 90 min. **Outdoor education:** N/P. **Grading:** A-F, beginning in G3. **Average nightly homework:** 15-30 min. for K; 30 min. for G1; 45 min. for G2; less than 60 min. for G3; up to 60 min. for G4-5; 2 hrs. for G6-8. **Posted on the Internet:** No. **Percentage of students participating in Johns Hopkins Center for Talented Youth Program:** N/P. **Other indicators of academic success:** N/P. **High schools attended by latest graduating class:** Lowell, Mercy-SF, SI, SHCP, Riordan, CSH, Lick, Stuart Hall, and SOTA, "as well as other public and private schools on the Peninsula and in San Francisco."

Faculty

Ethnicity: N/P. **Percentage of teachers with graduate degrees:** N/P. **Percentage with current California credential:** "N/P but all of our teachers hold a teaching credential. Some have both the Lutheran and State credentials. Some have Masters degrees." **Faculty selection/training:** N/P. **Teacher/student ratio:** N/P. **Special subject teachers:** N/P. **Average teacher tenure:** N/P.

Middle School

Description: G7-8, departmentalized. **Teacher/student ratio:** 1:30. **Elective courses offered:** Foreign language in G 7-8; art, humanities, and public speaking in G8. **Achievement tracking in:** N/P. **Student social events:** N/P.

Student Support Services

No. of Licensed Counselors on staff: One part-time. **Counselor/student ratio:** N/P. **Learning specialists on staff:** N/P. **Learning differences/disabilities support:** N/P. **High school placement support:** A meeting is held for parents in G6-7 in the spring, G8 in the fall. Private meetings are held with the principal.

Student Conduct and Health

Code of conduct: " Very strict, but loving and nurturing in a Christian environment." **Prevention education and awareness addressed in:** Drugs are addressed. In G6-8, awareness of the body from a Christian perspective is also addressed.

Athletics

Sports offered/team play begins in: Soccer, basketball, baseball for boys; volleyball and basketball for girls. Instructional play for basketball and volleyball begins in G3 and league play begins in G4.

Campus/Campus Life

Campus description: "A safe and secure environment for academic learning." **Library:** One on each campus. A librarian is on campus weekly. **Sports facilities:** Each campus site has a gym. **Theater/Arts facilities:** N/P. **Computer lab:** Yes. **Science lab:** Yes. **Lunch program:** No. **Bus service:** No. **Uniforms/dress code:** Uniforms. **Opportunities for community service:** Junior High school students have the opportunity to do community service hours in conjunction with the Church community.

Extended Day

Morning care: Begins at 7 a.m. **After-school care:** Until 6 p.m. **Grade levels:** K-8. **Cost:** Approx. $3/hr. **Drop-in care available:** Yes. **Coverage over major holidays:** No. **Homework help:** Yes. **Snack:** Provided. **Staff/student ratio:** 1:20. **After-school classes:** Art, music (orchestra, choral, handbells, instrumental), Mandarin. Cost: Varies; contact school.

Summer Programs

The school offers a 4-week summer school. The morning academic program (8:30 a.m.-12:15 p.m.) includes 1 hour of reading, 1 hour of mathematics, and 1 hour of language arts. The afternoon recreation program (1-4 p.m.) includes age-appropriate field trips, movies, playground activities, on/off campus activities, music, and arts and crafts. Before school care is available starting at 7 a.m. After-school care is available until 6 p.m. **Cost:** N/P.

Parent Involvement

Parent/teacher communication: Parent/teacher conferences are held twice a year; mid-quarter and quarterly grades are given; newsletters, Principal's Notes, and notices are distributed. **Participation require-**

ments: 20 hours of volunteer work for families with 1 student; 30 hours for families with 2+ students. **Parent education programs offered?:** At some Parent Teacher League meetings.

What Sets the School Apart From Others

"West Portal Lutheran School has been in existence since 1951. We are a multi-cultural, Christian, highly academic, traditional school. We value the partnership that has developed between the church, home, and school and strive to maintain open lines of communication. In developing our curriculum, we strive to educate the spiritual, academic and physical aspects of our students. Our students, upon graduation, are accepted into the most desired high schools in San Francisco and the Upper Peninsula. We treasure each student for his/her abilities and work with our families to provide the best education possible so that each child may reach his/her potential and become a productive member of society. Respect for individual differences and tolerance for all cultures are important aspects in the curriculum."

How Parents/Students Characterize School: N/P.

Zion Lutheran Day School

495 Ninth Ave. (between Anza and Geary) (Inner Richmond Dist.)
San Francisco, CA 94116
(415) 221-7500   fax (415) 221-7141
www.zionsf.org

Carolyn J. Grundt, Head of School and Director of Admission,
cgrundt@zionsf.org

General

Coed K-8 day school. Founded in 1946. Lutheran. Nonprofit. **Member:** Lutheran Church, Missouri Synod. **Enrollment:** Approx. 200. **Average class size:** 25. **Accreditation:** WASC/NLSA (6-year term: 2000-06). **Endowment:** N/P. **School year:** Late Aug.-June. **Instructional days:** 180. **School day:** 8:30 a.m. to 3 p.m.

Student Body

Ethnicity: 65% Asian, 15% multi-racial, 12% Caucasian (non-Latino), 5% Latino, 3% African-American.

Admission

Applications due: Jan. (call for date). **Application fee:** $30. **Application process:** Call for appointment, receive individual tour and application at that time. **No. of applications:** 60. **No. of K spaces:** 25. **Percentage of K class made up of school's preschool class:** N/A. **Admission evaluation requirements for K:** Must be 5 years old before Dec. 2nd of entering school year. **Other grades:** Provide copy of most recent report card, SAT scores, and one-day visit to the school. **Preferences:** Siblings and church members are automatic enrollments. **What sort of student do you best serve?** "Although we cannot serve the child with special education needs, we serve the children and community around us."

Costs

Latest tuition: $6,000. **Sibling discount:** $1,000 per year for the 3rd child in the family. **Tuition includes:** Lunch: No; Transportation: No; Laptop computer; No. **Tuition increases:** Approx. 4% annually. **Other costs:** Approx. $300 uniforms, $250-350 for Outdoor Education in G6-8. **Percentage of students receiving financial aid:** 6%. **Financial aid application deadline:** N/P. Financial aid is based on need. **Average grant:** N/P. **Percentage of grants of half-tuition or more:** N/P. **Donations:** N/P.

School's Mission Statement

"The school's goals are that students will be 'Active Christians who develop and maintain beliefs and behaviors rooted in the Bible; develop the values of love, kindness, patience, forgiveness, self-discipline, responsibility, friendship, compassion, courage perseverance, honesty, loyalty, and faith in the Triune God; become an active and effective member of church and effective member of the church and community; display a strong sense of Christian community and commitment to serving others; cultural empowered youth who recognize and affirm the dignity and worth of all; understand and appreciate ethnic and cultural diversity; learn from and co-exist with the diverse people in our changing world; healthy individuals who use communications skills to promote adaptability, integration, friendliness and politeness; recognize the benefits of fitness and wellness; display good sportsmanship; academically proficient learners who have mastered essential skills in reading, writing, speaking, spelling and listening; have developed math, science, social science, art, music and technological literacy; research, organize, and use information; demonstrate the ability to reason and think critically; strive to be creative and productive; demonstrate the ability to solve problems; and score at or above grade level norms on annual standardized achievement tests.'"

Academic Program

Philosophy: "Our curriculum follows and expands upon the curriculum required by the state of California and the Core Knowledge Sequence for Lutheran Elementary Schools. Our graduates and transfers are gladly accepted into parochial, private, and public schools. The curriculum subjects are Religion, Reading, Spelling, Language Arts, Creative Writing, English Grammar and Mechanics, History and Geography, Science, Math, Computer Technology, Art, Music and Physical Education. Special subjects are added depending upon the grade level." **Foreign languages:** Spanish beginning in G6. **Computer training:** Computer classes begin in K with students going to the computer lab for 1 hour a week. **No. of computers available for students:** "In the computer lab, one per student; in addition, each classroom has computers." **No. of hours weekly of:** Art- 1; Drama- 1; Music (jr high)- 1-1.5 and 1 hr. of choir; Computers- 1; Foreign language- 2 (G6-8); PE- 1-1.5. **Outdoor education:** G5-8. **Grading:** A-F, beginning in G3. Posted on the Internet: No. **Average nightly homework:** .5 to 1 hr. in K-2; 1-2.5 hrs. in G3-5; 2.5-4 hrs. in G6-8. **Percentage of students participating in Johns Hopkins Center for Talented Youth Program:** N/A. **Other indicators of academic success:** "Ninth grade surveys indicate that our school is accomplishing its goals. Of this year's 8th grade class, 14 applied to Lowell High School and 11 were admitted." **High schools attended by latest graduating class:** Lowell, SI, SHCP, Mercy-SF, SOTA, Urban, Lick, Lincoln, and Washington.

Faculty

Ethnicity: 80% Caucasian (non-Latino), 10% Asian, 5% African-American, 5% other. **Percentage of teachers with graduate degrees:** 45%. **Percentage with current California credential:** "100% with State Certification." **Faculty selection/training:** BA and MA. **Teacher/student ratio:** 1:25 in G1-8, 1:12.5 in K. **Special subject teachers:** Spanish, computer, PE. **Average teacher tenure:** 14 years.

Middle School

Description: G6-8, departmentalized. **Teacher/student ratio:** 1:25. **Elective courses offered:** Art and music appreciation, performing arts, choir, handbells. **Achievement tracking in:** All subject areas. A high school level algebra class is also offered to eighth graders who display high achievement in math. **Student social events:** Youth group events, dances, community service involvement.

Student Support Services

No. of Licensed Counselors on staff: N/P. **Counselor/student ratio:** N/A. **Learning specialists on staff:** N/P. **Learning differences/disabilities support:** Private tutoring is available after school. An after-school homework center is offered twice a week (for an additional fee). If necessary, recommendations are made to obtain outside evaluations and support. **High school placement support:** The principal conducts high school information night each fall.

Student Conduct and Health

Code of conduct: "Students will show respect toward all staff members and each other." **Prevention education and awareness addressed in:** Life Issue Classes.

Athletics

Sports offered: Basketball and volleyball for G5-8; all-school track meet in the spring. **Team play begins:** N/P.

Campus/Campus Life

Campus description: The school has two buildings. The main building houses the church, Parish Hall, K-6 classrooms, offices, and a gym. The

Jr. High Building includes G7-8 classrooms and a computer lab/media center. **Outdoor facilities:** The school has a fenced yard with a play structure, as well as an outdoor basketball court. **Library:** "Numerous print volumes located in each classroom." **Sports facilities:** Gym and outdoor basketball court. **Theater/Arts facilities:** N/P. **Computer lab:** 50 computers for student use, 15 with internet access. **Science lab:** N/P. **Lunch program:** Hot lunches may be purchased in advance ($4 each) for the school year. **Bus service:** No. **Uniforms/dress code:** Uniforms. **Opportunities for community service:** N/P.

Extended Day

Morning care: Begins at 7 a.m. **After-school care:** Until 6 p.m. **Cost:** $2/day for morning; $10/day for after-school. Late pick up after 6 p.m. is $15/per day per child. **Grade level:** N/P. **Drop-in care available:** As needed at the same rates as extended care. **Coverage over major holidays:** No. **Homework help:** Students are encouraged to do their homework each day while in extended care but it is not mandatory. **Snacks:** N/P. **Staff/student ratio:** N/P. **After-school classes:** Program offerings such as arts/crafts, cooking, music and games. Older students may attend study hall. Academic Chess on Mondays. **Cost:** N/P.

Summer Programs

The school offers a 4-6 week Summer Enrichment Program as well as a one-week Vacation Bible School. The programs are open to all. **Cost:** $100/week for the Enrichment Program and $20/week for Vacation Bible School. Extended care is available for an additional fee.

Parent Involvement

Parent/teacher communication: Two mandatory conferences during the first two quarters, voluntary after that. **Participation requirements:** Twenty five hours of volunteer time are required (field trips, Wednesday Lunch helpers, spring musical helpers, etc.) to receive a $200 reimbursement on the Parent Volunteer fee of $300. Last year, 68% of parents volunteered. **Parent education programs:** Sunday morning Bible classes deal with parenting issues. Parent Teacher League (PTL) sponsors guest speakers for discussions.

What sets school away from others?

"Although we are a high academic school, we are first and foremost a Christian school, seeking a nurturing Christ-centered community."

How Parents/Students Characterize School

Parent comment(s): "Zion is a loving, caring place where children are educated both mentally and spiritually."

Student comment(s): "I like a small class where I can ask lots of questions. My school is like a big family."

ADDITIONAL PRIVATE SCHOOLS

The schools listed below were not included in the front of the book for various reasons, the most common being that they chose not to provide all of the information requested or didn't provide it by the publication deadline.

SAN FRANCISCO

Ecole Notre Dame des Victoires

659 Pine Street (at Stockton) (Chinatown/Financial District)
San Francisco, CA 94108
(415) 421-0069
www.ndvsf.org

Mary K. Ghisolfo, Principal, principal@ndvsf.org
Coed K-8 parochial day school. Founded in 1924. Catholic. Nonprofit. **Latest tuition:** $5,880 plus fees of $800 in K-3 and $400 in G4-8. **Mission Statement:** "We embrace the values of the Marists and the Sisters of St. Joseph of Orange and continue our tradition of teaching the French language and culture. As a faith-filled community, the faculty and staff of NDV are committed to nurturing our students spiritually, academically, socially, and physically. We support a diverse group of learners who endeavor to develop an inclusive and compassionate world vision." **Foreign languages:** French. **Outdoor education:** G6 in Yosemite. **Sports offered:** Soccer, basketball, volleyball, cross-country,

track. **Team play begins in:** G3. **Sports facilities:** Gymnasium. **The-ater/Arts facilities:** Yes. **Extended day:** Until 6 p.m.

Hillwood Academic Day School

2521 Scott Street (at Broadway) (Pacific Heights/Cow Hollow)
San Francisco, CA 94115
(415) 931-0400
www.hillwoodschool.com

Mr. Eric Grantz, Head of School, ericgrantz@yahoo.com
Coed K-8 day school. Founded in 1949. Proprietary. **School year:** Sept.-June. **School day:** 9 a.m. to 3 p.m. **Latest tuition:** $500/month, $5,000/year. **Mission Statement:** "Beginning in kindergarten and con-tinuing through our junior high, it is our goal to guide our students in developing their skills and talents to the best of their individual abili-ties. We create a student-centered learning environment in which stu-dents are challenged to think critically, exhibit creativity, communicate effectively, and educated to become life-long learners. With much dedi-cation and encouragement, it is our hope for our students to graduate Hillwood having acquired a foundation and the confidence in which to build a future." **Extended day:** Morning care from 7:30 a.m.; after-school care to 6 p.m. **Summer programs:** July camp. Uniforms.

Holy Trinity Orthodox School

999 Brotherhood Way (at 19th Ave.) (Lake Shore/Park Merced)
San Francisco, CA 94132
(415) 584-8451
www.holytrinitysf.org

Father Michael Pappas, Principal
Coed K-8 Orthodox day school. Founded in 1971. Independent. Religious. **Enrollment:** Approx. 40. **Average class size:** 8-10. **School year:** Sept.-June. **Applications due:** Ongoing. **Application fee:** $50. **Application process:** Call church for appointment. **No. of K spaces:** 15. **Latest tuition:** $3,550 for new students, $3,350 for returning students. **Sibling discount:** Yes (amount N/P). **School's Mission**

Statement: "Holy Trinity Orthodox School provides children with the educational and social tools to make learning, critical thinking, questioning and creating into enjoyments of a lifetime." **Foreign languages:** Greek. **Summer program:** None.

Megan Furth Academy at Sacred Heart/St. Dominic

Grades K-4
2445 Pine Street (at Steiner) (Western Addition/Pacific Heights)
San Francisco, CA 94115
(415) 346-9500 *fax (415) 346-8001*

Grades 5-8
735 Fell Street (between Webster and Fillmore) (Western Addition)
San Francisco, CA 94117
(415) 621-8035
www.shsdschool.org

Norma Dahnken, Principal
Savita Sahi Roberts, Director of Admission
Coed K-8 parochial day school. Catholic. **Enrollment:** Approx. 175. **Average class size:** Approx. 20. **Accreditation:** WASC/WCEA. **Latest tuition:** $3,000 per child (+ fees). **Mission Statement:** "We strive for each child to become self-motivated toward individual excellence, reflected in community service and participation as lifelong contributing citizens." **Uniforms. Extended day:** Until 6 p.m. Cost is included in tuition.

Our Lady of the Visitacion School

795 Sunnydale Avenue (at Sawyer) (Visitacion Valley)
San Francisco, CA 94134
(415) 239-7840 *fax (415) 239-2559*
www. Olvisitacion.com

Sister Chris Maggi, DC, Principal, visitacionsf@yahoo.com
Coed K-8 parochial day school. Founded in 1964. Catholic. **Enroll-**

ment: Approx. 241. **Average class size:** Approx. 27. **Accreditation:** WASC/WCEA. **Latest tuition:** $3,900. **Mission Statement:** "It is the mission of Our Lady of the Visitacion School to provide its diverse student population with the educational opportunities for academic achievement that are necessary to fulfill the basic Archdiocesan elementary curriculum requirements for entrance into secondary school. All learning experiences are fostered within a faith community that has as its model the person and Gospel of Jesus Christ. Animated by the spirit of St. Vincent de Paul, St. Louise de Marillac and St. Elizabeth Ann Seton, education and teaching are seen as the vision of service that manifests the daughters of Charity's consecration to God, to the Church and to the Community and the vision of service (Philosophy of Education, Daughters of Charity, Western Province)." **Uniforms. Extended day.**

St. Anthony Immaculate Conception

200 Precita Ave. (at Shotwell) (Bernal Heights/Mission)
Francisco, CA 94110
(415) 648-2008 *fax (415) 648-1825*
www.saicsf.org

Sister Carolyn Marie Monehan, O.P., Principal, scmarie@saicsf.org
Coed K-8 parochial day school. Catholic. Nonprofit. **Enrollment:** Approx. 242. **Applications due:** Rolling. **Latest tuition:** $4,000 for participating families, $4,368 for non-participating.

St. Brendan School

940 Laguna Honda Blvd. (at Portola)(Twin Peaks)
San Francisco, CA 94127
(415) 731-2665 *fax (415) 731-7207*
www.stbrendansf.com

Sister Diane Erbacher, O.P., Principal, srdiane@stbrendansf.com
Coed K-8 parochial day school. Founded in 1947. Catholic. Nonprofit. **Enrollment:** Approx. 340. **School year:** Aug.-June. **Latest tuition:** $4,000 for participating parishioners, $4,200 for non-participating.

Saint Charles Borromeo School

3250 18th St. (btwn. Shotwell and South Van Ness)(Mission Dist.)
San Francisco, CA 94110
(415) 861-7652 fax (415) 861-0221
www.sfstcharlesschool.org

Sister Bankal, Principal, smcbancal@sfstcharlesschool.org
Coed K-8 parochial day school. Founded in 1894. Catholic. Nonprofit. **Application fee:** $40. **Latest tuition:** $3,400 for 1 child, $4,400 for 2, $5,400 for three. **Sibling discount:** See above. **Other costs:** $350 Registration fee. Financial aid is based on need. Faculty includes Dominican Sisters. Americorps volunteers work as teaching assistants. **Learning differences/disabilities support:** Remedial math and reading instructors. Title 1 funding for special needs students. Other: Tutoring with USF students and mentoring program with SOMA Scholars of UC Berkeley. **Team sports:** Basketball beginning in G4. Interactive digital library. Computer lab. Lunch program. **Uniforms.** **Extended day:** "Available." **Parent Participation:** 40 parent volunteer hours required for 2 parent families. **What sets school apart from others:** "We provide safe, caring and family-oriented environment."

St. Elizabeth School

450 Somerset Street (btwn. Bacon and Wayland) (Excelsior District)
San Francisco, CA 94134
(415) 468-3247 fax (415) 468-1804
www.stelizabethsf.org

Gena Babdoub, Principal
Coed K-8 parochial day school. Founded in 1949. Catholic. Nonprofit. **Accreditation:** WASC/WCEA. **Application fee:** $30. **Application process:** Application form, birth certificate, and baptismal certificate if applicable. **Admission evaluation requirements for K:** Testing, teacher recommendations. **Other grades:** Testing, previous report cards. **Latest tuition:** $3,840 for active parishioners, $4,730 for inactive/non-parishioner. **Sibling discount:** Yes, 53%. **Other costs:** $330 registration fee. **Donations:** "Mandatory participation in scrip, raffle

calendars, service hours, festival pledge, entertainment book." **Mission Statement:** "The mission of St. Elizabeth School is to form young disciples of Christ through a Gospel-oriented, contemporary, catholic education marked by a spiritually-vibrant, academically-rich, and emotionally-nurturing environment, which encourages students to realize their intellectual potential and to lead moral lives of service to others." **Academic philosophy:** "The students of St. Elizabeth School are children of God, all possessing unique gifts. We believe that through the education of our students, we celebrate their uniqueness as they are called to the mission of Jesus. The administration, faculty, and staff in partnership with the parents, help to form the spiritual, moral, social, and intellectual development of our students. Through the education at St. Elizabeth School, students realize their potential to be life-long agents of change in society." **Campus description:** St. Elizabeth School has 9 classrooms, 3 resource rooms, a library, administrative offices, a faculty room, an auditorium with a stage, a special education room, daycare area, kitchen, and a gymnasium. **Extended day:** Morning care from 7 a.m.; after-school care until 6 p.m. **Grade levels:** K-8. **Parent Participation requirements:** 40 volunteer hours each year for 2-parent families and 20 for single parent families.

St. Finn Barr School

419 Hearst Avenue (near Monterey Blvd.)(Outer Mission District)
San Francisco, CA 94112
(415) 333-1800
www.stfinnbarr.org

Thomas Dooher, Principal, tdooher@stfinnbarr.org
Coed K-8 parochial day school. Founded in 1962. Catholic. Nonprofit. **Accreditation:** WASC/WCEA. **School day:** 7:55 a.m. to 3 p.m. **Applications due:** Rolling. **Latest tuition:** $4,400 for contributing families, $5,150 for non-contributing. **Mission Statement:** "We are dedicated to meeting the needs of the whole child, embracing his or her potential to become an independent thinker and productive member of society in accordance with gospel values and Catholic tradition." **Academic program:** "Integrated music, drama, art, and choir

program." **Uniforms. Extended day:** Until 6 p.m. After-school Spanish classes available.

St. Stephen School

401 Eucalyptus Drive (at 22nd Avenue) (Lakeshore)
San Francisco, CA 94132
(415) 664-8331 *fax (415) 242-5608*
www.st-stephen.org

Sharon Allen, Principal
Coed K-8 parochial day school. Founded in 1952. Catholic. **Enrollment:** 310. **Average class size:** 35. **Accreditation:** WASC/WCEA. **Latest tuition:** For participating families, $4,080 for 1 child, $6,095 for 2, and $8,450 for 3; for non-participating, $4,470 for 1 child, $7,600 for 2, and $9,480 for 3. **Mission Statement:** "It is the mission of St. Stephen School community to educate children in a nurturing faith filled environment that addresses the whole child, spiritually and intellectually. We believe that it is our mission to provide students with an opportunity to grow in their relationship with God as they pursue academic excellence. As we enter the next millennium, students in this community are encouraged to be mindful of the dignity of all persons, and to actively work for peace and justice in the world. Instructional programs designed to reflect the Gospel teachings of Jesus Christ prepare students to become caring, responsible members of society who are committed to working within their diverse community and the global society." **Uniforms. Extended day:** Until 5:45 p.m.

St. Thomas More School

St. Thomas More Way (at Brotherhood Way) (Lakeshore)
San Francisco, CA 94132
(415) 337-0100 *fax (415) 452-9653*
www.stthomasmoreschool.org

Joe Elsbernd, Principal
Coed K-8 Archdiocesan day school. Catholic. **Philosophy statement:** "Catholic education is intended to make one's faith become living,

conscious and active through the light of instruction. It is the unique setting within which this ideal can be realized in the lives of Catholic children and young people. ... As Catholic educators, we at St. Thomas More School hold as primary: belief in God, Christ, Church, the value of the human person and commitment to a mission of service, that every person as a child of God has equal dignity and an inalienable right to an education. ...That parents have the primary responsibility for the education of their children. Therefore ... we support, enhance and complement this role." **Uniforms. Extended day:** Until 6 p.m.

St. Thomas the Apostle School

3801 Balboa Street (at 39th Avenue) (Outer Richmond)
San Francisco, CA 94121
(415) 221-2711 *fax (415) 221-8611*
www.stthomasapostle.k12.ca.us

Thomas Lambre, Principal
Coed K-8 parochial day school. Catholic. **Enrollment:** Approx. 307. **Average class size:** 34. **Mission Statement:** "St. Thomas the Apostle School is dedicated to making Christ a vital part of the lives of its students by providing a strong Catholic/Christian community, a solid doctrinal foundation in the Catholic tradition, academic excellence, and an environment in which each child, respected and valued as a unique individual, is encouraged to achieve his/her full potential. In community with the parents, the primary educators, all school personnel respond to this challenge by providing a Christ-centered atmosphere and opportunities in which the dignity and worth of each child is valued and respected by all." **Uniforms. Extended day:** Until 6 p.m.

Sts. Peter and Paul Elementary School

632-666 Filbert Street (at Washington Square) (North Beach)
San Francisco, CA 94133
(415) 421-5219 *fax (415) 421-1831*
www.stpeterpaul.san-francisco.ca.us

Lisa Harris, Principal
Coed PreK-8 parochial day school. Catholic. Founded in 1925. **Enrollment:** 280. **Accreditation:** WASC/WCEA. **Latest tuition:** For participating families, $4,675 for 1 child, $9,350 for 2, and $14,025 for 3; for non-participating, $5,675 for 1 child, $10,350 for 2, and $15,025 for 3. **Uniforms. Extended day:** Until 6 p.m.

San Francisco Adventist School

66 Geneva Ave. (at Mission) (Outer Mission)
San Francisco, CA 94112
(415) 585-5550 *fax (415) 585-4155*
www.sfja.org

Rob Robinson, Principal, office@sfja.org
Co-ed K-8 day school. Founded in 1912. Seventh Day Adventist. Nonprofit. **Accreditation:** National Council for Private School Accreditation, the North American Division of Seventh-day Adventists, and the Pacific Union Conference of Seventh-day Adventists. **School year:** Aug.-June. **School day:** 8 a.m. to 2:15 p.m. for K, 8 a.m. to 3:30 p.m. for G7-8. Applications accepted year-round. **Application process:** The family interviews with the principal and presents achievement/grade report info. The child is interviewed and has basic testing with the classroom teacher. **What sort of student do you best serve?** "San Francisco Adventist School is open to young people who desire a Christian education. Only students and families who support the principles of conduct of Christian education, to grow physically, mentally, and spiritually, and wish to contribute to the development of a Christian community should apply. The school will not knowingly admit or retain those who are not in harmony with these principals." **Latest tuition:** $3,070-$4,960. Financial aid and scholarships are available. **Mission statement:** "The mission of San Francisco Adventist School is to provide a learning environment that fosters a growing Christian experience in each child and also nurtures and encourages optimum cognitive, physical, social, emotional, spiritual, and creative development in each child, that will result in increased personal self-esteem needed for a happy, productive life." **Extended day.**

School of the Epiphany

600 Italy Street (near Geneva) (Excelsior)
San Francisco, CA 94112
(415) 337-4030 *fax* (415) 337-8583
www.sfepiphany.org

Diane Elkins, Principal
Coed K-8 parochial day school. Catholic. Founded in 1938. **Enrollment:** Approx. 635. **Average class size:** Approx. 33. **Accreditation:** WASC/WCEA. **Latest tuition:** For participating Catholics, $3,825 for 1 child, $6,925 for 2, and $10,219 for 3+; for non-participating or non-Catholics, $4,717 for 1 child, $9,434 for 2, and $14,151 for 3+. **Mission Statement:** "The School of the Epiphany is a Catholic, Parochial school serving the youth of Epiphany Parish and its surrounding areas. We challenge students to achieve educational excellence within a Catholic tradition. The School of the Epiphany operates in service to Epiphany Parish and in the spirit of the Presentation Sisters." **Academic program:** "Various in-curriculum programs are offered in Spanish, computer, music and PE. The middle schools exploratory program includes classes in advanced computers, card making, wood working, cooking, Tagalog, music, library, tutoring, journalism, choral singing, nutrition, fashion design, karate, photography and drama. After-school services include piano and drama classes." **Uniforms. Extended day:** Until 6 p.m. Cost: $175/month.

Star of the Sea School

360 9th Avenue (at Geary) (Inner Richmond)
San Francisco, CA 94118
(415) 221-8558 *fax* (415) 221-7118
www.starsf.net

Terence Hanley, Principal
Coed K-8 parochial day school. Founded in 1909. Catholic. **Accreditation:** WASC/WCEA. **Enrollment:** Approx. 230. **Average class size:** 15-20 in lower school, approx. 32 in middle school. **School year:** Aug.-June. **Instructional days:** 180. **Ethnicity:** 49% Asian, 27%

Caucasian (non-Latino), 12% multi-racial, 7% African-American, 5% Latino. **Applications due:** Rolling. **Application process:** "Please call." **What sort of student do you best serve?** "Families who value a solid, basic education and want Christian values for their children." **Latest tuition:** $4,500 with 5-7% increase annually. **Sibling discount:** Yes. **Mission Statement:** "Star of the Sea School is a unique, loving Christian community of caring persons who enthusiastically strive to instill Christ-like values and academic excellence in a way that challenges ourselves, our students and our parents. Our school is about people, with the rich ethnic backgrounds of those entrusted in our care, we strive to bring out the uniqueness and potential of each child. We see the parents as the primary educators. As parents work to develop their child holistically (spiritually, academically, psychologically, physically and culturally) we, as educators, are here to reinforce what has begun in the home. We dedicated to guiding our students to form a thinking conscience, and to learn to make sound decisions, so that they may be responsible adults of tomorrow. Star of the Sea Catholic School exists for people; it is our desire to lead each other, and our students and parents to real love and respect for each individual. Each person has been gifted by God with life, and in turn shares personal gifts with others." **Philosophy:** "Star of the Sea exists as part of a thriving faith community over 100 years old. Under the advocacy of Mary, our patroness, we guide families who trust their children's education to our care. Inspired by the educational tradition of the Sisters of St. Joseph of Carondelet, we meet students where they are, in order to lead them on the path toward Christ. As dedicated educators we realize that parents are the primary educators of their children. In choosing Star of the Sea they show us the commitment they have. In turn we pledge ourselves to work with parents to prepare children to become responsible, contributing member of the community. We see effective education as stewardship. As gifted individuals we share knowledge and resources available in order to make the world a better place through our academic curriculum we strive to call forth the very best each student has to offer. Our students' gifts find affirmation through our holistic educational program that addresses religious, intellectual, social aesthetic, emotional and physical needs. Star of the Sea School exists for people. We are rich in ethnic diversity. We strive to educate so that real love and respect for the uniqueness and potential of each individual will be evident in our school community." **Academic program:** "Star of the Sea is known for its strong academic curriculum. Students receive daily instruction in religion, English, social studies, math, science, and reading. Art, music, computer training, and PE are also part of our well-rounded curriculum. Spanish and Chinese language classes are available on the premises after school hours." **Athletics:** "Students in G3-8 have the opportunity to participate in soccer, basketball, and girls volleyball in the newly renovated gym. Teams play in the Catholic Youth Organization. Cheerleading is available for G4-8." **Middle School:** "G6-8 are departmentalized. The Student Council is an active and productive group of students meeting on a weekly basis with a faculty moderator. Students can be involved in the production of the school newspaper under the guidance of a faculty advisor. Students in G4-8 have the opportunity to become Altar Servers." **Campus description:** The campus consists of a school building, library and extended care building, and a gymnasium. **Parent/teacher communication:** "Star of the Sea promotes open and active communication between school and home. A weekly envelope is sent home with a letter from the Principal and notification of upcoming events. A yearly calendar is provided, as well as updated monthly calendars. Student work packets are sent home on a regular basis to keep parents abreast of their child's work, and report cards are sent home four times a year. In addition to regular scheduled parent/teacher conferences in November, the faculty is available for consultation whenever necessary."

Voice of Pentecost Academy
1970 Ocean Avenue (West of Twin Peaks)
San Francisco, CA 94127
(415) 334-0105 *fax* (415) 586-3990

R. Sherwood Jansen, Principal
Coed PS-12 day school. Pentecostal. Founded in 1974. **Enrollment:** Approx. 150. **Ethnicity:** "93% students of color." **Instructional days:** 180. **Teacher/student ratio:** 1:16. Uniforms.

Marin County

North Bay Christian Academy

6965 Redwood Blvd.
Novato, CA 94945
(415) 892-8921 *fax (415) 893-1750*
www.nbcs.com

Pam Carraher, Principal
Coed K-12 day school. Christian. School day: 8 a.m. to 4 p.m., early dismissal on Mondays. **Latest tuition:** $2,950 for K, $3,200 for G1, $2,950 for G2-5, $4,850 for G6-8. **Sibling discount:** Families may deduct $30 per month from the total monthly tuition due for the second child, $120 from the monthly tuition for the third child. Fourth children are $50 per month. Fifth children and beyond receive the third child discount. **Mission Statement:** "North Bay Christian Academy is a diverse, caring community dedicated to imparting a Christ-centered education that cultivates students, in partnership with the home and the church, to become transforming influences in the world." **What sets the school apart from others:** "A unique feature of our school is the range of ages that learn and play together. While the elementary program is housed in one wing and the middle school and high school in another, between classes students of all grades interact. This atmosphere fosters valuable interpersonal skills across generational lines."

Our Lady of Loretto School

1811 Virginia Street
Novato, CA 94945
(415) 892-8621 *fax (415) 892-9631*
www.ollnovato.org

Sue Maino, Principal
Coed K-8 day school. Accreditation: WASC/WCEA. **Latest tuition:** For in-parish families, $5,064, for out-of-parish or nonparticipating $5,864. **Sibling discount:** Yes (amount N/P). **Mission Statement:** "OLL is committed to: Forming whole persons who can apply for Gospel values; recognizing parents and guardians as the primary

educators of the students; involving the students as active members of the Christian community; developing self-esteem and respect for the dignity of others; enabling the students and staff to grow in their love and knowledge of Jesus and the Gospel teachings within the curriculum and extracurricular activities; presenting students with an awareness of cultures and encouraging them to express their own inherent uniqueness." **Uniforms. Extended day.**

St. Anselm School

40 Belle Avenue
San Anselmo, CA 94906
(415) 454-8667 *fax (415) 454-4730*
www.stanselmschool.com

Odile Steel, Principal
Coed K-8 parochial day school. Founded in 1924. Catholic. Nonprofit. **Accreditation:** WASC/WCEA. **School year:** Aug.-June. **School day:** 8:15 a.m. to 3:15 p.m. (2 p.m. dismissal for K). **Applications due:** March 1 (for K). **Application fee:** $10. **Application process:** Submit application fee, schedule interview and tour. **Admission evaluation requirements for K:** Testing, teacher recommendations. **Other grades:** Half- or full-day visit, teacher recommendations, test scores, grades. **Preferences:** Parish members first, then members of other Catholic churches. **What sort of student do you best serve?** "We offer a strong academic curriculum with several co-curricular programs geared to the average and above-average student." **Latest tuition:** $5,360 with scrip, $5,110 without scrip. **Sibling discount:** Yes (amount N/P). **Mission Statement:** "St. Anselm School strives to prepare students for a truly Christian life to develop programs of educational excellence, and to provide quality leadership." **Academic philosophy:** "St. Anselm is more than an academic institution. It provides an educational system that emphasizes the spiritual, intellectual, and personal development of the students. Our goals are to compliment the home in developing the whole child, and to instill in each child a sense of closeness to and love for God and His Church. We hope to foster a love for learning and to encourage an enthusiasm for academic excellence. St. Anselm encourages an appreciation for the intrinsic value of life, a respect for

the dignity of others and a commitment to social justice. In promoting in each child a positive self-image, we aim to achieve the ultimate goal that each child will realize his/her full potential with a sense of duty to God, Church, self, family, peers and community." **Foreign languages:** Spanish. **Special subject teachers:** Science, technology, PE, music, Spanish. **Uniforms. Extended day:** From 7:15 a.m.; after-school care until 6 p.m. **Grade levels:** K-8. **Cost:** $3.25/hour. **Snacks:** Provided. **Parent Participation requirements:** 40 volunteer hours.

St. Hilary School

765 Hilary Drive
Tiburon, CA 94920
(415) 435-2224 *fax (415)435-5895*
www.sainthilary-school.org

Janet Lovette, Principal
Melissa Addleman, Director of Admission, admissions@sainthilary-school.org
Coed K-8 parochial day school. Catholic. Nonprofit. **Enrollment:** Approx. 237. **Accreditation:** WASC/WCEA. **School year:** Aug.-June. **Instructional days:** 180. **Application fee:** $50. **Application process:** Call the school for application packet and schedule a tour. **Admission evaluation requirements for K:** Teacher recommendations, assessment. **Other grades:** Testing, teacher recommendations. **Latest tuition:** $6,010 for participating parishioners, $7,106 for non-parishioner/non-participating. **Percentage of faculty with current California credential:** 100%. **Sports offered:** Basketball, volleyball. **Campus description:** Recently remodeled with library and technology center, gymnasium, and science lab. **Uniforms.**

St. Isabella School

1 Trinity Way
San Rafael, CA 94903
(415) 479-3727 *fax (415) 479-9961*
www.stisbellaschool.org

Cynthia Bergez, Head of School, cbergez@marincounty.net
Coed K-8 parochial day school. Founded in 1962. Catholic. Nonprofit. **Enrollment:** Approx. 270. **Average class size:** 32. **Accreditation:** WASC (3-year term). **Instructional days:** 182. **School day:** 8 a.m. to 3 p.m. **Application due date:** Accepted year round. **Application fee:** $50. **K application process:** Submit application, then attend a school tour. Students applying to K attend a screening after which parents are notified by mail of their child's status. **Other grades:** After completing the application process, students attend school in their present grade. Parents are called with their child's status and notified by mail with a confirmation letter. **No. of applications:** 80. **No. of K spaces:** 35. **Admission evaluation requirements for K:** Screening, recommendations. **What sort of student do you best serve?** "Students with good academic skills and appropriate behavior." **Latest tuition:** $5,676. **Sibling discount:** Yes (amount N/P). **Tuition increases:** Approx. 8% annually. **Other costs:** Approx. $473 for books, $80 other fees. **Mission Statement:** "St. Isabella Parish school is committed to providing an education that challenges students to live out the Catholic faith in service to God, family and society responsibly. We provide a solid foundation for the spiritual, psychological, and academic development of our students. St. Isabella educates tomorrow's leaders." **Uniforms.**

St. Patrick School
120 King Street
Larkspur, CA 94939
Phone (415) 924-0501 *fax* (415) 924-3544
www.stpatricksmarin.com

Ann Kalayjian, Principal
Coed K-8 parochial day school. Catholic. **Enrollment:** Approx. 259. **Average class size:** Approx. 29. **Accreditation:** WASC/WCEA. **Latest tuition:** For participating families, $5,856 for 1 child, $10,548 for 2, and $14,352 for 3; for non-participating, $6,026 for 1 child, $10,718 for 2, and $14,522 for 3. **Mission Statement:** "To instill in our students a love and respect for our Catholic tradition, a strong academic foundation, and a reverence for themselves, others and the world

around them." **Uniforms. Extended day:** From 7:15 a.m. until 8 a.m. and from dismissal to 6 p.m.

St. Raphael School

1100 Fifth Avenue
San Rafael, CA 94901
(415) 454-4455 fax (415) 454-5927
www.saintraphael.com

Maureen Albritton, Principal
Coed PS-8 parochial day school. Founded in 1889. Catholic. **Enrollment:** Approx. 180. **Average class size:** 22. **Accreditation:** WASC/WCEA (6-yr. term: 2003-09). **Ethnicity:** "46% non-Caucasian." **Latest tuition:** $5,255 for parishioners, $5,605 for non-parishioners. **Tuition increases:** Approx. 2-9% annually. **Mission Statement:** "Saint Raphael's School, rooted in the Dominican tradition, is dedicated to living out Catholic values in a richly diverse population while providing a strong academic education for all students." **Uniforms. Extended care.**

St. Rita School

102 Marinda Drive
Fairfax, CA 94930
(415) 456-1003 fax (415) 456-7946
www.strita.edu

Marilyn Porto, Principal
Coed K-8 parochial day school. Catholic. Founded in 1957. **Enrollment:** Approx. 200. **Accreditation:** WASC/WCEA. **Application process:** Call for a registration package/curriculum guide and to make an appointment to meet with the principal and visit classrooms. Applicants to K must be 5 by September 1. **Latest tuition:** For participating families, $5,820 for 1 child, $9,840 for 2, $12,900 for 3, and $15,180 for 4+; for non-participating, $6,720 for 1 child, $11,340 for 2, $14,700 for 3, and $17,180 for 4+. **Mission Statement:** "As pro-

fessional educators at St. Rita's, a unique and special Catholic school, we are called to share in the educational mission of the Church. Accordingly, we endeavor to teach as Jesus did, practice what we teach, and challenge our students to live their lives in imitation of Christ. We are committed to providing our students with an innovative and comprehensive curriculum. We envision their education as one that will prepare them to make a difference, not only in the Church and their local communities, but also the international society of the twenty-first century." **Campus:** Located in downtown Fairfax. The campus includes a science and computer building. **Uniforms. Extended day.**

APPENDIX

At parents' request in response to the prior editions of this book, certain statistics from the schools' profiles are compiled below.

School Size

Holy Trinity Orthodox School	40
Cascade Canyon	66
Kittredge School	85
The Laurel School	85
Ring Mountain Day School	95+
Lisa Kampner Hebrew Academy	100
Montessori de Terra Linda	130+
Adda Clevenger Junior Preparatory and Theater School	150
Krouzian-Zekarian-Vasbouragan Armenian School	150
Voice of Pentecost Academy	150
The Discovery Center School	160
San Francisco Friends School	160+
Megan Furth Academy at Sacred Heart/St. Dominic	175
St. Raphael School	180
Synergy School	185
Presidio Hill School	186
Saint Monica School	190
Brandeis Hillel Day School – Marin	200
Marin Christian Academy	200
Marin Waldorf School	200
St. Rita School	200
Zion Lutheran Day School	200
St. Philip School	205
Marin Montessori School	207
Mission Dolores Catholic School	210
St. James School	210
Live Oak School	225
Star of the Sea School	230
St. Hilary School	237
Mount Tamalpais School	240
St. Mary's Chinese Day School	240

School of the Epiphany	635
Lycée Français La Perouse	655

N/P: Ecole Notre Dame des Victoires, Hillwood Academic Day School, North Bay Christian Academy, Our Lady of Loretto School, St. Anselm School, Saint Charles Borromeo School, St. Elizabeth School, St. Finn Barr School, St. Thomas More School, San Francisco Adventist School.

Average Class Size

Holy Trinity Orthodox School	8-12
The Laurel School	9
The Discovery Center School	12
Lisa Kampner Hebrew Academy	12
Mount Tamalpais School	12
Marin Montessori School	12-30
Adda Clevenger Junior Preparatory and Theater School	14
Cascade Canyon	14
Kittredge School	14
Presidio Hill School	14-17
Ring Mountain Day School	15
Marin Primary & Middle School	15
Convent of the Sacred Heart Elementary School	15-20
Lycée Français La Pérouse	15-20
Saint Monica School	15-20
Stuart Hall for Boys	15-20
Star of the Sea School	15-30
French-American International School	16
Krouzian-Zekarian-Vasbouragan Armenian School	16
Chinese American International School	16-18
The Hamlin School	16-22
Cathedral School for Boys	16-24
Marin Christian Academy	17
Brandeis Hillel Day School – Marin	18
Marin Country Day School	18
Live Oak School	18-22
Marin Horizon School	20

N/P: Children's Day School, Ecole Notre Dame des Victoires, Hill-wood Academic Day School, Katherine Delmar Burke School, North Bay Christian Academy, Our Lady of Loretto School, St. Anselm School, St. Anthony Immaculate Conception, St. Brendan School, Saint Charles Borromeo School, St. Elizabeth School, St. Finn Barr School, St. Hilary School, Sts. Peter and Paul Elementary School, St. Rita School, St. Thomas More School, San Domenico School, San Francisco Adventist School, Voice of Pentecost Academy

Latest Tuition or Tuition Range

The Hamlin School	$19,275
Marin Country Day School	$18,825-$21,800
Katherine Delmar Burke School	$18,805-$19,460
San Francisco Day School	$18,760
San Francisco Friends School	$18,245
Mount Tamalpais School	$18,000
Marin Primary & Middle School	$16,700-$18,100
Town School for Boys	$17,950
Convent of the Sacred Heart	$17,450-17,850
Stuart Hall For Boys	$17,450-$17,850
Brandeis Hillel Day School-Marin	$17,400-$18,400
Brandeis Hillel Day School-SF	$17,400-$18,400
Cathedral School for Boy	$17,400
Saint Mark's School	$16,850
French-American International School	$16,570-$17,880
Children's Day School	$16,500
Live Oak School	$16,100-$16,950
Chinese American International School	$16,050-$17,000
Ring Mountain Day School	$15,950-$16,830
Presidio Hill School	$15,900-$16,975
The San Francisco School	$15,600-$16,820
The Laurel School	$15,400
San Domenico School	$14,712-$16,636
Lycée Français La Pérouse	$12,930-$14,375
San Francisco Waldorf School	$12,530-$13,830

Adda Clevenger	$12,000
Marin Waldorf School	$11,675-$13,035
Kittredge School	$11,300-$11,900
Synergy School	$10,900
Marin Montessori School	$10,830-$14,990
Marin Horizon School	$10,720-$18,000
Montessori de Terra Linda	$10,550
Cascade Canyon	$10,200
The Discovery Center School	$9,000
St. Hilary School	$6,010-$7,106
Krouzian-Zekarian-Vasbouragan	$6,000
Zion Lutheran Day School	$6,000
Ecôle Notre Dame Des Victoires	$5,880
St. Patrick School	$5,856-$6,026
St. Rita School	$5,820-$6,720
St. Isabella School	$5,676
St. Raphael School	$5,255-$5,605
West Portal Lutheran School	$5,148-$5,373
St. Anselm School	$5,110-$5,360
Our Lady of Loretto School	$5,064-$5,864
Saint Vincent de Paul School	$5,000-$7,750
Hillwood Academic Day School	$5,000
St. Gabriel School	$4,980
St. John's School	$4,750
Sts. Peter and Paul Elementary School	$4,675-$5,675
St. Philip School	$4,609
St. Mary's Chinese Day School	$4,500
Star of the Sea School	$4,500
St. Finn Barr School	$4,400-$5,150
Saint Monica School	$4,390-$4,990
Marin Christian Academy	$4,210-$4,820
Holy Name of Jesus School	$4,200-$5,100
St. Cecilia School	$4,175-$5,000
St. Paul's Elementary School	$4,107-$4,557
St. Stephen School	$4,080-$4,470
St. James School	$4,050-$4,502

St. Anthony Immaculate Conception	$4,000-$4368
St. Brendan School	$4,000-$4,200
Mission Dolores School	$3,950-$5,150
Saint Brigid School	$3,950
Our Lady of the Visitacion School	$3,900
St. Elizabeth School	$3,840
School of the Epiphany	$3,825-$4,717
St. Anne School	$3,600-$4,950
Corpus Christi School	$3,600
Saint Charles Borromeo School	$3,400
Holy Trinity Orthodox School	$3,350-$3,550
San Francisco Adventist School	$3,070-$4,960
Megan Furth Academy	$3,000
North Bay Christian Academy	$2,950-$4,850
St. Peter's School	$2,700

N/P: Lisa Kampner Hebrew Academy, St. Thomas More School, St. Thomas the Apostle School, Voice of Pentecost Academy,

Percentage of Students Receiving Financial Aid

Lisa Kampner Hebrew Academy	88%
St. Peter's School	60%
Children's Day School	40%
Mission Dolores Catholic School	40%
Marin Waldorf School	34%
Synergy School	33%
Brandeis Hillel Day School – Marin	30%
Brandeis Hillel Day School – San Francisco	30%
Corpus Christi School	30%
Krouzian-Zekarian-Vasbouragan Armenian School	30%
French-American International School	28%
San Francisco Friends School	28%
Live Oak School	27%
Lycée Français La Pérouse	25%
The San Francisco School	25%
Chinese American International School	23%

Marin Country Day School	23%
Presidio Hill School	23%
St. James School	23%
Katherine Delmar Burke School	22%
San Francisco Day School	21%
The Laurel School	20%
Ring Mountain Day School	20%
Cathedral School for Boys	18%
Marin Horizon School	18%
Saint Mark's School	17%
Saint Brigid School	16%
San Francisco Waldorf School	16%
Mount Tamalpais School	15%+
Saint Monica School	15-20%
The Hamlin School	15%
Marin Primary & Middle School	15%
St. Paul's Elementary School	15%
Stuart Hall for Boys	15%
Convent of the Sacred Heart Elementary School	14%
Marin Montessori School	14%
St. Gabriel School	11%
The Discovery Center School	10%
Marin Christian Academy	10%
St. Cecilia School	10%
St. John's School	10%
St. Mary's Chinese Day School	10%
Holy Name of Jesus School	8%
Montessori de Terra Linda	7%
Zion Lutheran Day School	6%
Kittredge School	5%
St. Anne School	5%
Saint Vincent de Paul School	5%
St. Philip School	2%

None: Adda Clevenger Junior Preparatory and Theater School, Cascade Canyon

N/P: Ecôle Notre Dame des Victoires, Hillwood Academic Day School, Holy Name of Jesus School, Holy Trinity Orthodox School, Megan Furth Academy at Sacred Heart/St. Dominic , North Bay Christian Academy, Our Lady of Loretto School, Our Lady of the Visitacion School, St. Anselm School, St. Anthony Immaculate Conception, St. Brendan School, Saint Charles Borromeo School, St. Elizabeth School, St. Finn Barr School, St. Hilary School, St. Isabella School, St. Patrick School, St. Raphael School, St. Rita School, St. Stephen School, St. Thomas More School, St. Thomas the Apostle School, Sts. Peter and Paul Elementary School, San Domenico School, San Francisco Adventist School, School of the Epiphany, Star of the Sea School, Town School for Boys, Voice of Pentecost Academy, West Portal Lutheran School

Percentage of Financial Aid Awards of ½ Tuition+

Marin Christian Academy	90%
Montessori de Terra Linda	90%
Mount Tamalpais School	90%
Saint Mark's School	89%
San Francisco Day School	80%
Katherine Delmar Burke School	79%
Ring Mountain Day School	75%
Cathedral School for Boys	70%
Marin Country Day School	68%
Marin Primary & Middle School	68%
Marin Montessori School	66%
The Hamlin School	65%
Marin Horizon School	65%
Presidio Hill School	62%
Lycée Français La Pérouse	60%
Children's Day School	50%
Corpus Christi School	50%
Synergy School	48%
San Francisco Waldorf School	40%

Mission Dolores Catholic School	30%
St. James School	25%
St. Mary's Chinese Day School	25%
Saint Monica School	10%
Saint Brigid School	6%
St. Paul's Elementary School	5%
St. Philip School	3%
Saint Vincent de Paul School	1%
Adda Clevenger	0%
Cascade Canyon	0%
The Discovery Center School	0%
Kittredge School	0%
Krouzian-Zekarian-Vasbouragan Armenian School	0%
St. John's School	0%

N/P: Brandeis Hillel Day School-Marin, Brandeis Hillel Day School -SF, Chinese American International School, Convent of the Sacred Heart Elementary School, Ecôle Notre Dame des Victoires, French-American International School, Hillwood Academic Day School, Holy Name of Jesus School, Holy Trinity Orthodox School, The Laurel School, Lisa Kampner Hebrew Academy, Live Oak School, Marin Waldorf School, Megan Furth Academy at Sacred Heart/St. Dominic, North Bay Christian Academy, Our Lady of Loretto School, Our Lady of the Visitacion School, St. Anne School, St. Anselm School, St. Anthony Immaculate Conception, St. Brendan School, St. Cecilia School, Saint Charles Borromeo School, St. Elizabeth School, St. Finn Barr School, St. Gabriel School, St. Hilary School, St. Isabella School, St. Patrick School, St. Peter's School, St. Raphael School, St. Rita School, St. Stephen School, St. Thomas More School, St. Thomas the Apostle School, Sts. Peter and Paul Elementary School, San Domenico School, San Francisco Adventist School, San Francisco Friends School, The San Francisco School, School of the Epiphany, Star of the Sea School, Stuart Hall For Boys, Town School for Boys, Voice of Pentecost Academy, West Portal Lutheran School, Zion Lutheran Day School.

Foreign Languages Offered in the Curriculum

Armenian
Krouzian-Zekarian-Vasbouragan Armenian School

French
Cascade Canyon
Convent of the Sacred Heart Elementary School
Ecôle Notre Dame des Victoires
French-American International School
The Hamlin School
Katherine Delmar Burke School
Lycée Français La Pérouse
Marin Primary & Middle School
Mount Tamalpais School
Saint Mark's School
San Domenico School
Stuart Hall for Boys
Town School for Boys

German
French-American International School
Marin Waldorf School
San Francisco Waldorf School
West Portal Lutheran School

Greek
Holy Trinity Orthodox School

Hebrew
Brandeis Hillel Day School - Marin
Brandeis Hillel Day School – San Francisco
Lisa Kampner Hebrew Academy

Latin
Cathedral School for Boys
Convent of the Sacred Heart Elementary School

French-American International School
Mount Tamalpais School
San Francisco Day School
Stuart Hall for Boys
Town School for Boys

Mandarin
Cathedral School for Boys
Chinese American International School
French-American International School
Katherine Delmar Burke School
Saint Monica School
Star of the Sea School

Sign Language
Cascade Canyon

Spanish
Cathedral School for Boys
Children's Day School
Convent of the Sacred Heart Elementary School
The Discovery Center School
French-American International School
The Hamlin School
Katherine Delmar Burke School
Kittredge School
Live Oak School
Marin Christian Academy
Marin Country Day School
Marin Horizon School
Marin Montessori School
Marin Primary & Middle School
Marin Waldorf School
Montessori de Terra Linda
Mount Tamalpais School
Presidio Hill School

Ring Mountain Day School
St. Anselm School
Saint Brigid School
Saint Mark's School
Saint Vincent de Paul School
San Domenico School
San Francisco Day School
San Francisco Friends School
The San Francisco School
San Francisco Waldorf School
School of the Epiphany
Star of the Sea School
Stuart Hall for Boys
Synergy School
Town School for Boys
West Portal Lutheran School
Zion Lutheran Day School

Foreign Language After School
Cantonese
Holy Name of Jesus School
St. Anne School
St. Gabriel School
St. Mary's Chinese Day School
Saint Monica School

French
Chinese American International School

Gaelic
Holy Name of Jesus School

Mandarin
Holy Name of Jesus School
St. Anne School

Spanish
Holy Name of Jesus School
St. Finn Barr School
St. John's School
St. Paul's Elementary School
St. Philip School

Schools with Learning Specialists on Staff
Brandeis Hillel Day School-Marin
Brandeis Hillel Day School-San Francisco
Cathedral School for Boys
Chinese American International School
Convent of the Sacred Heart Elementary School
The Discovery Center School
French-American International School
The Hamlin School
Holy Name of Jesus School
Katherine Delmar Burke School
Live Oak School
Lycée Français La Pérouse
Marin Country Day School
Marin Horizon School
Marin Montessori School (Consultant)
Marin Primary & Middle School
Marin Waldorf School
Mount Tamalpais School
Presidio Hill School
St. Anne School
Saint Brigid School
St. Cecilia School
St. Gabriel School
St. James School
St. John's School
Saint Mark's School
St. Mary's Chinese Day School
Saint Monica School

St. Paul's Elementary School
San Domenico School
San Francisco Day School
San Francisco Friends School
The San Francisco School
San Francisco Waldorf School
Stuart Hall for Boys
Synergy School
Town School for Boys

Extended Day Programs

Adda Clevenger Junior Preparatory and Theater School
Brandeis Hillel Day School – Marin
Brandeis Hillel Day School – San Francisco
Cathedral School for Boys
Children's Day School
Chinese American International School
Convent of the Sacred Heart Elementary School
Corpus Christi School
The Discovery Center School
Ecôle Notre Dame des Victoires
French-American International School
The Hamlin School
Hillwood Academic Day School
Holy Name of Jesus School
Katherine Delmar Burke School
Kittredge School
Krouzian-Zekarian-Vasbouragan Armenian School
The Laurel School
Lisa Kampner Hebrew Academy
Live Oak School
Lycée Français La Pérouse
Marin Christian Academy
Marin Country Day School
Marin Horizon School
Marin Montessori School

Marin Primary & Middle School
Marin Waldorf School
Megan Furth Academy at Sacred Heart/St. Dominic
Mission Dolores Catholic School
Montessori de Terra Linda
Mount Tamalpais School
Our Lady of Loretto School
Our Lady of the Visitacion School
Presidio Hill School
Ring Mountain Day School
St. Anne School
St. Anselm School
Saint Brigid School
St. Cecilia School
Saint Charles Borromeo School
St. Elizabeth School
St. Finn Barr School
St. Gabriel School
St. James School
St. John's School
Saint Mark's School
Saint Monica School
St. Patrick School
St. Paul's Elementary School
St. Peter's School
St. Philip School
St. Raphael School
St. Rita School
St. Stephen School
St. Thomas More School
St. Thomas the Apostle School
Saint Vincent de Paul School
Sts. Peter and Paul Elementary School
San Domenico School
San Francisco Adventist School
San Francisco Day School

San Francisco Friends School
The San Francisco School
San Francisco Waldorf School
School of the Epiphany
Stuart Hall for Boys
Synergy School
Town School for Boys
West Portal Lutheran School
Zion Lutheran Day School

None: Cascade Canyon, Holy Trinity Orthodox School, St. Mary's Chinese Day School (Study hall until 5 p.m.)

N/P: Holy Trinity Orthodox School, North Bay Christian Academy, St. Anthony Immaculate Conception, St. Brendan School, St. Finn Barr School, St. Hilary School, St. Isabella School, Star of the Sea School, Voice of Pentecost Academy

Summer Programs

Adda Clevenger Junior Preparatory and Theater School
Brandeis Hillel Day School – San Francisco
Cathedral School for Boys
Children's Day School
Chinese American International School
Convent of the Sacred Heart Elementary School
Corpus Christi School
The Discovery Center School
French-American International School
The Hamlin School
Hillwood Academic Day School
Holy Name of Jesus School
Katherine Delmar Burke School
Kittredge School
Krouzian-Zekarian-Vasbouragan Armenian School
The Laurel School
Live Oak School

Lycée Français La Pérousea
Marin Christian Academy
Marin Country Day School
Marin Horizon School
Marin Montessori School
Marin Primary & Middle School
Marin Waldorf School
Montessori de Terra Linda (K only)
Mount Tamalpais School
Presidio Hill School
Ring Mountain Day School (K-4)
St. Gabriel School
Saint Mark's School
St. Mary's Chinese Day School
Saint Monica School
St. Peter's School
San Domenico School
San Francisco Day School
San Francisco Friends School
The San Francisco School
San Francisco Waldorf School
Stuart Hall for Boys
Synergy School
Town School for Boys
West Portal Lutheran School
Zion Lutheran Day School

None: Cascade Canyon, Holy Trinity Orthodox School, Lisa Kampner Hebrew Academy, Saint Brigid School, St. James School, St. Paul's Elementary School, St. Philip School, Saint Vincent de Paul School

N/P: Brandeis Hillel Day School-Marin, Ecôle Notre Dame des Victoires, Megan Furth Academy at Sacred Heart/St. Dominic, Mission Dolores Catholic School, North Bay Christian Academy, Our Lady of Loretto School, Our Lady of the Visitacion School,

St. Anne School, St. Anselm School, St. Anthony Immaculate Conception, St. Brendan School, St. Cecilia School, Saint Charles Borromeo School, St. Finn Barr School, St. Hilary School, St. Isabella School, St. Patrick School, Sts. Peter and Paul Elementary School, St. Raphael School, St. Rita School, St. Stephen School, St. Thomas More School, St. Thomas the Apostle School, San Francisco Adventist School, School of the Epiphany, Star of the Sea School, Voice of the Pentecost Academy

ABOUT THE AUTHORS

Betsy Little and Paula Molligan offer school placement for preschool through high school throughout the Bay Area with offices in Marin and San Francisco. Website: www.littleandmolligan.com. E-mail: betsy@littleandmolligan.com or paula@littleandmolligan.com.

Little and Molligan, 4040 Civic Center Drive, Suite 200, San Rafael, CA 94903, (415) 492-2877.

OTHER BOOKS AVAILABLE FROM PINCE-NEZ PRESS

Private High Schools of the San Francisco Bay Area (3rd Ed.)
by Betsy Little, MBA, MS and Paula Molligan, MBA, MS. 60 schools from
Sonoma to San Jose and the East Bay and expert advice about the high
school admission process. 1-930074-14-X, $24.95

Getting Into the High School of Your Dreams!
by Susan Vogel. A workbook to organize the high school admission process.
1-930074-04-2, 54 pages, $16.95

Finding a Preschool For Your Child in San Francisco & Marin (3rd. Ed.)
by Lori Rifkin, Ph.D., Vera Obermeyer, Ph.D., Irene Byrne, MS, and Me-
linda Venable. Covers more than 150 public and private preschools in San
Francisco and Marin and advises parents on how to choose a preschool.
1-930074-12-3, $23.95

Finding a Nanny For Your Child in the San Francisco Bay Area
by Alyce Desrosiers, LCSW. Essential advice if you hire child care providers. Information about background checks, interviews, and sample contracts.
Lots of Bay Area resources. 1-930074-00-X, $19.95

*Learning Disabilities from a Parent's Perspective: What You Need to Know
to Understand, Help and Advocate for Your Child*
by Kim E. Glenchur, MA, MBA. Essential information for any parent who
suspects or learns their child may have a learning disability. 1-930074-07-7,
$23.95

*Birthing: Choices You Have to Create the Best Birth Experience for You and
Your Child*
by Irene Byrne, MS. An objective guide to making your own healthy, informed decisions about your baby's birth. 1-930074-06-9, $19.95

These books as well as other works of fiction, nonfiction, poetry, and humor,
are available on our website at www.pince-nez.com as well as in bookstores.
To order directly from the publisher, please call 415-267-5978 or e-mail
susan@pince-nez.com.